the Street-Smart Writer

Self-**Defense** Against Sharks and **Scams** in the **Writing** World

Jenna Glatzer and Daniel Steven

To Travis Tea

Nomad Press

A division of Nomad Communications

10 9 8 7 6 5 4 3 2

Copyright © 2006 by Jenna Glatzer and Daniel Steven

All rights reserved.

ISBN: 0-9749344-4-5

Questions regarding the ordering of this book should
be addressedto Independent Publishers Group

814 N. Franklin St.

Chicago, IL 60610

Nomad Press

2456 Christian St.

White River Junction, VT 05001

www.nomadpress.net

Contents

Acknowledgments

Lauri Berkenkamp is the only editor who will dish about *American Idol* with me, and that's not even my favorite thing about her. I'd tell you how great she is, but I'd use up my quota of adjectives for the book. If only it weren't for her one tragic flaw: not letting me put a shark bite on the book cover.

Somewhere along the way in my writing career, I earned the title "writers' advocate," but I'm not the first to deserve that title. My scam-hunting hero is Victoria Strauss, an author who's been fighting injustice on behalf of writers for almost a decade. Not only is she tireless in her efforts, she's a remarkable human being who is as classy and caring as she is devoted. A. C. Crispin, James D. Macdonald, Dave Kuzminski, Teresa Nielsen Hayden, and C. E. Petit are all well-deserving of respect and appreciation for all they've done to help keep writers out of trouble. You've been my role models and, I'm honored to say, my friends.

Thank you to my co-author, Daniel Steven, for your enthusiasm, insight, and dedication to this project from the start. Your wisdom added much to this book.

The rest of the thanks belong to:

- The folks on the AbsoluteWrite.com forums, for the constant amusement and camaraderie. Thanks, in particular, to the moderators, who set terrific examples.

- The Cletians, who are so close to world domination. You are my sanctity.

- Professor John Schulz, who told me to "be tough as nails, but never lose your sensitivity."

- Amy Brozio-Andrews, my right-hand woman.

- The Glatzers and the Policastros for their never-ending support and love.

- The writers who psychically email me just at those moments when I'm ready to throw in the towel, to let me know that I made a difference.

- Everyone at Nomad Press for being terrific to work with.

- Anthony, who says "I love you" a hundred times a day and always finds my shoes.

Introduction

I wish there were no need for this book. Truth is, when my publisher approached me with the idea for this book, I was hoping to say, "Sorry, there's not enough material on this topic for a whole book." But after reflecting on it for, oh, ten minutes, I realized I could write a book the length of *War and Peace* about scams and unsavory characters in the writers' world. And that made me realize I had to do it.

The first time I got scammed, I was a ten-year-old budding writer. I had written a poem that I was very proud of, from the point of view of a dying fetus. (Clearly I was a tortured artist in the making.) I sent the poem to a contest I'd found that advertised in the back of a magazine. It offered a big financial grand prize and the possibility of publication.

Imagine my delight when the organization running the contest wrote to tell me that my poem was selected as a semi-finalist based on its fine literary merit! As such, it was selected for publication in a gorgeous hardcover anthology of award-winning poetry. I could pre-order my copy right now.

"Mom!" I screamed down the hall. "I'm going to be a published writer! I need some money!"

Reality took a while to sink in, and in the meantime, I entered many more contests of the same caliber.

But my writing career began in earnest when I was 21. By then, I thought I was wise enough to sidestep the potholes in the publishing pavement. Apparently not, because my first "agent" rooked me out of $250, another turned out to be the laughingstock of the industry, and several of my early publishers got away with stiffing me out of the fees they had promised me.

Along the way, I started AbsoluteWrite.com, which became the most popular online magazine for writers. I also started a message board where writers could report their experiences with deadbeat publishers, producers, agents, contests, editors, publicists, and so on. What I found was that the same companies that had rooked me so many years ago were not only still in business, they were thriving. And what was worse was that the scams were obviously multiplying.

Perhaps because would-be scammers saw how profitable others had been when they preyed on the dreams of unsuspecting writers, whole new categories of rip-offs against writers were born. The Internet seemed to be a birthing center of some of the most insidious and deceptive practices, and unfortunately, despite the individuals and writers' organizations working hard to bring down the unscrupulous companies, or at least warn writers about potential pitfalls, the scams remain on the rise. Now they're just even more cleverly worded and harder to spot from a distance.

Because I'm now well-published and well-known in the online writing community, writers frequently come to me for advice when they're unsure of whether or not the company they're dealing with is legitimate. It breaks my heart when I have to tell them that someone who's shown an interest in their work has a bad agenda. Often, it's so exciting for writers to find anyone who takes an interest in their work that they remain blind to warning signs, even when they seem, to an outsider, to be flashing in neon colors.

Scammers seize the opportunity to take advantage
of a writer's weakness: hope.

I don't need to tell you that writing is a competitive business, and that there's usually a lot of rejection along the path before a novel is bought, a screenplay gets produced, an article is published, or a poem winds up in *The New Yorker*. Scammers know this, and they seize the opportunity to take advantage of a writer's weakness: hope.

Writers dream. We dream of making it to best-seller lists, of our future Academy Awards speeches, of our Nobel Prizes. We also dream of sharing our stories with the world one way or another, and maybe even getting paid to do so. It's common understanding that we need to pay our dues to get there, so when someone—anyone—tells us our work is good, we tend to latch on and let the praise cloud our judgment.

We want to believe that people have good intentions. And, just to put things in perspective, the majority of industry professionals I've dealt with throughout my writing career do have good intentions, and my experiences have been positive the vast majority of the time.

However, just as in any other field, there are sharks. There are even people who don't mean to be sharks, but are so clueless about the business that they'll do you more harm than good. And there are businesses that exist "on the edge"—fulfilling some sort of legitimate role for writers, but misleading writers along the way about the limits of what they offer and the downsides of working with them. My co-author, Daniel Steven, has seen firsthand the financial and emotional wreckage caused by these sharks, semi-sharks, and fellow travelers.

That's what this book is all about—the sharks and how to avoid them. In these pages, you'll find descriptions of various species that could maim or even kill your writing career. You'll learn what to watch out for as well as what sorts of questions to ask. You'll learn how to spot a good offer, what to do if you've already been scammed, how to research a company or individual, and much more.

I hope it will help you navigate a clear path toward your writing goals. The more education and knowledge writers acquire about this industry, the easier it will be to knock the scammers out of business—they'll have no one left to fool! So let's get started, and get you on your way to a successful writing career.

Chapter 1

Agents and Managers: Hone Your Shark-Spotting Skills

Do You Need an Agent?

What a Good Agent Can Do for You

How a Bad Agent Can Hurt You

Deadbeat Agent Warning Signs

How to Research an Agent

As soon as a writer types "fade out" on a screenplay or "the end" on a manuscript, someone, somewhere, tells the writer, "You need an agent!" It's half true.

The Myth

First, let me tell you my own situation: I have a literary agent and a screenwriting manager. I've sold fifteen books to publishers. My agent handled three of those deals for me; I got and negotiated the remaining twelve deals on my own. That includes the authorized biography of Céline Dion—my editor never even asked if I had an agent. I've also had almost all of my screenplays optioned, and my manager negotiated one of those options for me. Again, I got the rest on my own.

So, do you need an agent? No. Would it be nice for you to have an agent? Probably, yes. Especially if you have no prior publication history and you're trying to sell a novel or screenplay. (Nonfiction is easier to sell on your own.)

Most reputable publishers and producers get inundated with unsolicited submissions from hopeful writers. Acquisition of new books and scripts is only one small part of a publisher or producer's work—the bulk of the work is editing, publishing, promoting, and marketing the company's already-bought works.

Thus, we have what's affectionately termed the "slush pile." This is where those unsolicited manuscripts get piled up in a publisher's office, to be dealt with eventually—perhaps during an eclipse on a Tuesday in a leap year. If you're an unknown and unagented writer and you haven't made any personal connection with someone at the company, it's likely that your prized manuscript will land in that slush pile. Sometimes it lives there for only a few weeks before someone gets around to reading it, sometimes months or years; sometimes it never gets read at all.

`A good agent can explain terms to you and do the arguing on your behalf.`

You'll often hear that reputable publishers won't look at unagented submissions. I can disprove that. Before I had an agent—and again after an agent had given up on one of my proposals—I had no problem getting editors at publishing houses to take a look at my work or consider me for assignments. That was true even of the publishers whose "official policy," as stated in Writer's Market or on their own web sites, was to consider agented writers only.

Perhaps twice I received a form letter by return mail to say, "Sorry, we can't read unagented submissions." The rest of the time my work got read and considered at big and small houses alike; all you really need is a terribly enticing pitch, and most editors will gladly take a peek. They just want some reassurance that reading your material won't be a waste of time. Having a good agent is one way to reassure them, but there are other ways—like writing an irresistible pitch, getting a referral from one of their authors, having excellent credits, or speaking to them at writers' conferences.

The Case for Agents

Wait, before you think I'm just insulting agents and telling you they're useless, let me set it straight. There are plenty of good reasons to want an agent, and plenty of things an agent can do for you.

A good agent can help move you out of that vast black hole of the slush pile. A big part of an agent's job is to get to know editors and their needs. Your agent should have a good idea of who's buying what and where your book might belong. And, if your agent has proven to editors that she can deliver what they need, having that agent's name on a cover letter atop your manuscript can be a big bonus. It'll get your work read faster, it'll often get it past the editorial assistants or readers who act as gatekeepers, and it may even influence an editor to give your work a shot if she was otherwise on the fence about it. After all, she trusts this agent's judgment.

The agent will also collect the money for you;
if payments are late, the agent will bug the publisher
and leave you out of it.

And, of course, there's the business end of things. An agent can help you negotiate a better contract—meaning a potentially higher advance and royalty rate, the ability for you to retain subsidiary rights or get a good share of the money from them, a lower reserve on returns, approval of the cover art, and so on. Publishing contracts can be mammoth documents filled with strange language a first-time writer couldn't possibly decode. A good agent can explain terms to you and do the arguing on your behalf.

The agent will also collect the money for you; if payments are late, the agent will bug the publisher and leave you out of it. And she'll decipher your royalty statements to make sure everything's accounted for.

Ideally, an agent will also intervene if you have any clashes with the publisher or producer along the way. The agent may chime in for you if your publisher-appointed publicist isn't returning your calls, if you hate the subtitle they've given your book, or if your book isn't getting the attention it deserves.

And another thing: Agents can find assignments for you without your having to come up with ideas to pitch all the time. My agents have frequently come to me with requests that have come straight from editors: "So-and-so needs a ghostwriter. Are you interested?" "This publisher wants to do a book about cat nutrition." "This publisher is looking for new titles in their series, *Tips from Utter Geniuses*." You probably won't find this information posted publicly; trusted agents get the inside scoop and can help their clients find this kind of work.

You should be able to trust your agent's editorial advice, too—the agent will be the first professional to read your new work and tell you what will make it stronger in the marketplace. The agent doesn't function as a line-by-line editor, but helps you get the proposal, synopsis, script, logline, pitch, novel, or sample chapters in marketable shape so that an editor will have an easier time championing your work.

On the Other Hand

It's not easy to land an established agent. Some will argue that it's harder to get an agent than it is to get a publisher. I may agree with that. Like publishers, good agents often have their hands full already and it's difficult for an unknown writer to get an agent's attention if the manuscript isn't an obvious slam-dunk.

This means that many excellent writers who write works that are tougher sells—short-story collections, children's picture books, memoirs, poetry, niche nonfiction books, cross-genre fiction, etc.—may have a tough time finding a reputable agent. Even writers with more mainstream work may get discouraged by how difficult it is to find solid representation.

But you always have options.

First, as I said earlier, you can send your work directly to publishers and producers yourself. No reason in the world not to. Don't send an entire manuscript or screenplay unsolicited. Instead, send a query letter.

A query letter is a synopsis of your work, armed with an attention-grabbing first sentence and the major beats of your story. It includes any important selling points, such as the specific target audience and how you can reach them, what your background is as a writer and/or any relevant life experience you have, any promised endorsements of your work, and why you think your work fits with their list. In short, it's your sales pitch.

In the case of novels, you may send the query along with a couple of chapters. In the case of nonfiction books, you may send the query with the book proposal (which includes your book's overview, a survey of the competition, information about the target market and how you'll reach them, your bio, an annotated table of contents, and sample material). Or you may choose to just send the query and wait for the editor or producer to request more. Don't waste time and money sending entire manuscripts before an editor requests them. They'll likely land in the trash or, at best, the slush.

You can also ask an attorney to submit your work for you—or to provide you with cover letters that you can send with your work. This appeases the producers and publishers who are afraid to touch unsolicited work because of lawsuit threats. Some producers will ask unrepresented writers to sign release forms that remove the production company's liability if they produce a similar work down the line, whereas others want to deal with a lawyer or agent only. Two screenwriters I know have entertainment attorneys on retainer for just this situation; when they encounter a producer

EDUCATE YOURSELF

Of course, you can also educate yourself. Check out sites like the following:

- **www.starvingartistslaw.com** "The launch pad for artists and writers looking for self-help legal information."

- **www.publishlawyer.com** As well as offering affordable flat-fee legal services for writers, this site also publishes legal articles for writers and editors in plain-speak from Daniel Steven.

- **www.ivanhoffman.com/helpful.html** Provides dozens of articles for writers and publishers about contracts, copyrights, and more.

- **www.nwu.org/bite/gloss.htm** A glossary of terms that may appear on your contract.

- **www.sfwa.org/contracts** The Science Fiction & Fantasy Writers of America provides "model contracts" for anthologies, agents, hardcover books, magazines, paperback books, and the Web.

who requires represented scripts, they have the attorney print off a cover letter on their behalves.

Once you're offered a contract, you can hire a literary or entertainment attorney to review it with you. An attorney will charge you a fee for this, but usually will not be entitled to a percentage of your future earnings for the work. A decent agent does not charge any up-front fees, but does take a cut (usually 10 percent for screenplays, 15 percent for books) of all of your earnings for that work.

Be careful to avoid the temptation of using the friend-of-a-friend attorney who doesn't specialize in publishing or entertainment law, but will give you a discount. That's not good enough. You need someone who is skilled at understanding every nuance of an intellectual property contract.

If you can't afford a lawyer, consider joining the National Writers Union (www.nwu.org) and asking for a free contract advisor. More than once on smaller deals, I've used the NWU's contract advisors' assistance to help me understand publishing contracts and know what changes to request. They will not do the negotiating for you, and they are not lawyers, but they are trained volunteers who have a good, solid understanding of publishing contracts.

You can also try contacting the Volunteer Lawyers for the Arts (www.vlany.org/res_dir.html); if you financially qualify, there are many lawyers who will work pro bono to assist you in situations like these.

How to Sniff Out a Fishy Agent or Manager

Having bad representation can be worse than having no representation at all. Unfortunately, anyone can call himself an agent or manager; there's no degree one must earn or test one must pass. That's why there are important steps a writer needs to take before trusting an agent or manager. Watch out for these warning signs:

Fees

Here's the big one, and I can't stress it enough. Don't ever, ever pay anyone to represent you. It's that simple.

When I began writing, many substandard agents charged "reading fees." Not knowing any better at the time, I paid them. But nowadays, there are plenty of watchdog organizations and individuals who have taught writers that reading fees are bad. It got harder to trick writers into paying a reading fee. So did the agents give up? Heck, no! They just changed the language so writers wouldn't recognize the red flag.

Yog's Law: "Money should flow toward the writer. The only place a writer signs a check is on the back."

You see, agents and managers are supposed to make their money one way: by selling their clients' work. They make money by keeping a percentage of what a writer earns from publishers and producers. They are not supposed to make money by charging a writer fees before work is sold!

Agents today may disguise fees in various ways. They may call it a "representation fee," a "retainer," a "set-up fee," an "evaluation fee," a "marketing fee," or even an "editing fee." They may find all kinds of great excuses to convince you that this fee is worth paying. They'll put up a web page for you! They'll send out lots of submissions on your behalf! They'll make you a big star, baby!

They may tell you that they'll refund your money when your work sells. They may tell you that you're getting charged because you're a first-time writer and it's more work for them to build your career from scratch.

A typical such agency's web site proclaims in capital letters that there are NO READING FEES, but a few sentences later, says this: "Clients pay a one-time $350 Marketing Fee to cover out-of-pocket expenses. Marketing Fees must accompany a signed and dated copy of my Rights Representative contract. Due to increased expenses, foreign writers are accessed a $500 Marketing Fee. This is a one-time fee; writers are never asked for another penny regardless of the amount of time or additional expenses it takes to place a manuscript."

(Nope, I didn't correct the grammar. Why in the world he would think the words "marketing fee" should be capitalized is beyond me.)

And to make it really convenient, right below the submission instructions is a button where you can pay his marketing fee by PayPal immediately! Act now and you'll never be asked for another penny even if he doesn't sell your manuscript for the rest of your life!

	Acceptable Agent Charges	Unacceptable Agent Charges
Types of Charges	• Photocopying • Long-distance calls • Postage • Courier service	• Editing fees • Web site fees • Set-up fees • Travel expenses • Publicity fees
How They Charge	• Itemized bill that's easy to understand and prove • Budget-conscious options • After expenses are incurred, preferably deducted from the advance instead of billed	• Vague categories like "postage" or "marketing" • Unnecessarily expensive options *(like sending every manuscript by FedEx)* • Up front

Pay no attention to "offers" like this. These are lame excuses to get into your wallet. I have trouble with agents who charge for any expenses at all, as, in my opinion, this is part of the cost of an agent's business and shouldn't be passed along to the writer. However, I'll admit that this is an idealistic viewpoint and many perfectly reputable agents do charge their clients nominal fees for submissions expenses. The major difference between what's acceptable and what's not is when and how you're charged.

An agent may charge you $4 for mailing your manuscript to a particular publisher. The agent may not charge you $300 for "postage expenses" without detailing how and when that money was spent. As an alternative to billing you for photocopying expenses, the agent may request that you send several copies of your proposal, manuscript, or script.

Also, you should have agreed to these expenses beforehand. Agents are not allowed to surprise you with bills if you never discussed or signed a contract allowing them to charge you for expenses. In a contract, allowable expenses should be spelled out.

An agent should not make a profit on these "expenses." I once encountered a so-called manager who wanted to charge me $20 per submission. Was he adding lead weights to the packages? I knew darn well I could mail the same script myself for $3.95 by Priority Mail, and even less if I sent it by Media Mail.

Agents who charge up-front fees or exorbitant fees for small expenses have no real incentive to sell your work. This "manager" who wanted to charge me $20 per submission didn't need to sell my work. He just had to find fifty gullible writers and tell them he sent their work out to one hundred producers over the course of a year. Wham—even if he does send all their work by Priority Mail, he's just turned an $80,000 profit.

An "agent" who charges a $200 up-front fee can easily lure in one hopeful writer a day and make $73,000 a year.

In both of these scenarios, the agent has no need to establish any relationships with editors or producers. He has no reason to target submissions well, or to make follow-up calls, do research, or help the writer improve. His only real mission is to keep luring in writers and occasionally throw them a bone that appears promising.

This "bone" can be totally made-up, half-true, or true but inconsequential.

The agent may say, "Hey, I'm sending your work to Random House today!" Sure, could be true, but it means nothing—you could send your work to Random House, too. Doesn't mean it'll get read, doesn't mean anyone's shown interest, doesn't mean a darn thing. Your three-year-old could draw a picture and send it to Random House, too.

The agent might say, "I spoke to an editor at Simon & Schuster about you today, and she's really excited to read your work." Hey, I could tell you the same thing. And maybe I did really get an editor on the phone and she said, "Sure, go ahead and send it" just to get me to stop pestering her. But it sounds good when it comes from a real-live agent, right?

The thing is, publishers and producers aren't fooled by bad agents. They know which ones send them garbage or, at best, completely inappropriate submissions. And having that bad agent attached to your name can only hurt you, because it looks like that's the best you could do.

Poor Writing and Speaking Skills

Once upon a time I leaped before I looked and wound up with a pretty lousy screenwriting agent. She didn't charge fees, so I figured I didn't have anything to lose. Another screenwriting friend of mine signed with her at about the same time I did. This friend took a trip to Los Angeles a few months later and set up some meetings with producers on her own. Boy, did she get an earful.

```
Having bad representation can be worse
than having no representation at all.
```

One of the producers was surprisingly candid with her. He asked her why in the world she signed with this horrible agent, and told her that the agent was a joke in the industry. Her cover letters were full of typos and egregious mistakes, her submissions were untargeted and usually unreadable, and she came across as a total airhead on the phone. Therefore, many producers had taken to "yessing" her to death when they were cornered into speaking with her, but secretly tossing the mail they received from her in the garbage.

I should have seen this coming when she misspelled both my name and my script's title on our contract. I should have seen it coming when she offered to help me edit my script and instead infused it with a ridiculous number of spelling and grammatical errors. I should have thought twice when I spoke with her on the phone and thought she sounded vaguely high on drugs. But I didn't think that hard about it; all I knew was that she didn't charge me any fees and she liked my work.

Until my friend came home with her story, I hadn't really thought about what kind of first impression she was making on my behalf. How unprofessional she must have seemed. If she made those bordering-on-illiterate errors on my manuscript and contract, of course her cover letters must have been shamefully embarrassing. What editor or producer would take her submissions seriously?

Lack of Credits

This same agent had one legitimate sale listed on her web site, as well as a few options, which is what convinced me to approach her in the first place.

I thought that was sufficient evidence that the woman knew what she was doing.

What I learned later was that the writer with the legitimate sale had actually made the deal on her own; she just called in the agent to negotiate after it was already in progress. I have no idea about the options, but I do know that none of those scripts have gone on to be produced, and that any writer can submit to the production companies she listed without having representation. For all I know, they may have been free options.

When you check out an agent, after determining that the agent doesn't charge up-front fees and is reasonably professional in her presentation, the next most important thing is to check out her credits. That is, what has she sold and to whom? This should never be a secret.

A new agent should be willing to be honest with you; if she has few or no sales yet, what does she have to prove to you that she is capable of selling your work? Maybe she's worked as an editor, sales director, or in another such position at a publishing house. Maybe she's an experienced author who has built up contacts with several publishers. Maybe she's worked at

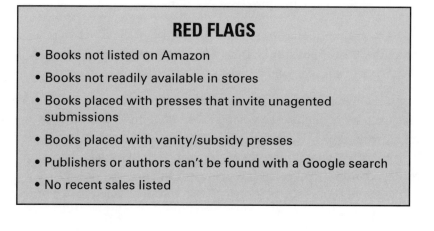

a book packaging firm, or as an agent's assistant, or as a publicist. In any case, ask her directly about any industry experience she has and take it into careful consideration. There's nothing wrong with being new to a career, there's just something wrong with pretending you're experienced when you're not.

Any agent who's been at it for a while and won't tell you about past book sales probably doesn't have any. There's no good reason to avoid naming names; the agent presumably wants her authors to sell books, right? And to sell books, people have to know the book exists. Most agents are thrilled to mention the names of clients' books at every chance they get; you may go out and buy the books, and that helps the author and the agent make more money. There's no issue of "privacy" at stake, so don't be fooled by an agent who says she doesn't divulge past sales out of respect for her authors' privacy. If you hear, "My client list is confidential," assume that means, "My past clients hate me."

Any agent who's been at it for a while and won't tell you about past book sales probably doesn't have any.

Now let's assume you have found a list of sales this agent has claimed. Don't stop there. Don't be wooed by a list of titles alone. It's up to you to do a little research now, and the Internet has made it easier than ever.

Hop on Amazon. Look up the titles.

First, be sure the titles are even there. Unless the books haven't been published yet, it's a really bad sign if a book isn't even listed on Amazon. It's not hard to get a book listed on Amazon.

Once you find listings, scroll straight down to "Product Details" and find out who the publisher is. If it's a big-name publisher you've heard of, great. Score one for the agent. If it's not, dig further.

Type the name of the publisher, in quotation marks, into Google or your search engine of choice. See what comes up. Is this a publisher with any sort of track record? Have they published more than one or two books? Is the author the owner of the company? (Bad sign; the agent didn't have to work too hard for that sale!) If they have a submissions link, check it out. Do they invite open submissions? (If so, you don't need an agent to get your work read there.) Do they ask for agented submissions only? (That's a better indicator that the agent was essential to the sale.)

Do this with several titles; check out what kinds of publishers the agent has sold to. If they're mostly small presses, decide for yourself if that's appropriate for your goals. There are plenty of reputable small presses, but be aware that they typically don't pay high advances or have much of a budget for publicity. However, if you have a niche book, a small press specializing in your niche may be your best option.

Don't be wooed by a list of titles alone.
It's up to you to do a little research now,
and the Internet has made it easier than ever.

Possibly the biggest red flag an agent can toss up is listing vanity-published or "co-op"-published titles in their sales. If an agent lists books published by iUniverse, Xlibris, Trafford, or Booklocker, for example, where authors actually pay to publish, this is not an agent you want representing you. Of course you could go to vanity presses on your own; there's absolutely no reason for an agent to get involved. Same for quasi-vanity publishers like PublishAmerica; again, there's no reason for an agent ever to list this as a sale.

One of the fee-charging agents has quite a list of "recent sales" on his web site. You might be tempted to pay his fee, considering his success rate, right? Except that when you look up the titles, you'll find that one after another was published by PublishAmerica, an author mill that's known to accept utter garbage without reading it and take pride in the fact that they churn out thousands of new books a year that typically sell fewer than one hundred copies apiece.

Any author can submit a manuscript to publishers like these, so it's a silly way for agents to make it look like they've made sales. If new writers have never heard of the vanity and subsidy presses and don't do their homework, they may not realize that the agent hasn't made legitimate deals.

On Writing-World.com, J. A. Hitchcock reports the sad tale of one author who got roped in by the pseudo-agency Canadian Literary Associates after seeing an ad of theirs in *The New York Times*. He got the call he'd always dreamed of: The agency told him they'd sold his book to Commonwealth

Publications. The author was thrilled to tears until he got the contract—which demanded money for publication. He questioned his agent; he was told that this was a legitimate new press that sought "cooperative publishing" with authors. So he signed and paid . . . to the tune of 61,000 Canadian dollars, before he discovered that Canadian Literary Associates owned Commonwealth.

His book never made it to bookstores, and he sued the company. They were ordered to pay back the money, but soon declared bankruptcy. Commonwealth lost a class-action lawsuit organized by their authors in 1998 and was ordered to pay plaintiffs a total of $10 million, but never did.

Legitimate agents never refer writers to vanity, co-op, or subsidy publishers. A literary agency that did this would quickly run out of money due to the lack of an advance and very low potential royalties unless they were receiving kickbacks from the company or had some kind of ownership, partnership, or other financial stake in the press.

You can also take a look at the sales ranks of the agent's titles. A rank in the millions is poor and means the author probably hasn't sold more than a handful of books on Amazon. If there's no rank listed at all, the book hasn't sold a single copy on Amazon. Anything better than 100,000 is respectable in my opinion, but 10,000 and under is where the action really is.

```
Legitimate agents never refer writers to vanity,
          co-op, or subsidy publishers.
```

Don't get too caught up in the Amazon ranks, though—they're not the end-all of the book sales world, and they're often hard to interpret. Some books sell a lot better off bookstore shelves, while others are heavily promoted online but may not appear on bookstore shelves at all. Just consider this one more factor in establishing whether or not the agent is for you. If all the books she's represented rank in the millions, that's a bad sign.

Referrals to Editing Services

If an agent or manager tells you your work could use some editing, fine. If the agent or manager suggests you hire an editor, fine. But if the agent or manager refers you to a specific editor, book doctor, packager, or editorial company, consider that a big red flag.

There have been several cases where an agent received a kickback for referring writers to editorial services. And usually, a fraudulent agent would refer all writers to these editorial firms in the hopes of making money off of the writers. Many times, the "agents" wouldn't even read the manuscripts—they'd just respond with a letter praising the writer, but suggesting editorial services. Hang around writers' message boards, and you'll find people comparing letters that appear personal on the surface, but turn out to be form letters.

"Your work has great potential," such a letter might start. "The characters are well-developed, but it has some structural problems and holes in the plot that will hinder its sales potential. It's very close to a publishable manuscript, but just needs a little professional fine-tuning. I suggest you bring this to XYZ Editorial services and work with an editor there. Then I'd be happy to reconsider it for representation."

The agent dangles the carrot: "If you hire this editor, there's a good chance I'll represent you and sell your book." Fat chance. An agent who needs to make money on kickbacks for referrals is not an agent you want. Again, the agent should make money solely when his authors make sales; relationships with editorial services like these are a conflict of interest. If an agent truly believes your work has great potential but needs professional editing, he should leave it up to you to decide if you want to spend that money—and to choose whichever editor you want—or to work on the editing yourself.

The agent dangles the carrot: "If you hire this editor, there's a good chance I'll represent you and sell your book."

One notorious case involved a New York editing firm known as Edit Ink. In 1997, New York State Attorney General Dennis Vacco knew something was amiss when he found out about this company through the complaints of several writers who realized they'd been scammed. He solicited affidavits from writers and even sent one writer on an "undercover mission" to prove the company was a fraud. He discovered that more than 3,600 writers had been referred to Edit Ink, and that the company grossed about $5.5 million dollars from these writers.

What's even worse is that the principals of Edit Ink had actually enlisted friends and family to pose as fake agents and publishers, soliciting authors' work online and even in reputable newspapers like *The New York Times*. When an author responded, the fakes would make the referral, send Edit Ink the writer's address (so they could send a brochure), and take 15 percent of the fee Edit Ink extracted from the hopeful writer.

For $5 a page, the underpaid and under-experienced "book doctors" at Edit Ink would . . . well, edit, to the best of their limited ability. Then, when the writer resubmitted the now-edited work, the agent would reject it for one reason or another.

The New York State Supreme Court convicted Edit Ink of fraud, false advertising, and deceptive business practices and ordered the five people who ran the company to pay millions of dollars in restitution and civil penalties. A state appeals court upheld the ruling, but the issue of refunding money to the duped writers was not resolved.

Advertising

Legitimate agents do not need to pay for advertising. Any agent with a solid track record already has more mail than he can handle coming in from writers seeking representation. On the slim chance that a reputable agent needs more writers, that agent may turn to publications for writers to ask them to post a call for submissions or list him in a directory. Editors of writers' publications are more than happy to post invitations for writers to submit to legitimate agents, and I can't think of any writers' publication that would charge for this kind of posting.

The warning lights flash on when an "agent" is paying for advertising with Google AdWords or similar services, or when an "agent" sends spam (unsolicited email) to members of online writing groups or message boards encouraging them to submit work, or paying for classified ads with headlines like, "You could get published! New authors wanted!"

You may even get direct mail solicitations from a fraudulent agent who bought your name from a mailing list sold by a contest or publication for writers. There are even reports of scammers who got their lists from the Library of Congress' Copyright Office. In short, any "agent" who sends you a generic letter seeking submissions is not someone you want to have representing you.

I'm not even an agent and I get requests for representation at least twice a month. So many writers are desperate for representation that they'll approach anyone vaguely connected to the publishing industry. No legitimate agent in his right mind would purposely pay to add more inexperienced writers to his slush pile.

Agents don't need flashy headlines and alluring web sites with "New writers welcome! Submit here!" buttons. Even new (legitimate) agents just need to put out the word to a couple of authors or editors, and submissions will pour in.

So avoid the temptation to submit to an agent just because he looks so welcoming. The agents you want are the ones you have to work to find, not the ones who come to unknown writers begging for submissions.

What it comes down to is that most agents who advertise all over the place are doing something seedy. Around the same time as the Edit Ink mess, a fraudulent agency called the Woodside Literary Agency was doing a fine job of luring in unsuspecting writers through advertising and sending spam to members of writers' lists.

Woodside charged a reading fee (up to $150), then praised the writer's work, while lying to writers about how selective they were. They claimed to accept only 5 percent of submissions when the truth was that they accepted any scribbling anyone sent their way (as long as it included payment!). They passed themselves off as industry insiders, but in fact had never sold anything.

They'd then offer a contract—which came with a $250 bill for "contract fees." Writers who attempted to warn others about this company became Woodside's targets for harassment and cyber-stalking.

New York State Attorney General Eliot Spitzer ordered Woodside out of business in 1999 and ruled that they make restitution to writers and penalties for breaking consumer protection laws. A year later, two of the people who ran Woodside were arrested on criminal charges of conspiracy to commit mail fraud and perjury.

This, of course, goes back to my first rule: Never, ever pay anyone for representation. No matter how they butter you up and no matter what they promise you.

General Incompetence

Then, too, there are the agents who aren't out to scam you and really do want to sell your work . . . but they have no clue how to do it. Some people just wake up one morning and decide, "Hey, I like to read. I could be a literary agent!"

They have no particular connections, they don't know what's selling and what's not, they live in Idaho and drive school buses by day and read manuscripts by night. Hey, everyone's entitled to a dream. But you don't need to get your dream wrapped up in theirs. In cases like these, once you've realized your agent isn't much of an agent, it's best to cut your losses as soon as possible, even if it means going it alone again.

Once you've realized your agent isn't much of an agent,
it's best to cut your losses as soon as possible,
even if it means going it alone again.

There's no good reason to tie up your work with an incompetent agent. It's generally not too difficult to get out of a contract with an agent, although it may take some time. Many agents require one- to six-months' written notice of termination; other agency agreements have terms of one to three years; still others just require that you submit the cancellation request in writing. The agent has the right to continue collecting commissions on any deals she's already made for you (which probably isn't a factor if you're ditching her for incompetence), and you're free to seek representation elsewhere.

One of the problems with bad agenting is that it makes the job of a good agent harder. Let's say your bad agent already submitted your work to several publishing houses. Even if the editors at those houses were prejudiced against your work because it came from a boob of an agent (or an unknown agent), even if no one actually read your work, a legitimate agent may hold this against you.

Your work has now been "shopped around," even if it was shopped incompetently. Agents don't like to represent work that's already been around the block. They're not likely to send it to the same houses the bad agent already sent it to, because it makes them look dumb if an editor remembers it was submitted (and rejected) earlier. Sometimes manuscripts are recorded, so even if the agent submits to a different editor at the house, she'll know that her company has already turned it down. This can jeopardize the agent's relationship with the editor; the editor doesn't want an agent to bother her with work that has already been rejected.

It's not always complete doom and gloom, though. One of my co-authors had an agent who was unable to sell his book proposal before he came to me for help. I spiffed up the proposal and sent it to a new agent. The new agent loved it. When he asked who had seen it already, a lump formed in my throat as I spilled the truth: It had already been represented and shopped around to most of the major houses. But, I was quick to add, they saw an old version of the proposal before I was on board, and the ex-agent was demanding too much money for the book.

The new agent appreciated my honesty, agreed to represent the book, and sold it to the first editor he sent it to at a great publishing house.

So all is not lost if you realize your agent isn't much help to you; just don't make the situation worse by allowing him to send your work to every publisher in America before you finally pull the plug. You and your new agent want to have some options left!

Mailing Address

Many writers assume that a real literary agent must be based in New York City, and a real screenwriting agent must be based in Los Angeles.

It's true that the bulk of the publishing world is in New York and the film world is in L.A. So it stands to reason that an agent who lives in those places has more opportunities to make connections, go to meetings, attend parties, and so on.

However, and this is a big however: it's not necessary for an agent to work in those cities to be successful. In fact, neither of the agents I work with are anywhere near New York—one's based in Dallas, Texas, and the other is based in Washington, D.C., and both frequently make deals with all the biggest New York houses.

The Dallas agent makes trips to New York often. He makes contacts over the phone and by email, and he flies into Manhattan to accompany clients on meetings and have lunch with important editors. His agency represents many top celebrities, and his location hasn't been any sort of problem.

My D.C. agent makes nearly all of her deals by phone and email. She's worked in other areas of the publishing industry, so she already had good contacts when she started. She doesn't find it necessary to move her business, and says the Internet has changed everything as far as deal making goes.

You're more likely to run into problems when you're dealing with a new agent who lives far from the hubs. If the person has few contacts to begin with, it's possible to network by phone and email alone, but it's certainly harder. Editors like a personal touch, and getting some face time with decision makers can boost an agent's stature. Editors are more likely to give priority to works hand-delivered by agents they know, or mailed by agents they've had lunch with and liked.

Aside from noting the city, though, look at the rest of the address. Is it a home address? Bad sign. Is it a post office box? Bad sign—this enables an agent to run off to Tahiti and be virtually untrackable.

Web Sites and Email

Not every good agency has a web site, but most do. The site may provide you with more clues as to how successful the agency is.

I would flat-out ignore any agency with a free site—you know, the kind hosted by Geocities or Homestead or AOL with the really long URLs and banner ads. A domain name is not expensive; an agency that can't afford to pay for its own domain and inexpensive hosting fees is probably not doing much business.

If a web site appears to be professionally designed, that's a plus in my book. A site that appears to have been created by the agent's twelve-year-old son is likely another clue that the business isn't booming.

The agency's site should not offer any services beyond agenting. If half of the web site is about the agency and the other half contains descriptions of paid services (coverage, manuscript evaluation, etc.), you'd best believe that the agency is not making enough money the right way—by selling clients' work. Agents shouldn't need a "side business" that involves profiting from writers.

The email address can be telling, too. One editor reports that she hates getting emails from agents who use personal addresses like "dougnkim@cyber.net." "It makes the agent look rinky-dink," she says. It's preferable for an agent to have a business domain-based email, and not a free address from Hotmail or Yahoo.

Put yourself in an editor's shoes. What image is this agency portraying? If an agency wants to be taken seriously, it had better project a professional image at every turn.

The Total Picture

When evaluating a potential agent, take all of these factors into account. One strike against an editor doesn't necessarily mean the agent is wrong for you. But if you add up these factors and begin to see an overall picture that looks crooked (lives in Iowa, past book sales are to small presses and not ranked well on Amazon, free web site, and so on), it's time to move on and keep looking for your match.

Chapter 2

Agents and Managers:
How to Spot a Good One

Where to Find Hot-Shot Agents

Online Agent Databases

What to Ask Before You Sign

Getting References

Now that we've talked about some of the warning signs
that should alert you to a bad agent, let's figure out
how to find a good one.

Directories and databases are a great place to research agents. While there is no definitive source that requires absolutely no cross-referencing or further research, there are several good guides that can start you on your quest. Guides provide far more reputable agents than disreputable ones. Understand that I found my first bum agent in one of these directories; at the time, I assumed that inclusion in a directory meant the agent was reputable. There are a small number of lousy agents who sneak into almost every one of these guides. Use them to pick up names and contact information, but always do further research on your own before signing with anyone.

DIRECTORIES AND DATABASES

- **Agent Query (www.agentquery.com)** A free, searchable directory of about 600 agents with verified credentials. Well-researched and includes extensive profile information. Don't miss this one!

- **Guide to Literary Agents** An annual directory published by Writer's Digest Books, this book provides contact information and guidelines for more than 400 literary and screenwriting agents who claim not to charge any up-front fees.

- **Jeff Herman's Guide to Book Editors, Publishers, and Literary Agents . . . Who They Are! What They Want! And How to Win Them Over!** Lists more than 150 agencies with information about what they represent and who the agents are; many listings are in-depth and personal.

- **Hollywood Representation Directory** Updated twice a year, this book is the one to get if your primary area of interest is screenwriting. Provides contact information for pre-screened agents, managers, and attorneys. it is also available online at www.hcdonline.com.

- **www.aaronline.org** This is the Agent Database of the Association of Authors' Representatives (AAR), a not-for-profit organization of literary and dramatic agents. As of this writing, there are 350 agents in the database, and it's free to search. Contact information includes postal addresses, web site addresses, and email addresses if the agent accepts email queries. The profiles tell you if they're accepting new clients and what they represent.

- **www.wga.org/agency/AgencyList.html** This is the searchable database of Writers Guild of America, west (WGAw) signatory agencies, and is a good place to look for basic contact information if you're a screenwriter. Agencies on this list have agreed not to charge reading fees or similar fees for dramatic work. You can call the WGA's Agency Department at (323) 782-4502 to ask about an agent's status or to report a fee-charging agent who claims to be signatory to the Guild.

- **Literary Market Place** This is an annually published book industry directory that contains information about agents, publishers, distributors, and so on. It's a mammoth reference book with a mammoth price tag (about $300), so check for it at your library.

Where to Look for the Hotshots

Publishers Weekly

I don't know many new writers who read *Publishers Weekly*. It's a shame, really, because all this great agent information is going to waste on people who are already industry insiders.

When a rep from a hot agency breaks out and starts his own agency, *Publishers Weekly* reports it. When a former editor hops the fence and becomes an agent, an agency expands into a new location, an agent switches houses, or a promising new agent appears on the scene, *Publishers Weekly* gets the scoop. And they get it long before the annual print directories could tell you about it.

The reason all of this is delicious information for writers is that agents who've moved, started their own agencies, or just been promoted from assistant-hood are much more likely to be open to submissions because their client lists are not yet full. A new agent at a well-known agency is hungry to make a name for himself, and the best way to do that is to discover an amazing new author who takes the literary world by storm. Find out who he is and what he wants in those first couple of months, before every other writer hears about him and his desk is piled to the ceiling with their pitches.

It's expensive to subscribe to *Publishers Weekly* (currently $225 a year if you subscribe on their web site, or $199 at Amazon.com), so if you can't afford it, check to see if your library carries it (they probably do, though it may be behind the desk). If they don't, ask them to carry it! You can also buy copies at most chain bookstores or access it online at www.publishersweekly.com.

On Acknowledgment Pages

Perhaps the very best way to find yourself a good agent is to figure out who represents authors whose styles or genres are close to yours. For example, if you write thrillers, look for successful thriller authors whose work bears some similarity to your own. If you write self-help books, check out self-help authors.

Many authors thank their agents on their acknowledgment pages or mention the agent on their web sites. See here for an example: www.authorsden.com/earlmerkel. Suspense novelist Earl Merkel mentions right at the end of his biography that his agent is Kimberley Cameron of the Reece Halsey Literary Agency. Better yet, he also mentions that his debut novel *(Final Epidemic)* hit national best-seller lists two weeks after its publication in 2002.

Now for the slightly tricky part: You don't want to approach the agents of your direct competitors. That is, if you've written a book proposal about how to get a better night's sleep naturally, you shouldn't approach the agent who represented the book *How to Sleep Soundly Tonight*. That puts the agent in a bad position, because if he takes you on as a client, two of his authors will be competing against each other in the marketplace.

However, you can certainly approach agents who've represented books about stress reduction, nutrition, meditation, and so on. These may be peripherally related topics, but not direct competitors. And if your writing style is strongly reminiscent of an already-established novelist—let's say Anna Quindlen—her agent probably isn't your best bet. Amanda Urban already has one Anna Quindlen. On the off-chance that you managed to catch Amanda's attention, you'd probably play second fiddle to her more-established client.

Perhaps the very best way to find yourself a good agent is to figure out who represents authors whose styles or genres are close to yours.

If you're a first-time author, your best bet is to look for recent books published by debut authors. In other words, if a new novelist makes a splash on the literary scene in a genre close to yours, pay attention to who represented that novelist and pounce quickly before the agent's list fills up. You've just figured out that this agent is (or recently was) open to previously unpublished authors and has the ability to launch an author's career. Double whammy.

Once you have a name of an agent who's captured your attention, you can type the agent's name into Google or look him up in the directories mentioned in the beginning of this chapter on page 27 to find contact information and further details.

From Editors

If you're fortunate enough to attract the attention of an editor before you have an agent, you can ask the editor for suggestions about which agents he trusts and likes working with. Often the editor will chime in with, "Oh, I'd be happy to refer you to so-and-so. I've worked with her on several books."

The editor doesn't mind doing this because it's a favor the agent will likely repay. By giving the agent a sure deal and a new client, the editor knows that agent will probably think of him when another client has a hot new project ready to market.

Of course, once you have a deal offer from an editor, it automatically becomes a whole lot easier to interest agents on your own. Usually, you can even bypass the whole query-and-wait procedure by making a few phone calls or sending emails to briefly introduce yourself and announce that there's a deal on the table.

Memberships

Membership in the AAR (Association of Authors' Representatives) or the WGA (Writers Guild of America) is a good sign. All agents who join the AAR are required to adhere to the organization's Canon of Ethics, which you can find at www.aar-online.org. Among other things, this canon states, "The AAR believes that the practice of literary agents charging clients or potential clients for reading and evaluating literary works (including out-lines, proposals, and partial or complete manuscripts) is subject to serious abuse that reflects adversely on our profession." Therefore, members are prohibited from charging these fees. Members also agree not to engage in any business that may be a conflict of interest or to receive "secret profits" in connection with any transaction involving a client.

In addition, AAR members promise that their books of account will be open to clients at all times, that payments will be made in a timely manner (within ten business days of a check's clearance, in most cases), and that they'll have separate bank accounts for money due authors.

If an agent claims to be an AAR or WGA member, be sure to double-check it with the associations' lists. There have been a few cases of fraudulent agents falsely claiming to be members.

Why Not a Member?

There may be legitimate reasons why an agent is not a member of the AAR or WGA. There are certain qualifications agents must meet before applying for membership. In the case of the AAR, some of the important qualifications are as follows:

- The agent must have been working as a literary or dramatic agent as a primary business for at least two years.

- The agent must have been responsible for authors' deals on ten or more literary properties in the preceding eighteen months, or five or more stage productions for playwrights in the preceding two years.

In other words, you may encounter a newer agent who does adhere to the AAR's Canon of Ethics and has made sales, but hasn't been in business long enough or made enough deals yet to qualify for membership. There are also some agents who choose not to belong even though they do qualify. There are annual dues and an initiation fee, and it's possible that some agents disagree with AAR's stances but remain trustworthy and capable agents.

If you encounter an agent you like, but that agent isn't an AAR member, it's worth asking why. Don't expect a seedy agent to come out and tell you, "It's because I rip off my authors and have made only two sales and refer writers to my wife for editing services." However, an honest agent may ease your mind by telling you that her membership application is in the works or that she's just a few months shy of qualifying.

Double-Checking

You'll notice I said earlier that you still need to do some research and cross-reference the listings you find in any of these publications or web sites. That's because of a few things: (a) a couple of sneaky bad agents usually worm their way into these directories because they're good at covering up their shady sides, (b) agents who used to adhere to AAR or WGA standards may decide to start charging fees or other such unsavory practices later, (c) previously decent agencies occasionally get sold to undesirable people, and (d) an agent's contact information and needs may change.

It's not often that a good agent goes bad, but it does happen occasionally. I ran into a WGA-signatory agency that had recently started charging up-front fees; the WGA had taken them off their official list, but hadn't revoked their membership. Instead, the Guild let them accumulate "warnings." The agency was still technically signatory because it had met all the requirements at the time they joined—so the agency's web site proudly declared that it was a WGA-signatory agency and the WGA didn't complain. A friend of mine was blinded enough by the "WGA-signatory" stamp of approval that he paid an agent about $4,000 before realizing he'd been scammed.

Similarly, a screenwriting agency that had some legitimate sales was apparently sold to a less-than-legitimate proprietor who promptly began charging representation fees. And more than one formerly reputable literary agent succumbed to the temptation of making some money "on the side" by engaging in editorial firms' kickback schemes.

So it's important to double-check the information you find anywhere, even from trusted sources. It's impossible for even the most savvy writers and editors of guides to do complete background checks on every agent, and even editors get lied to when compiling directories like these. An editor may ask straight-out, "Do you charge any up-front fees?" and the agent may respond, "No," based on whatever technicality he's devised to rationalize the practice. ("It's not an up-front fee . . . it's a retainer!")

Where to Do Your Homework

Luckily, there are many ways for writers to check on an agent's track record and reputation, and most are free.

Agent Research & Evaluation

www.agentresearch.org

Provides free "agent verification." Click on their "services" link and you'll find various agent-related research they'll do for you. The more in-depth research is a paid service, but they'll be happy to check public records for you to find out if an agent has a track record of sales. They'll also tell you if they've received any complaints about that agent. In addition, you can subscribe to their (paid) newsletter, which includes in-depth information about reputable agents ten times a year.

Writer Beware

---

www.writerbeware.com

Sponsored by the Science Fiction & Fantasy Writers of America, this organization maintains extensive databases of agents, publishers, and editors, with the intention of helping to expose bad practices and steer writers away from fraud.

The site includes alerts for writers, general tips about what to look out for, and case studies. You can write to the volunteers who run this web site to ask for background information about an agent you're interested in, or to report shady practices you've encountered in the literary world. They'll tell you what they know—free. Victoria Strauss and A. C. Crispin, both well-published authors who are dedicated to helping writers, run the site.

Publishers Marketplace

---

www.publishersmarketplace.com

Publishers Marketplace is a service of PublishersLunch. PublishersLunch is a free daily newsletter that tracks literary and film deals; it reports on what was sold to whom and which agent sold it. Publishers Marketplace offers premium services by paid subscription ($15 per month as of this writing). Both services can be tremendously beneficial to writers.

At Publishers Marketplace, it's free to view member profiles. As of this writing, 192 agents have profiles on this site. Profiles show an agent's contact information, bio, specialties, clients, best-known projects, most recent sales, sub-agents, and submission requirements. Agents are listed here voluntarily, so if they've provided submission guidelines, they're open to new clients. This is an easy way to check on an agent's track record. Take note of who the clients are and which publishers the agent sells to.

If you sign up for the paid version, you can search their deal archives. I've found this particularly helpful when friends have asked me for agent recommendations. I'll ask them which authors they identify with, then look up those authors' names to find out which agents have represented them.

Reading PublishersLunch will give you an idea of who the "hot" agents are and what they're selling. Deals are categorized into fiction, nonfiction, and film rights, then sorted according to the rate of advance the author receives; a "nice deal" is anything up to $100,000, and a "major deal" is $500,000 and up, for example. By taking note of these categories, you can figure out which agents command the highest advances, and which ones don't seem to move beyond the "nice" distinction. A huge added bonus is that most of the time, the agent's email address is included with each listing.

It's impossible for even the most savvy writers and editors of guides to do complete background checks on every agent, and even editors get lied to when compiling directories like these.

Even this service is imperfect; anyone can report a deal, and the listings are not verified. Therefore, a few bum deals do make it through to the listings. For example, when I posted a list of recently announced deals, Victoria Strauss (scam-hunter extraordinaire) noted that one was by an agent who charged up-front fees, and the publisher didn't pay an advance and had "issues" about missing royalty payments. However, the majority of deals reported here are legitimate and to large and mid-size publishing houses.

Absolute Write "Bewares & Background Check"

---

www.absolutewrite.com

Click on "forum," then scroll down to "Bewares & Background Check." This is where writers can read and post information and warnings about agents, editors, producers, publishers, etc. Toward the top, there's an index to the entire board, or you can use the "search" box to check the archives to find out if the agent or agency you're researching has been mentioned before. If not, feel free to post a question to ask if others have experience with the agent or agency.

Preditors and Editors

www.anotherealm.com/prededitors

This is a mammoth site maintained by author David L. Kuzminski on a volunteer basis. Here, you can search through listings of agents, publishers, and other industry professionals worldwide. The listings are alphabetized and web site links or contact information is provided when known. David puts a dollar sign ($) in the listings when he has been able to confirm that the agent has made legitimate sales.

If he has received complaints about a particular person or company, he investigates—and if it turns out that the company has violated any of the criteria he sets forth in his evaluation form, he'll mark the person or company "Not recommended," often with a reason noted (such as "charges fees"). If he has a particularly positive experience with a company, he'll mark it "Recommended." Many listings have neither designation, and some include author notes. There aren't any bios or submission guidelines here, but it's definitely a spot to check when you're ready to investigate an agent.

Had this site been around when I began writing, it would have saved me some heartache: Nearly every shady company I've ever dealt with in the literary and screenwriting world has a "Not recommended" tag. Don't ever sign with an agent before checking here first.

SFF Net

www.sff.net

This is a site with reliable information for writers. It's populated by a high proportion of published pros who write genre fiction, but new writers are welcome. Here, you can participate in discussions with professional authors, publishers, and editors in personal newsgroups that can be read with a newsreader rather than exclusively on the Web. You're welcome to ask questions about agents or publishers.

Better Business Bureau (BBB)

www.bbb.org

I left this one for last because first, few agencies are listed here, and second, they let a lot of bad companies slip through. The BBB is nearly useless for writers. Often, companies I know are disreputable and sleazy are listed as having a "satisfactory" record with the BBB. It can often take many, many complaints before a business gets an unsatisfactory rating. Why? Membership in the BBB is paid; once a business pays its membership fee, it seems the company holds a "get out of jail free" card when it comes to ratings. And even if they receive numerous complaints, as long as the company responds (not resolves the situation—just responds to it!), the BBB considers it solved. It's also easy for some companies to escape formerly bad ratings. PublishAmerica had an unsatisfactory listing, but somehow ditched it when they became BBB members in 2005.

However, it's always worth a check; when I searched for Creative Literary Agency in Michigan, for example, I found that the company has an unsatisfactory rating due to an unresolved complaint alleging the company didn't live up to terms of their contract.

When to Start Your Homework

I'm not suggesting that you do a thorough background check on every agent you plan to query. After all, you'll probably need to query many agents before finding one who's right for you. It's a waste of time to spend hours checking every possible resource to make sure an agent is a saint, only to get back a form letter that says, "Sorry, I'm not taking on any new clients right now."

If you've found an agent's profile or contact information in a reputable place (not just from a random Internet search or in a classified ad), just a few minutes of digging around to make sure the agent isn't a notorious scammer and has some legitimate credits is fine for the time being.

But once the agent has shown some sort of an interest or requested more material from you, that's the time to do a more in-depth search. Don't wait until the agent has offered you a contract before figuring out you wasted your time and postage. Not to mention that the excitement of the possibility of representation may put a rose tint on those detective glasses of yours. To put it another way, the time to figure out if your boyfriend is a criminal is before he flashes the shiny engagement ring. Shininess can be blinding.

Questions You Need to Have Answered Before Signing

Don't treat an agent to an in-depth inquisition before she's determined she wants to represent you. A legitimate agent will usually be put off if you ask her a hundred questions about her background before she's even read your work. Not only does she not have time to field these inquiries from every prospective writer, but it can make you look lazy or ignorant if the answers are easily available with a little research.

QUESTIONS TO ASK A PROSPECTIVE AGENT

- How long have you been an agent? (If less than three years, what did you do before you were an agent?)
- How many clients do you have?
- How many properties have you sold this year?
- Which publishers have you sold to?
- Have you sold much work in my genre before?
- Where do you think my work belongs?
- Realistically, what kind of deal do you hope to get for my book?
- What's your commission?
- Do you charge for expenses, and if so, which expenses, when, and about how much?
- Do you have any sub-agents or foreign rights associates?
- Will you keep me apprised of all submissions and responses?
- How often should I expect to communicate with you, and how do you prefer to communicate (phone or email)?
- Are you signing me for one project, or will you represent all of my work?
- What happens if I get an offer on my own? Are you still entitled to a full commission?
- If our relationship doesn't work out, how is the contract terminated?

Begin with doing as much of your homework on your own as you can; the answers to many of these questions should be easy to attain by searching the Web, looking at the agent's own web site, reading agent guides, or asking fellow writers.

Get References

Finally, after you've been offered representation and before you accept, check in with a couple of the agent's current clients. It's best not to ask the agent for references—if she gives you any, of course it'll be clients who are happy with her. Better to take a look at the agent's list of clients or sold properties and hunt down the authors yourself. Many authors today have web sites of their own, or an email address listed somewhere or other on the Internet. Write brief and cordial notes to these authors along these lines:

"Mary Canary has just offered me representation, and I'm thrilled. Before I accept, though, I wanted to check in with you to ask if you've been happy with her. I noticed on her profile that you're a client of hers. Please forgive me if this is too personal a question, but I'd love to hear your impressions of her."

If her clients rave about her and say she's made lucrative deals for them, you can now rest easy. All your homework is done, and all that's left is gut instinct: Is this agent right for you? Are you ready to commit? If so, it's time for you to get back to writing and let the agent do the selling!

When Caution Turns to Paranoia

Janet Reid of JetReidLiterary applauds when writers take time to learn what to look for in a literary agency. "Lord knows there are some fishy people out there who really want to separate authors from their hard-earned cash," she says. "Sometimes, however, wariness can slip over into unproductive cynicism. For example, I had a prospective client rewrite the offer contract I sent him (in and of itself a very bad move). He wanted to include a clause that said 'the agent won't do anything to damage the value of the book.' Now, when you think about that statement, it's clear he's coming at this process with the idea that he has to fend off villains left and right.

"Most agents, and certainly the good ones, are on your team. We want you to succeed. In fact, our income depends on it. Yes, there are sharks in the water, but it's still safe to swim."

Chapter 3

Paying to Publish: Vanity and Subsidy Presses

What Is a Vanity Press?

Watch Out For Fringe Publishers

What About Print On Demand?

The Truth About Vanities

Self-publishing As an Alternative

"Publishing houses are evil! They won't give new writers
a chance and they want to rip off writers and steal
all the profits! It could take years for them to publish
your book even after you have a contract. You'll lose
all editorial control. They won't help you publicize
your book, either, and unless you're Stephen King, you
can't get a decent advance. They're trying to keep new
writers out of their own little elitist club!"
Any of that sound familiar?

It's the rhetoric espoused by many of today's vanity and subsidy presses. Mind you, they rarely call themselves vanity or subsidy presses anymore. They may call themselves POD publishers, on-demand publishers, co-op publishers, independent publishers, or self-publishing companies.

Regardless of what they call themselves, vanity presses are usually easy to recognize: You have to pay them to publish your work. This payment may be in the form of up-front set-up fees, copyright fees, cover art fees, editing fees, printing fees, or even the cost of purchasing copies of your own book.

The Trendy Way to Publish

Vanity publishing is not a new concept. It's just that years ago, the printers who would take authors' manuscripts and turn them into bound books charged a lot more to do so because they used offset printing processes. This meant that they had to print many books all at once to make it cost-effective—usually a thousand or more—which required a pretty big investment on the writer's part. Then the writer would have hundreds or thousands of books piled up in his garage, a big debt, and a desperate prayer that he'd be able to sell the books somehow.

However, in the late 1990s, vanity presses had a breakthrough: They began using print-on-demand (POD) publishing processes. Using POD, books are stored on a computer and printed one at a time as customers order them. Hence, the up-front costs are minimal. This made it much more affordable for aspiring authors, and vanity POD presses cropped up all over the place.

Not only did they advertise in reputable writers' publications, but they had seemingly great credentials to boot: iUniverse, for example, was backed in part by Barnes & Noble. Xlibris had a partnership with Random House. Of course, this made writers hopeful that Barnes & Noble stores would stock books published by iUniverse and that Random House might republish books that did well with Xlibris.

And the publishers didn't exactly dispel this notion; iUniverse's web site declares, "We act like a 'farm team' for traditional publishers. Our authors have gone on to major publishers such as Kensington, Random House, and McGraw-Hill."

So began the vanity press craze.

According to their web sites, Trafford has published more than 5,000 titles since 1995, Xlibris has published more than 8,000 titles since 1997, iUniverse has published more than 12,000 titles between 1999 and June 2003 (and continues to publish 400 new books a month), and AuthorHouse (previously known as 1st Books) has published more than 23,000 titles since 1997 with 500 new titles a month. Keep in mind there are just four of the players in the vanity press game; there are dozens of others.

According to Powell Books, all commercial publishing houses combined publish about 60,000–75,000 books a year that are meant for bookstore sales (as opposed to textbooks, technical books, etc.). I'm not sure if vanity and self-published books have yet outnumbered commercially published titles, but if not, my bet is that we're heading that way.

The Misfit Vanities

Recently, there's been an upsurge in what I'd call "fringe" publishers. They don't fit the primary definition of vanity or subsidy press—that is, they don't charge the author an up-front fee to publish. However, they fit the rest of the profile. They accept nearly every submission that comes their way, they use print-on-demand technology, they do little or no editing (the author has "complete editorial control"), and they rely on the author as the book's personal salesperson instead of aiming for bookstore and library sales.

They can also be much more dangerous for writers than the easily identified vanity presses because some of the fringe companies are the most misleading of all. The worst offenders, like PublishAmerica, insist to prospective authors that they're "traditional" publishers and are not in any way associated with POD or self-publishing. This is not true.

PublishAmerica does not developmentally edit manuscripts, does not have a distributor to sell to bookstores, does not offer a catalog, offers a $1 advance, asks for a list of friends and family who will receive order forms, and has never had a book stocked nationally in any chain bookstores. They require authors to pay for their own copyrights and hold authors to a seven-year contract.

Literally hundreds of authors have written to me after being taken in by the very convincing sales pitch they read, only to find that the "traditional publisher" was nothing like a traditional publisher. Authors have written to me with heart-breaking stories about all the time, money, and effort they spent trying to market their books, only to get a royalty report that showed they sold a dozen books in a year. This is unacceptable, yet fringe publishers abound and continue to deceive unsuspecting writers.

Just like unscrupulous agents, you'll often find these fringe publishers paying for advertising with Google AdWords and similar directories. They invite new authors to submit and promise you'll see your work in print quickly, at no cost to you, if they approve your manuscript. (Ha! Approval is all but guaranteed at some of these companies, considering that they often don't even read the manuscripts. One author, Kevin Yarbrough, turned in the same thirty pages of a manuscript copied over and over again until it was long enough to look like a real novel, and it was happily approved by an "editor" at PublishAmerica. Another author, Dee Power, just repeated the same ten pages over and over.)

Authors are highly encouraged to buy mass quantities of their own books for resale and to divulge addresses of friends and family so a sales pitch can be sent to them, too. Rarely do fringe publishers supply an author with more than five free copies of their books. (Commercial publishers have always given me at least twenty.) They may even have sales and promotions aimed at the author instead of the readers: Buy at least 201 copies of your own book and they'll give you a 5 percent discount and a free copy of the company president's book!

I have never been pressured in any way to buy my own books. My publishers make their profits from readers, not from the authors. In many cases, I'm not even permitted to resell my own books.

PublishAmerica sent its authors an email with one such promotion:

"*The New York Times* contacted us this week to propose a partnership," PublishAmerica wrote. "We are now working with *The New York Times* to bring a new era of marketing services to our authors. It appears that our authors are being taken very seriously by *The New York Times*."

Interesting. When contacted, *The New York Times* was utterly baffled by this "partnership." It turns out that all they did was have their sales department convince PublishAmerica to pay for some advertising. Does that mean it's a partnership and the *Times* is taking PublishAmerica seriously?

This email ended with a "special promotion" where authors would get discounts if they bought their own book in bulk. They had to buy a minimum of fifty books, but wouldn't get the best discount unless they bought at least two hundred books.

In the next email, they detailed their "partnership" plan. For three months, they would take out ads in *The New York Times* book review section. In the ads, they'd list their ten best-selling titles.

"The list will be determined by the number of sales in the preceding four weeks. All sales will be counted, since publishers don't distinguish between bookstores and individuals buying their books. Even books bought by the authors count!"

What a telling last line. And I bet it won't surprise you to find that authors bought their own books by the hundreds in the hopes of landing on this top-seller list.

Unfortunately, being on the list apparently did nothing for the authors who got there. As tracked by popular novelist James Macdonald, Ingram showed no boost in sales following the books' appearances in the *Times* ads. Many of the books that appeared in the ads had no sales whatsoever through Ingram, which is one of the two major book wholesalers. Booksellers and libraries order their books from Ingram or Baker & Taylor, primarily.

Nevertheless, PublishAmerica continued sending out "offers" for the authors to buy their own books in mass quantities, and authors reported buying up to a thousand copies at a time.

Simply put, this is not the way traditional presses operate. I have never been pressured in any way to buy my own books. My publishers make their profits from readers, not from authors. In many cases, I'm not even permitted to resell my own books.

There are a couple of fringe publishers that are honest about what they offer and what they don't: Lulu.com and CafePress.com. They do not claim that your books will be available "from sea to shining sea," they do not pretend that they will help you market your work, they do not pretend to be selective, and they don't even set the price. You do. The others I'm aware of are money-making machines that can wreak havoc on an author's dreams and bank accounts.

For the purposes of this book, I will lump the fringe publishers in the vanity category as well, because their authors face the same problems as the pay-to-publish authors and the rhetoric is usually the same.

JAMES D. MACDONALD'S THREE TESTS

- A useful agent has sold books you've heard of.
- A useful publisher is one whose books you've seen with your own eyes on the shelves of your local bookstore.
- A useful contest is one that you've seen mentioned on the cover of a published book.

Does POD Always Mean Vanity?

No. There are some legitimate small presses that use POD technology but don't share the vanity press business model. That is, they're traditional publishers in every way other than their printing method.

What does this mean? They are selective about the books they publish, they employ real editors, they have publicity staffs and distributors, and they don't try to profit from the author—they count on sales to readers to make a profit. Also, they normally have returnable policies with bookstores and offer standard discounts.

Using POD technology allows presses with small budgets to make smaller investments in printing. The trade-off is that they have a smaller profit margin this way.

Other publishers—even major houses—sometimes use POD to keep backlist titles in print if they're not selling enough to warrant an offset print run (and storage of books).

Lynn Price, acquisitions director of Behler Publications, a new small press, says, "It's not our intent to become rich off the backs of our authors."

Lynn, who was once a PublishAmerica author herself, was so disappointed by her experience that she decided to start her own company and treat authors the way she wished she had been treated. Although they use POD technology, Behler's books all have print runs (in other words, they print hundreds of books at a time, not one at a time), returnable policies, and standard bookstore discounts. They're selective about the books they publish, but are more open to new authors than many of the big traditional houses.

"First off, we pay an advance to our authors. It isn't much, but it isn't a dollar, either," she says, referring to the "symbolic" one-dollar advance PublishAmerica offers. "Low three figures is all we can afford at the moment. As we grow we plan on raising the bar on that as well.

"We have a real living, breathing, editing department who are all passionate about developmental and copyediting. Our editors have experience with Bloomsbury and Simon & Schuster. All of them have master's degrees. Since it's our goal to get reviewed by big-time reviewers, our editors don't allow our authors to get away with anything. This is the most important part of publishing in our way of thinking and we don't rush this process.

"We have a marketing department that works very hard at obtaining reviews for every one of our titles and setting up a book-signing schedule for our authors (with the belief that requests for signings sound more legit coming from the marketing department of a publisher than from the author). Our marketing team also works at getting our books into stores at the national level. We see it as our job to sell our author's books, not the other way around. We do request that our authors be available for the local signings we schedule for them, but we do the work, not the author."

> Most often, writers turn to vanity presses
> after having their work rejected by agents
> and/or traditional publishers.

Reasons Writers Use Vanity Presses

If my perceptions are to be believed, most often, writers turn to vanity presses after having their work rejected by agents and/or traditional publishers. They get tired of the rejection, or they just feel they've run out of options, and vanity publishing offers something new: easy acceptance.

However, there are other reasons. Some writers are so eager to see their work in print that they'd rather go with the sure bet and have a book in their hands in a few months instead of hoping to find a publisher that will release it in a year or two. Some just don't know any better. Some think it's the path to riches, or want total editorial control, or figure they'll have an easier time attracting a major publisher once they have a book printed.

Then there are the better reasons—and here's why I don't think vanity publishing is an evil entity that should be eradicated. Some people get into this type of arrangement knowing just what they're doing and with reasonable expectations.

There are the rare writers who educate themselves about the entire process and do wind up using vanity publishing as a stepping stone to commercial success. When I say "rare," I mean rare. Because iUniverse and AuthorHouse wouldn't give me numbers, I can use only Xlibris as a measuring stick. They say about thirty of their eight thousand books were picked up by commercial houses, which translates to 0.375 percent.

WHEN SELF-PUBLISHING OR VANITY PUBLISHING MIGHT BE A GOOD OPTION

- If your commercially published books have gone out of print, and you want to give readers a way to order them again.
- If you've written a niche nonfiction book with too small an audience to attract a mainstream publisher.
- If you've written a book of poetry or a short-story collection (both notoriously hard to sell to commercial presses).
- If you've written a timely manuscript (something related to an upcoming election or event, for example) and can't afford to wait for a commercial publisher to get it in print.
- If you have a built-in audience of your own (on the Internet or at speaking engagements, for example) and want to hand sell your books.
- If you want to use a book to attract or supplement other types of business—a nutritionist who just wants to have a book to give or sell to clients to outline her system, for example.
- If you just want the sheer pleasure of holding a book of yours in your hands and sharing it with friends and family—not expecting a profit or mass sales, but just an outlet for your labor of love.

The Less-Than-Truths

Vanity presses vary in their insistence on stretching the truth—or in some cases, telling outright lies. It is to be expected that any business will highlight its attributes and downplay its weaknesses, of course, and some vanity presses walk the line pretty honorably. Others use the most misleading language possible to deny their shortcomings or even to twist their shortcomings to sound like positive attributes. Here, we'll call them on some of their bluffs.

You'll Get Bookstore Placement

Bar none, this is the lie that hurts authors the most. Many vanity presses mislead authors into believing that their books will be stocked on bookstore shelves just like commercially published books.

The fact is that even commercially published books have to compete for bookstore shelf space. There's no way that even the biggest bookstores could stock every one of the millions of books currently in print.

But vanity-published titles? Good luck.

Reputable commercial publishers have established channels of distribution. That is, they have distributors and sales reps who show their books to booksellers. They also mail catalogs to booksellers, and usually have an online catalog.

Vanity presses vary in their insistence on stretching the truth—or in some cases, telling outright lies.

Many factors are against vanity-published authors: First, because anyone can type up a manuscript and have it turned into a book, much of the work published in this manner is awful. No editor has given it a seal of approval, and in many cases, no one's even looked it over for spelling and grammatical errors. This creates a bias against all self-published books, because booksellers don't have time to find those rare ones of professional quality.

Second, many print-on-demand books are priced higher than commercial counterparts and have non-returnable policies. Commercial books are sold on consignment to bookstores, meaning that if books don't sell, stores can return them.

Third, vanity presses typically offer a far lower discount to bookstores than their traditional brethren. They may offer bookstores a 20–40 percent discount while bookstores are accustomed to a 50–55 percent discount. Booklocker states up front, "If the primary way you want to sell your print book is through bookstores, we're not the right company for you. No POD company is. Most bookstores will not stock POD books because they want a 50 percent discount to do so. Given the cost structure of POD, it is not possible to offer such a deep discount." Bookstore sales, they say, are a small percentage of their authors' earnings. "Authors making the most money on our system are selling directly to the customer through Booklocker.com or their own sites."

Fourth, many vanity presses require bookstores to pay them in advance to order books, while traditional presses expect payment a few months after the books are delivered, payable through the distributor.

Finally, self-published books have fewer available publicity channels, so distributors and stores hesitate to carry books that won't get "buzz."

To test bookstore placement of vanity presses, visit the web site of a vanity press. Note ten of their book titles. Not the few best-sellers they show on their home page, but random titles you find in their online catalog. Now visit a bookstore and search for these titles on shelves. Chances are you won't find any of them. Try this exercise with a major book publisher and the difference will be obvious.

You can even try a variation of this test from home. Just go to www.bordersstores.com and you can check store inventory; click "My Stores" and type in a zip code. It'll show the locations of stores closest to that zip code. Choose six of them, then go to "Search Store Inventory." Plug in some titles and within seconds, you can see if they're on the shelves at Borders. "Yes" means the item is stocked, "order" means it's not. You can change the locations and check as many stores as you want.

How do vanity presses get away with misleading authors like this?

You have to look at the language carefully. Some say that your book will be "available" at bookstores nationwide. Translation: Your book won't be in stock, but if someone walks in and specifically places an order for it, the bookstore can probably get it and deliver it to that customer. Often they'll make the customer pay in advance. The more honest vanity presses say the book will be "available for order" at bookstores nationwide, which basically means the same thing.

Some vanity presses also boast that their authors' books are stocked in bookstores. Sure, if an author goes to his local bookstore and begs the acquisitions manager to buy his book, it's possible he'll get what he asks for. Bookstore owners do sometimes try to support local authors and overlook their store policies if an intrepid author walks in with a good sales pitch or teary-eyed plea. This is more common with independent bookstores; chains have stricter policies against stocking vanity-published books.

Some authors even find a way to get around their publisher's non-returnable policy: They offer their books on consignment to independent bookstores. This means that the author pays the publisher for the books, gives them to the bookstore, and gets a percentage of the retail price if the books sell. If not, the author has to come back to pick up the unsold books and gets nothing.

Even if the author sells a few books this way, her profit margin (if any) is extremely low and it requires a lot of legwork. And it can take store owners several months to pay back the author for books sold.

So let's pretend that a vanity house has five thousand authors. Half of the authors manage to convince one bookstore to carry one copy of their book. Ta-da! The vanity press can now claim that its authors' books are stocked in thousands of brick-and-mortar stores all over the country! They can even say that they get orders from bookstores every day! But think about the truth of that statement: All that means is that they've gotten orders for 365 books in a year. If they have five thousand authors, they'd darn well better sell more than 365 books in a year.

The truth is that the vast majority of vanity-published books are sold to the author and the author's friends and family, and an average vanity-published book sells fewer than one hundred copies. Some place the average closer to fifty.

I applaud Xlibris for offering one of the most honest assessments of the bookstore issue in its FAQ section. In part, it reads, "In the current book-selling climate, it is difficult to place any books on bookstore shelves. This is an industry-wide statement, but applies to print-on-demand books in a particular way . . . Xlibris books are sold on a non-refundable basis."

Likewise, in an interview on www.girlondemand.blogspot.com, the CEO of iUniverse, Susan Driscoll, said, "If an author isn't traditionally published, then his/her title is not likely to get stocked nationally on bookstore shelves. Anyone who tells an author otherwise isn't telling the truth."

I abhor PublishAmerica for its opposite rhetoric: "PublishAmerica books have the same chance of making it onto a bookstore shelf as do the books of any publisher." Yeah, right. Test out that statement for yourself. How many Simon & Schuster books can you find on your local bookstore shelf, and how many PublishAmerica books?

The truth is that the vast majority of vanity-published books are sold to the author and the author's friends and family, and an average vanity-published book sells fewer than one hundred copies.

You'll Have Editorial Control

"While most people have a pretty realistic sense of how well they can sing or draw, pretty much anyone able to jot down a grocery list thinks that he or she ought to write a book, and that this book ought to be published," writes Laura Miller in her book column on Salon.com.

Many people who self-publish do so because they don't want anyone else touching their words. Vanity presses happily mention this as an attribute: The author has total editorial control. They won't change a single word of your precious manuscript; even if you have a misspelling in the title, they won't fix it. I mean this literally—I once received a book for review that had three grammatical errors in the title and subtitle. As you can imagine, I didn't read any further. The lack of editing is one of the major reasons vanity-published books have such a hard time in the marketplace.

In my opinion, all writers need editors. A few plot inconsistencies or aimless tangents really do matter to reviewers and readers, and it can be hard to spot problems in your own work. Developmental editors at commercial publishing houses are not in business to strangle your voice or mess up your vision. They're there to make suggestions to strengthen and tighten your manuscript. You can always disagree with an editor's suggestions. There's a give-and-take process where writers and editors hash it out and decide what's best for the book. Working with editors has certainly helped me to improve my craft. A great editor can become a teacher and mentor.

Then comes the copyediting. Copyeditors are there to spot things like misplaced apostrophes, awkward sentence structure, places where you've accidentally written "to" instead of "too," and lapses in logic (for example, if you wrote that your main character was wearing a green hat, and in the next scene, it's blue—or if your character was in Pennsylvania in one scene and Texas in the next, with no explanation as to how he got there so quickly).

Proofreaders are the last people to check through a manuscript before it gets printed. They're there to spot any last-minute typos, check to see if any web site addresses are out-of-date, and make sure the formatting held up properly between your computer and the printer's layout—are all of the paragraphs still indented and the headings still in bold, for example?

The lack of editing is one of the major reasons vanity-published books have such a hard time in the marketplace.

Those are three separate and essential steps. Some fringe publishers claim that they'll assign an editor to your work—however, they don't actually mean that your book will go through all three steps. Typically, what they mean is that someone will run your manuscript through spellcheck and perhaps look it over to make sure there aren't any obvious grammatical errors. This just isn't enough, not to mention that the "editors" hired by fringe publishers are typically unqualified, with no prior industry experience.

If you publish with a vanity press, you'll have to pay for outside editorial services. Seek editors with experience in your genre, and be sure to ask for references and credits. You might start at the Editorial Freelancers Association (www.the-efa.org), Book Editing Associates (www.bookediting.com), or the Editors' Association of Canada (www.editors.ca). Search these before you submit your work; some companies charge high fees if you want to make corrections to the manuscript after they've accepted it.

We'll Help You Market Your Book

Excuse me while I wipe the tears of laughter from my eyes.

Vanity presses, on the whole, do as little as possible to help authors market their books. Most don't even send out review copies to the media—the author must pay for and send review copies. Some charge additional fees to send out a press release on the author's behalf, which is all but a complete waste of time if it doesn't come with a review copy or industry buzz. Some will send free press releases by email, which is even more futile.

Vanity presses, on the whole, do as little as possible to help authors market their books.

What else do they do? They list your book in their online catalog. Big whoop. How many readers do you know who purposely go to vanity press's web sites to search for new books to read? Plus, take a look at most vanity press sites and tell me who they're targeting: new writers or readers? You got it—most are geared toward luring in more and more writers, and the actual book listings are buried in a little link somewhere that potential readers are unlikely to find.

Many also tell you that they'll give you a free guide to teach you how to publicize your book. If this guide was effective, do you really think the average vanity-published book would still be selling fewer than a hundred copies?

They downplay what real publishers do by telling writers that publishing houses today expect the author to handle publicity themselves. Again, this is misleading. A commercial house will expect the author to contribute to publicity efforts, but they share the responsibility and provide "muscle" for the author's efforts.

Commercial publishers typically have a publicity staff to set up reviews, interviews, radio shows, book signings, and other appearances. They subscribe to ProfNet and other such services where journalists go to look for experts—and they let you know whenever a journalist is about to cover a topic related to your book. They use services like Bacon's Media Directories (www.bacons.com) to keep on top of editorial contacts to help target the right audience for your book. They have media and bookstore connections and experience writing material such as press releases and media kits to gain attention. They'll often send out postcards or fliers announcing your book to potential readers, or print some up so you can hand them out. They may also provide you with bookmarks, bookplates, or other promotional doodads at no cost to you. Sometimes they set up author tours or, at least, bring books to the major book fairs. Most publishers send out hundreds of review copies; my last publisher has already sent out 350 and is still going strong. I didn't have to pay for those copies or postage.

Expect to spend at least half
of your time on publicity and marketing,
particularly if you can't get a distributor.

If you go with a vanity press, you could hire a publicist (expensive), pay for the marketing services the press offers (usually worthless), or do all this on your own—and spend the money to print and send all your own media kits and books, as well as to make follow-up calls and pay all travel expenses. Expect to spend at least half of your time on publicity and marketing, particularly if you can't get a distributor.

Some publicists won't even represent self-published books. "Occasionally I will take on self-published authors if they have distribution channels set up and, preferably, if they've been through the publishing process before so that they know the ins and outs of the business," says Joanne McCall of McCall Public Relations.

Without publicity, a book is invisible. Even if you have decent distribution, people have to know to go look for your book.

Publishing Increases Your Credibility

Using vanity publishing as a stepping-stone to break into traditional houses rarely works. Most agents and publishers are not impressed that you have a vanity-published book on your resume. To them, it often means the book wasn't good enough to sell to a "real" publisher. You can change this impression with strong sales. Agents may think, "If he sold all those books by himself, imagine what he could do with a big house behind him."

> Using vanity publishing as a way to
> break into traditional houses rarely works.

"That's my dream—to find someone who has self-published and actually has a track record," says agent Michael Broussard of Dupree, Miller & Associates. "But you have to be careful if you intend to get them a book deal with a major publisher. If they sell too few copies (1,500 or less), it really doesn't matter, but if they sell too many—like 60,000, the publishers will think the market is saturated . . . so a nice number is 15,000–30,000 copies sold."

You can also overcome the stigma of vanity publishing by winning a major competition, like the Writer's Digest Self-Published Book Award. Kenny Kemp won this contest with *Dad Was a Carpenter* in 1999 and sold the rights to HarperSanFrancisco in a three-book deal. By the way, PublishAmerica books are eligible for the Writer's Digest Self-Published Book Award, yet more proof that the industry does not see PublishAmerica as the "traditional" press it claims to be.

Professional writers' associations don't consider vanity-published books as legitimate credits, either. You won't get into the Authors Guild, the Science Fiction and Fantasy Writers of America (SFWA), the American Society of Journalists and Authors (ASJA), the Mystery Writers of America, or most other writers' organizations by having a vanity-published or fringe-published book to your name.

Right on their application form, the Authors Guild states, "A contract with a vanity press or any press that requires the author to bear the expense of publication or buy copies of his or her own book does not qualify as a writer for membership in the Guild."

Many writers who initially self-publish go so far as to use a pseudonym and omit old books from their bios when pitching a new manuscript to commercial houses; a weak sales record can haunt you. Major publishers are unlikely to buy a book from an author whose other books tanked.

Agent Sam Stoloff at Frances Goldin Literary Agency advises that authors whose self-published or vanity-published books haven't sold well not list these books in their credits when approaching him for representation.

The Publishing Door Is Closed to New Authors

Some vanity presses make it sound like commercial houses have all locked their doors and are doing their best to keep fresh talent away. Know what? This is utter rubbish.

First, keep in mind that every successful author was once an unpublished writer. Someone let them into that tight little clique, right?

It's really easy to dispel this myth. Subscribe to PublishersLunch (www.publishersmarketplace.com) for one week.

Why? Because PublishersLunch reports book deals, and if you read the details for just one week, I'm betting you'll be amazed by how many debut authors are listed. If you prefer, pick up an issue of *Publishers Weekly* for the same reason. Look for the words "first-time novelist" or "debut author." Look for authors who are described by other professions (journalist, political analyst, nutritionist, swimmer, professor)—this often means they don't have any other book credits; otherwise, they'd be listed with titles like "Nutritionist and author of *XYZ*."

I counted fourteen first-timers in my latest weekly issue of PublishersLunch, and those are just the ones I could verify—I'm certain there are other authors mentioned in their deals listings who aren't jumping up and down to mention that they've never had a book published before.

First-time novelists and nonfiction authors make deals at well-known publishing houses literally every day. Big and small deals alike. Agented and unagented. I've personally spoken with first-time authors who've gotten million-dollar advances. My first advance was considerably more modest (I think it was $2,500), but it was a small press and I've had no problem building my way up from there.

We'll Get Your Book Into Print Fast!

It is faster to publish with a vanity POD press. (Mostly because you're skipping many steps commercial publishers consider necessary.) This may matter to you if your book is timely, such as a book about a news event. Otherwise, rushing to print is usually a poor idea. The trade magazines that publish book reviews for an audience of libraries and book sellers want galleys several months before a book's official publication date. You'll increase your book's potential for getting picked up by bookstores and libraries if you get positive reviews in these trades, such as *Booklist, Library Journal, Publishers Weekly, New York Review of Books,* and *School Library Journal.*

Further, experienced publishers know when books in your category sell best. Did you know that romance books do well in February and children's titles are hot in September? Do you know when another house is going to release a highly promoted competing book? Your publisher should know— and plan an appropriate launch date.

Look at Our Reviews!

Many vanity presses brag about all the positive reviews their books get. And certainly, I'm not telling you that you can't get a review of a vanity-published book. What I am telling you is that you will face a huge uphill battle to get it reviewed anywhere worthwhile (major newspapers, national consumer magazines, trade magazines, etc.). This isn't my opinion; it's a fact supported by many, many book review editors and disgruntled vanity-published authors (many of whom couldn't even get their home-town papers to take a peek). I'll show you what I mean:

Patti Thorn of *Rocky Mountain News* wrote a column about her Christmas wish list. One of her wishes? "A way to stop the avalanche of self-published books. I've gotta be honest with you, Santa, internet publishers such as iUniverse, 1st Books and Xlibris are making my life miserable. Now every Tom, Dick and Harry can self-publish a book relatively cheaply, then call me up to demand I review their 'book.' Given that more than 60,000 titles are published legitimately every year and the space we have for, oh, say 500 of them, it's just not possible to tackle these vanity titles."

Suffice it to say there are very few significant print publications that welcome vanity titles for review.

Bob Hoover of the *Pittsburgh Post-Gazette* wrote in 2003, "For reviewers, these on-demand books pose the same challenges that self-published titles do: They have not passed muster by professional editors and marketers or been found good enough to carry a company's brand . . . Not all books are created equally . . . Because [vanity-published] books do not go through the rigorous examination, editing and guarantees of a trade publisher, the *Post-Gazette* chooses not to review them."

Heather Lee Schroeder of Wisconsin's *The Capital Times* writes, "On *The Capital Times* books page, we have a pretty strict policy about self-published books. Only in rare cases do we review or write about them. Over the years, I have been accused of snobbery, elitism, and downright meanness . . . Everyone needs an editor, and to be blunt: Most self-published books have not been adequately edited. In fact, most are almost unreadable."

Publishers Weekly, one of the most influential places a book can be reviewed, notes, "We do not review self-published books unless there is a first printing of 2,000 or greater, and an arrangement with a reputable distributor, in which case we will take the book under consideration."

Who else blatantly states that they will not review self-published or vanity-published titles? *School Library Journal, Kirkus Reviews, The New York Times* . . . I could go on and on, but suffice it to say there are very few significant print publications that welcome vanity titles for review. No, that's too generous. I don't know of any significant print publications that welcome vanity titles.

We Have Distribution Through Baker & Taylor and Ingram!

Yes, Baker & Taylor and Ingram are great big companies, but they're not distributors, no matter what they call themselves. They're wholesalers. The difference?

Distributors have sales forces. These salespeople visit booksellers and pitch the books they represent, usually by bringing copies of the books and media kits or at least the cover art and book details. They tell the chain's buyers or individual store managers about the publishers' promotional plans for the books and any other key selling points that may entice book sellers to buy multiple copies. Then they take orders. Sometimes they'll do this bookstore round only once in a book's life, but often they'll re-pitch backlist books (that is, books that are not in the current season's publishing slate) that are gaining momentum or are expected to be more in-demand for one reason or another. About 75 percent of all books on store shelves are backlist books. When you have no distributor pitching to stores, you don't get to benefit from that momentum of repeated publicity.

Wholesalers like Baker & Taylor and Ingram do not employ sales representatives. They do not visit bookstores and pitch books. They just have warehouses where they'll store copies of your book until someone calls them to place an order. In the case of vanity presses, these wholesalers will typically order just a copy or two on the off chance that a bookstore calls in a special order. They do not do the legwork. Don't let a press mislead you into believing that association with these wholesalers will help you get books onto bookstore shelves. All it really means is that your aunt Mimi in Wichita, Kansas, can walk into a bookstore and place a special order for your book, then come back to the bookstore in a month or two to pick it up.

Wholesalers like Baker & Taylor and Ingram
do not employ sales representatives.

Or maybe not even. Several vanity-published authors caused a stir in the fall of 2004 when they complained that customers went to order their books at stores and were told the stores couldn't even place the order on their system. The problem? Ingram, one of the two powerhouse wholesalers, had decided to stop stocking POD books altogether. They were flooded by so many vanity-published POD books that never sold that they decided even one or two copies of each title was taking up too much warehouse space.

Therefore, if a bookstore tried to place an order, it would show that the wholesaler had none in stock in their warehouses. They'd then have to place a back-order, and many bookstores won't do this because back-orders can take ages to arrive.

Currently, Ingram is trying to remedy the situation to allow bookstores to order POD books again, but they do seem firm on their decision not to stock them in their warehouses anymore.

We'll Get You Listed on Amazon!

Oh, I'm so impressed. Any book with an ISBN can be listed with online booksellers. You can get yourself listed on Amazon and BN.com with minimal effort. This isn't a big selling point. Plus, many vanity presses don't even get cover art shown on book listings.

We Have Big-Name Affiliations!

Go ahead, take a look at how far those big-name affiliations have gotten authors. Random House invested in Xlibris in 2000. Since that time, how many Xlibris titles has Random House purchased? None. How many iUniverse titles are stocked at your Barnes & Noble? Take a look and tell me how many you find.

In early 2003, iUniverse announced its "Star Program," where they promised to invest in and promote books that demonstrated strong initial sales. Thus far, only eighty-three titles have qualified. In March 2005, *Publishers Weekly* reported on their findings in the article "iUniverse by the Numbers." They stated that in 2004, iUniverse published 18,108 titles. Of those, only fourteen were stocked nationally in Barnes & Noble stores. The total number of copies printed was 792,814, which means an average of 43.2 sales per book if all of the printed books sold (as opposed to being given away to authors' family, reviewers, or currently sitting in the author's garage).

As a book reviewer, I groan every time I get a pitch that reads, "My book is published by Xlibris, a partner of Random House." Do they think they're fooling me with the name-dropping? Or do they really believe that Random House's financial investment in the company constitutes endorsement of its books' literary merit?

Although I don't know how they presented themselves to authors when they debuted, I do know that Xlibris is now honest about the Random House partnership. The media director was forthright with me when I asked if Random House had picked up any of their titles yet. They haven't. I also asked how many of their books had been picked up by any commercial publishers, and he responded, "About thirty." No one at iUniverse or AuthorHouse would answer the same question.

You'll Make Big Bucks!

Some vanity presses try to woo authors with crazy "look how rich you could get" figures. They try to make it sound like you'll earn far more money with a vanity press (with their "higher than industry standard" royalty rates) than you would with a traditional press.

Riiiight. So what are these giant earnings vanity press authors actually report? One of my sources said, "$12.50." Another said, "$3.59." I'd weep in my cornflakes.

> It's true that it's rare for an
> author to get rich by writing books.
> But it should never create a
> financial loss for the author!

Let's say you managed to sell a hundred copies through bookstores. How much would you earn on a 250-page paperback book printed as cheaply as possible with a retail price of $20? About $240. Which means, if you paid a print-on-demand company to publish your book and didn't even spend a dime to have it edited or promoted, you still wouldn't even have recouped your initial investment, let alone made any profit from your hard work.

Wait, no, let's say you're a better marketer than the average vanity press author and you manage to sell three hundred books through bookstores. Now you've made $720. Subtract whatever it cost you to publish, hire an editor, pay for postage and books for review copies, pay for cover art, etc. How is this in any way worth it financially for you?

In a commercial publishing arrangement, publishers pay authors an advance against royalties. For first-time authors, an advance may be just hundreds of dollars, or it may be hundreds of thousands of dollars. (My informal surveys show that most new authors make $2,000–$10,000 on their first advances.) Then, once the royalties have surpassed the amount of the advance, authors begin collecting checks from publishers, usually twice a year. Authors are not expected to spend a cent on anything—not on copyright registration, not on cover art, editing, ISBN registration, press release distribution . . . nothing. The publishers pay for all of this. They don't do it out of the goodness of their hearts—they do it because it's an investment for them. They believe the authors will be successful, and they invest in the authors' success.

It's true that it's rare for an author to get rich by writing books. But it should never create a financial loss for the author!

Other Options

You do have other options, in between the major publishers and vanity publishers.

Conventional Self-Publishing

On the "respectability" scale, old-fashioned self-publishing is a step above publishing with a vanity press. With conventional self-publishing, the author truly takes on the role of publisher, and takes a bigger financial risk.

The author is in charge of every step of the process, from finding a cover artist to securing distribution. Self-publishers hire printers and usually use off-set printing, which means that hundreds (or thousands) of books will be printed at once. Self-publishers may also use POD methods, contracting directly with a digital printer like Lightning Source rather than an intermediary company. The author buys an International Standard Book Number, better known as an ISBN (actually, the author buys a block of numbers, because you can't currently buy just one), copyrights the book in his name, and names his "publishing company" anything he wishes.

It's somewhat easier to get bookstore placement and legitimate reviews of conventionally self-published books, and the profit margin is higher if the self-publisher sells well.

One of my friends, Peter Bowerman, made a full-time living off his first self-published book, *The Well-Fed Writer*, for more than two years. He didn't treat it as a get-rich-quick scheme; he educated himself about the process heavily before he leaped into it. And because he did such a good job, most reviewers never even realized his book was self-published. They just thought Fanove Publishing (his company's name) was a commercial small press.

If this interests you, do yourself a favor and check in with the experts before you begin. Here are resources that I recommend:

The Self-Publishing Manual **by Dan Poynter.** Dan is the best-known "guru" of self-publishing. At 432 pages, this book gives a comprehensive overview of the steps you'll need to take. (See www.parapub.com for details and other resources for self-publishers.)

1001 Ways to Market Your Books **by John Kremer.** A mammoth of a book that teaches self-published and commercially published authors alike the ins and outs of getting a book publicized and sold in retail stores, libraries, catalogs, book clubs, and even alternative outlets like shopping channels.

Small Presses

Small presses publish between two and fifty titles annually, often in niche categories. If you're unable to sell to major publishers, they provide a nice alternative.

Without the overhead of big publishers, they have freedom to print titles by authors with less-established platforms, or more controversial or creatively risky material. While small-press authors don't always get paid advances, they can take their newly published books and land major publishing deals, or use the sales to establish a track record to sell the next

IS THE SMALL PRESS RIGHT FOR YOU?

- Are they listed in Writer's Market? (Not necessary, but a good sign.)
- How long have they been in business?
- Does their catalog look professional?
- Do their books get national bookstore distribution?
- What other books have they published?
- How many copies have their best-selling titles sold?
- Do they have a web site?
- Do they have a solid plan for marketing your book?
- Will they provide you with promotional materials such as postcards, fliers, or bookmarks?
- Will they actively help you set up signings, speaking engagements, and interviews?
- Is there a limit to how many review copies they'll send out?
- Have they sold foreign rights or serial rights for a comparable title?
- Have they sold to book clubs?
- Have their books been reviewed in major trade publications and high-circulation newspapers?
- Are they members of any small press associations, such as Publishers Marketing Association (PMA)?
- What kind of experience does your editor have?

title. Mainstream publishers do look for the next hot small-press book to "discover"—especially those that are proven in the marketplace, selling upwards of twenty thousand copies.

However, you must do your homework before you sign with a small press. Above all, make sure they have a deal with a major book distributor like Independent Publishers Group or National Book Network. (You can find more in *Literary Market Place*, a library resource book.) There are many other questions that will verify legitimacy and allow you to determine if the press can meet your needs.

As a final acid test, contact authors published by this press and ask about their experiences. (Do a Google or Yahoo search to locate these authors.)

In publishing, bigger isn't always better. After fifteen books with large, mid-size, and small presses alike, know which one's my favorite to work with? Nomad Press, the small press that published the book you're holding. At larger publishers, authors can sometimes feel like numbers, and can get lost in a sea of bigger fish. Smaller publishers may work harder to cultivate relationships with authors and to promote books long-term. Why? They can't afford to have a book fail. If a major house sees that a book isn't selling well, they can drop it and focus on new titles that have blockbuster potential. At a press that publishes fewer than fifty books a year, each one has to do well or the publisher is in trouble!

For an extensive list of small presses, visit the Small Press Center at www.smallpress.org.

Chapter 4

What to Do If You've Been Screwed

How to Terminate a Publishing Contract

Where to Report Deadbeats

Despite all I've just told you about the misleading
statements many vanity presses make, all of the major
POD vanity presses are still going strong, and none
have been convicted of fraudulent or unethical business
practices. (Not that I'm implying that all of them are
fraudulent or unethical, mind you. But some of them
. . . well, don't get me started.)

However, the precursor to today's POD companies were the more expensive offset vanity companies, and the principals of some of them have, indeed, been convicted of crimes. Consider the case of Sovereign Publications: This was a vanity press run by Dorothy Deering (an unemployed ex-bookkeeper with a felony embezzlement conviction) and her family. Dorothy, who also ran a fee-charging fake literary agency, convinced hundreds of writers to spend thousands of dollars on "co-op" publishing fees before she and her partners were caught and imprisoned for fraud. Not only were her clients misled by her false claims about the industry, but the vast majority of them never even got the books they paid her to publish. Instead, they were fed excuse after excuse about why the books were delayed—primarily pity-inducing stories about bad health and deaths in the family.

Northwest Publishing of Utah, also advertising itself as a "joint venture" publisher, took in millions of dollars in author payments, assuring writers that they were selected based on the merit of their manuscripts. Utah's Attorney General launched an investigation and the founder, James Van Treese, and his son, Jason, went to jail for fraud and failure to pay taxes.

How did these unscrupulous companies go down? The authors took action. They wrote letters, got the FBI interested, and filed class-action lawsuits. After numerous letters, the right special agent took an interest and investigated thoroughly. In similar cases, authors have filed civil lawsuits or hired publishing attorneys to fight to get their rights (and money) back.

Your Options

You don't have to roll over and play dead if you feel you've been misled. There are several steps you can take. Many vanity presses do not claim the rights to authors' books and will not put up a fuss if you ask to end your agreement with them, provided you're not trying to get your money back.

Others, however, are not so author-friendly. If you have one of these publishers, and you're truly unhappy with your publishing arrangement, you need to pull your publishing agreement out of the file cabinet or desk drawer and read it.

First, check on the term of the contract—the length of time it remains in effect. Some vanity publishing contracts have very long terms (PublishAmerica's contracts at one point were life terms and are currently for seven years). If the term is near its end, simply wait it out and you're home free. Just make sure of two things: (1) that the term does not automatically renew (if so, follow the notice provision to prevent automatic renewal) and (2) that all of your rights (copyright ownership) revert to you on termination.

If the term of your agreement isn't about to expire, check the contract to see if there are any provisions for "termination without cause," simply by giving thirty, sixty, or ninety days' notice. If so, give the notice by certified mail, return receipt requested (or by some other method to prove receipt) and you are free. Again, just make sure that the rights to your book revert to you upon termination. If the publisher fails to give you a written reversion, you can record a copy of the applicable contract provision with the Copyright Office.

What if neither of these options applies? Then you have to evaluate whether you can terminate the contract "for cause," because the publisher has, in legal language, breached its agreement.

A breach of contract is the failure by one party to live up to his or her responsibilities under a contract, without a legal defense or excuse (or a note from their mother). Usually, a breach involves either a substantial or material failure to perform as promised or keeping the other party from performing as promised. After a breach occurs, the other party can seek remedies for the failure, including money damages, and/or declare the contract terminated.

A breach of contract is the failure by one party to live up to his or her responsibilities under a contract, without a legal defense or excuse.

If you believe your publisher breached the agreement in a substantial way, such as by not publishing your book in the time required, or failing to edit, or failing to promote your book as promised, you may choose to declare the contract terminated by the breach.

Unfortunately, the publisher may not see things as you do, and may continue publication of your book and/or refuse to revert your rights in the book as required by the agreement.

If so, your only alternative is to file a court action—if you can. Many publishing agreements include arbitration clauses requiring that an arbitration panel must settle all disputes (usually under the auspices of the American Arbitration Association).

Despite public perception that arbitration (rather than court action) is a good thing, arbitration usually favors the publisher. Arbitration awards are historically more conservative than those given by judges and juries, arbitrators are industry members sympathetic to the publisher, and the cost of the arbitration often is prohibitive. Arbitration clauses, however, are enforceable, and if you have such a clause in your publishing agreement, you must abide by it—you cannot file a lawsuit, even in Small Claims Court.

What if you do nothing? Unless you arbitrate or file a court action that results in a favorable decision, you may be in legal limbo regarding your copyright.

Example 1

You signed an agreement with Gouge-em Publishing Company. Gouge-em promised to publish your book using print-on-demand technology within three months for a fee of $500, and you assigned all copyright for three years. You paid the fee, submitted your manuscript, and six months have passed with no publication, despite repeated inquiries by you. The agreement has an arbitration clause.

You send Gouge-em a certified letter stating that you consider the contract breached and terminated and demand a written reversion of your rights. Gouge-em does not respond.

Soon afterward, you meet an agent at a writers' conference who would like to represent your book. The agent tells you, however, that you must get your rights back from Gouge-em before he can market the book to publishers.

In this example you must file an arbitration action against the publisher. If you do not, but simply take the position that your rights reverted to you, there is always the possibility that Gouge-em could file a copyright infringement action against your new publisher—a sure way to ruin a relationship.

Example 2

Same facts as in Example 1, but Gouge-em agrees with you that the contract is terminated. However, it fails to send you a written reversion of rights. In this case, your options are better: You may record with the Copyright Office a copy of the termination page of the agreement or other document that supports your reversion of rights. Some publishers may still demand a formal reversion from Gouge-em, but others will accept this.

If all this seems a bit overwhelming, you should seek help from a publishing attorney. In my experience, most publishers are no more interested in incurring legal fees than you are, and once you show you are serious about enforcing your rights, they will comply with the agreement.

WHAT ELSE CAN YOU DO?

If you feel you've been treated unfairly, misled, or ripped off, you owe it to yourself and to other writers to report your experiences. Here are several places you can do so.

The Attorney General www.naag.org

Use the drop-down menu to locate the Attorney General in the state where the publisher is located.

The Better Business Bureau www.bbb.com

Provides an online form to report complaints; they will contact the publisher with your report. Don't count on this to be effective, but it's always worth filing a report.

Federal Trade Commission www.ftc.gov
They don't resolve individual consumer complaints, but they do investigate fraud.

Writer Beware www.writerbeware.com
Investigates writer complaints; keeps records of publishing industry frauds, scams, and problems.

Preditors & Editors www.anotherealm.com/prededitors
Submit reports here to help warn writers about unscrupulous companies.

Absolute Write Bewares & Background Check
www.absolutewrite.com/forums
Warn other writers by posting your experiences in the forum here.

The Rip-Off Report www.ripoffreport.com
Consumers can report complaints publicly here.

Letters to the Editor
Send letters to newspaper editors to draw media attention to problems you've experienced.

Chapter 5

Trouble Spots in Book Contracts

Consulting Contract Experts

Those Confusing Clauses, Explained

Your Money, Your Rights

Negotiating: What to Expect

Book contracts are written by the publisher's lawyers, and as such, are always written with the publisher's best interests in mind, not the author's. This doesn't mean that book contracts are purposely written against the author's best interests, but it does mean that they require close scrutiny for clauses that favor the publisher and may harm you.

It always is best to have a publishing attorney go over your book contracts. I know it can be a significant investment, but it can save you from major mistakes and headaches down the line.

Several publishing attorneys offer flat-rate contract review services. My co-author, Daniel Steven, currently charges between $375 and $650, depending on whether you want him to negotiate the contract terms for you, or just advise you about what to change or negotiate on your own.

Qualified agents also can vet contracts for you; the ones who've been around the block and made plenty of deals should know what to look for.

They also often work with lawyers who advise them, especially if they belong to sizeable agencies. But be aware that not all agents (even experienced ones) have the legal savvy to know what language is dangerous, or what some clauses mean.

It always is best to have a publishing attorney go over your book contracts. I know it can be a significant investment, but it can save you from major mistakes and headaches down the line.

I've also had good experiences with the National Writer's Union's contract committee: If you become a member, a volunteer will examine your contract and advise you about any problem spots by phone or email. These are not lawyers; they're fellow writers who've gone through training and can advise you in a peer-to-peer capacity, which is not as good as legal advice, but is certainly better than nothing. Every advisor I dealt with was knowledgeable and taught me what to ask for. (They don't negotiate for you; they highlight problem areas and tell you what to ask for.)

But when I mention a "publishing attorney," I mean exactly that. I've heard of too many problems from people who hired a "contract lawyer" (a general term that means almost nothing—all lawyers work with contracts in some capacity, but that doesn't mean they know anything about what a book contract should look like), a friend-of-the-family lawyer, or just the first lawyer they found in the phone book. Many lawyers will tell you that they've handled book contracts before, but that doesn't mean they've handled them well. It takes special knowledge and training to catch the nuances of publishing contracts, which are often mammoth documents with confusing clauses.

Regardless of whether you consult an expert, you can and should empower yourself to understand the main problem spots so you have a better idea of what matters to you and what to negotiate. Lawyers are human and may not spot every questionable term; I've sometimes spotted problematic language that even my lawyer and agent didn't. There are a number of general terms to be aware of.

> Regardless of whether you consult an expert, you can and should empower yourself to understand the main problem spots so you have a better idea of what matters to you and what to negotiate.

Manuscript Acceptance

Of course the publisher will want the right to ask for changes to your manuscript before accepting it for publication, and in most cases, the editor and author have no problem working this out. However, you need a "cover your butt" provision to make sure that the publisher doesn't unreasonably delay production of the manuscript or payment of your advance by never getting back to you about what changes the editor wants. This means you need a time limit, such as: "If, within sixty days of receipt of the complete manuscript, Publisher has not sent Author a written statement requesting corrections or revisions, the manuscript will be deemed to have been accepted. Author will submit changes to the manuscript within thirty days of such statements."

Keep in mind that the editor who acquired your book may not be the same editor who sees it through to publication; editors change publishing houses with surprising frequency. If a new editor comes in before your manuscript has been accepted, this provides the assurance that he can't just sit on your book while his own pet projects take priority. He must read it and make suggestions within sixty days of the date you turned it in.

> You should have the right to see and approve any changes: After all, the book is in your name, not the editor's.

Also, who gets the final say on the manuscript? Can the editor make changes to the manuscript (aside from copyediting) without your approval? Be sure to insert a clause (if there isn't one already) that says the author must approve all material changes to the manuscript before publication. Otherwise, an editor could add something with the belief that she's clarifying something you've written, but she's actually written something factually incorrect. Or she could add in extra resources that you don't approve of. Or she could chop out a section of your novel that you thought was integral to the conclusion. You should have the right to see and approve any changes: After all, the book is in your name, not the editor's.

Royalties

Authors are paid for their work through royalties—a percentage of the amount the publisher receives from the sale of each book. Publishing contracts typically include an advance against these royalties. This means that the author gets paid a certain amount of money before publication, but this amount is charged against (deducted) from the royalties due the author after the book is released.

Royalty rates are negotiable, will vary based on the book's intended market and format (hardcover, trade paperback, or paperback), and generally are on a sliding rate. For example, a hardcover book meant for general readership might have royalties of 11 percent of the cover or retail price on the first 5,000 copies sold, 12.5 percent on the next 5,000, and 15 percent thereafter (paperback royalties are generally in the 6 to 9 percent range).

Don't fixate just on the royalty percentage, however; the key to royalties is not only the royalty percentage but what price the percentage is based on. You must understand the implications of your formula before you can understand your proposed royalty rate.

Royalties for novels and general interest or "trade" nonfiction books usu-

---

DEFINING NET RECEIPTS

Not only are royalties based on net receipts generally less lucrative than royalties based on list or cover price, they often are difficult to figure out. Some publishers don't define "net receipts." What will be deducted before you start making money?

If it's not in your contract, try to insert this clause: "'Net Receipts' means actual cash receipts from all sales of the Work in any media or format less shipping costs, returns, and sales or value-added taxes remitted to Publisher by the purchaser."

Otherwise, if net receipts are undefined, you may be paying for the publisher's electric bill, phone bill, editors' salaries, company cars, etc. The publisher could argue that these expenses are part of the "cost" of your book.

ally are paid on the cover price of the book (also called list or retail price). Nonfiction books for limited markets, such as academic or professional texts, usually are paid on "net receipts" or "net revenue." For authors, assuming the percentage is equal, cover price always is preferable—not only is it more profitable, but you always know exactly how much money you make per book sold. If you're getting 10 percent royalties on the list price of a book that costs $10, you're getting $1 per book.

The key to royalties is not only the royalty percentage but what price the percentage is based on.

"Net receipts" or "net revenue" royalties are based on the wholesale price—which is the amount actually received by the publisher from the bookseller or purchaser, and are also used for subsidiary rights like foreign or audio rights retained by the publisher and sold to a third party. (These usually are split fifty-fifty with the author). A third formula, "invoice price," is also sometimes used. Invoice price differs from retail price or cover price by not including the "Freight Pass Through" to compensate the publisher for the cost of shipping, and thus the invoice price is less than the list or cover price.

Payment on Publication

Advances typically are not paid in one lump sum, but rather, divided into two to four payments.

You should get part of your advance on contract signing, but the other parts may come when you've finished half the manuscript, when you've turned in the full first draft, after the final manuscript is approved, once it's been scheduled for release, on publication, and/or six months after publication.

This is negotiable. Keeping in mind that it may take more than a year before the book is released, ask yourself if you want to (or can) wait that long for your final payment. Remember that you're putting in the work up front; if you don't have other sources of income, you may not be able to wait for that check.

From the publishers' perspective, they'd like to hold on to their money as long as possible. One editor reports that she prefers to hold the final payment until six months after publication to have more money available for marketing.

I always try to negotiate so that my advance is entirely paid up when the final manuscript is accepted. Generally, my contracts stipulate one-third payment on contract signing, one-third at the halfway mark, and one-third on approval of the final manuscript (not after copyediting and proofreading; just after the developmental editor has signed off and sent it to the next stage).

Indemnities and Warranties

These purely "legal" clauses are frequently skimmed over by authors and not fully understood either by agents or editors. These paragraphs set forth the respective responsibilities of the parties in the event of claims by third parties against the book, such as for defamation, copyright infringement, or invasion of privacy. Drafted by the publisher's lawyers, they often can be overbroad to a ludicrous degree.

In general, the "warranty" clause is the author's promise to the publisher that her work is original and does not defame (libel) any individual, nor invade anyone's right of privacy. To give this promise "teeth," the publisher also includes an "indemnification" clause, which is the author's agreement

MODEL WARRANTY AND INDEMNIFICATION CLAUSE

Author represents that he is the sole owner of the Work and has the exclusive right and power to enter into this Agreement, that the Work to the best of his knowledge does not contain any libelous matter and does not violate the rights of any person or persons, does not infringe any existing copyright and has not heretofore been published in book form. Author shall hold harmless and indemnify the publisher from any recovery finally sustained by Publisher by reason of any violations of copyright or other property of personal right; provided, however, that Publisher shall with all reasonable promptness notify Author of any claim or suit which may involve the warranties of Author hereunder. The warranties contained in this paragraph do not extend to drawings, illustrations, or other material not furnished by Author.

to reimburse the publisher for any damages suffered by the publisher if the author's warranties are false. This is required even though all but the smallest publishers carry "publisher's perils" insurance policies that cover the publisher for such damages.

What can you do about it? As a first-time author, realistically, not much. You can, however, try to make the clause less one-sided by asking that your indemnities take effect only upon a "finally sustained" judgment. Adding these words means that you would not have to pay the cost of a frivolous or unjustified claim—only claims that are proven in court and upheld on appeal. You also should obtain a "best of your knowledge" standard for your warranties. Under this standard, you would be responsible only for claims that you knew or reasonably should have known about (for instance, if you knowingly included a lengthy quotation without the author's permission).

Once you are an established author, you may be able to limit your indemnification to those damages the publisher can't recover under its insurance policy or even have the publisher make you an "additional insured" on the publisher's insurance policy, so that you, as well as the publisher, are covered.

Reserve Against Returns

The book publishing world works on consignment. That is, nearly all commercial publishers offer books to bookstores on a returnable basis. (This is part of what separates commercial publishing from print-on-demand publishing). The bookstore may order five copies of your book. In a couple of months, if there are still three copies sitting on the shelf, they may return the books to the distributor or publisher for full credit. In the case of mass-market paperbacks (the so-called "rack-sized" books usually printed on low-grade paper and released in high quantity at a lower price than a "trade" or full-size paperback, often distributed through drugstores, airports, and supermarkets in addition to bookstore placement), they just have to strip off and return the covers, then dispose of the books through the trash or recycling. (Unfortunately, these missing-cover books often turn up for sale at garage sales and book fairs. This deprives the author of her royalty; don't buy them.) With hardcovers and trade paperbacks, the bookstore returns the whole books.

You earn a royalty as soon as the bookstore has ordered the book, not when the book is actually sold to a customer—but that royalty is taken back if the book gets returned. Therefore, most publishers have a "reserve against returns" clause, where the publisher can hold back some of your royalties in anticipation of some copies being returned.

The problem comes when the contract allows the publisher a "reasonable" reserve against returns—an intentionally vague provision. Try to get a "cap" on the reserve of between 10 and 25 percent, the lower the better; also try to limit the time that the publisher can hold the reserve to no more than one, six-month accounting period.

Option on Next Work

These clauses give the publisher the right to either buy or make an offer for the author's next book or books. Best advice: don't accept any option clause. Most publishers will yield on this issue.

It's not in your best interest to promise any publisher the first right on your next work, especially when you haven't even seen how well they'll handle the current one. Of course, everyone goes into his or her first contract with high hopes and expectations, but what if you wind up disappointed by the experience? What if they do a lousy job editing or marketing your first book?

```
You earn a royalty as soon as the bookstore has
ordered the book, not when the book is actually
            sold to a customer.
```

Further, what if your next book isn't appropriate for this publisher? I write on many topics. If I signed an unrestricted option clause with a health publisher, I'd have to give them the first look at my children's picture book, even if I know they don't publish children's picture books, and they can hold me up from submitting it to appropriate publishers.

If you can't eliminate an option clause entirely, then make sure it imposes no real burden (see section 13 of form 5—Trade Publishing Agreement—in the appendix). Get rid of any contract language requiring you to submit a completed manuscript, rather than a proposal; requiring lengthy (more than sixty days) consideration periods for the publisher; or requiring that you offer your next book to the publisher on the same terms as the current book. (What if your first book is a bestseller and you can now command much higher fees?)

Best advice: don't accept any option clause.

Ideally, you should aim for a very limited period during which the publisher may bid on your next book ("right of first negotiation"), permitting you to sell the book to other publishers if you don't accept the terms. I've read clauses that state that even if the publisher has refused to make an offer, the author still must allow them a month or two to decide if they want to make an offer after another publisher does so. In other words, let's say Publisher A tells you they don't want your book. After you shop it around, Publisher B makes you an offer. You want to accept it, but you can't, because now you have to go back to the publisher that already rejected it and give them a chance to change their minds!

Some clauses also stipulate that you can't accept an offer from another publisher if it's not on "better terms." That may sound logical to you now, but there are intangibles you may not be aware of yet. Maybe Publisher A is offering you more money up front, but you trust Publisher B to do a better job with the marketing. Or you felt like a number at a large publisher that can offer a higher advance, and you'd prefer to try a smaller publisher that can't pay as much, but can show you more personal attention (big fish in the small pond). You should always have the right to refuse the publisher's offer, no matter what the terms are, if you choose. All the first option should give them a right to do (if you have to include it) is to read the work and make an offer.

You'll also want to restrict the clause as much as possible: Instead of allowing them the first option on your next work, make sure it's the next work in the same genre, in the same series, or the next work that's in categories the publisher deals with. And make sure it doesn't give them the first option on more than one more book.

I've never had a problem getting publishers to strike the clause altogether. The publisher of the book you're reading right now included an option clause in my first contract with them (for *Make a Real Living as a Freelance Writer*). I didn't sign it. I said something to the effect of, "If all goes well, I'd be happy to offer you my next book, but I can't commit to that yet." And you're holding the evidence: It worked out well. I happily offered them my next book in the genre even though I wasn't contractually obligated to do so.

You should always have the right to refuse the publisher's offer, no matter what the terms are, if you choose.

If your book does sell well, there's something to be said for loyalty to the press that helped you get there. Publishers and agents alike complain that writers tend to jump ship after they've helped make the writers successful. The option clause is a bit of an insurance policy for the publisher—a guarantee that you'll give them another shot after their initial investment in you. It's not usually an evil clause in its intent, but there are too many situations where the clause becomes impractical.

Even a well-restricted clause can be an annoyance because it wastes your time. Let's say I started by writing a fantasy book for a small press, and I signed an option clause that said I'd offer them my next fantasy novel. They paid me a $2,000 advance and I earned modest royalties. After that, I wrote three mainstream novels for major publishers. By then, I made $20,000 advances. If I ever wanted to write another fantasy book, I'd have to go back to that small press and offer it to them, even if Random House had already expressed interest. I might have to wait two months before the small press offered me another $2,000 before I could turn it down and go back to Random House, and by then, their enthusiasm might have cooled. So think long-term, and never be afraid to negotiate, even if you don't see what the "big deal" is yet.

Copyright Registration

Unless the book is a work-for-hire (which it shouldn't be, unless you've been hired by a book packager, for a series book, or as a ghostwriter), the copyright should always be in your name, and the publisher should be responsible for registering it. If you're dealing with any legitimate publisher, you never will have to pay for copyright registration.

Timeframe to Publication

There always should be a limit to the amount of time a publisher has to publish your work. If no timeframe is listed, you run a significant risk: What if the publisher runs into monetary problems or reorganizes the types of books they publish and decides to put your book on the back burner for years?

What if they're not even really sure if they want to publish it anymore, but they've already paid your advance, so they think they should hang onto it just in case? What if—and here's a lousy one—they bought it to keep it off the market? That's an unusual one, but not unknown. Every now and then, a publisher will purposely buy a book that stands to compete with a book they're about to publish (or have already published), then they purposely don't release it, or don't market it, because it may interfere with the success of the other book.

Sometimes the problem isn't even the publisher's "fault," but a shift in the market. For example, many books about terrorism were delayed after 9/11. Three novelists I know had their books fall in limbo for several months; I'm not even sure if one was ever released. A book about technology may become obsolete before publication. A biography of a movie star may get shelved if the star gets arrested.

Then there are the "force majeure" ("act of God," unavoidable catastrophe) problems: What if the publisher's building burns down, or there's a flood, earthquake, hurricane, or other such emergency that forces the publisher to delay your book's production?

There are many reasonable causes for a project to be delayed, but the author should have the right to take the book back if the publisher doesn't show plans to get the book released right away once the immediate problem has ended.

Generally, a contract will stipulate that the publisher has somewhere between twelve and twenty-four months to release the book after the publisher has accepted the manuscript. Always aim for the shortest time possible (do you want to wait two years before the book hits shelves and you can begin earning royalties?) while understanding that you probably don't want the publisher to rush your book to print in less than six months. There are many steps that need to be taken care of before a book is released: editing, copyediting, typesetting, proofreading, (possible) indexing, cover design, endorsements, catalogue inclusion, listing with Books in Print, press releases, advance review copies to the trade, etc. To get reviewed in most major trade magazines, the publisher will have to send copies of your book months in advance of the release date; you don't want them to skip this step because they're rushing to get the book out too quickly. Twelve to eighteen months at maximum is plenty of time, and most publishers hit this timeframe.

MODEL FAILURE TO PUBLISH CLAUSE

If Publisher does not publish the Work within the time specified above for reasons other than first serial or book club use, delays of Author in returning the copyedited manuscript or proofs, Author's failure to comply with requests made by Publisher's counsel or delays caused by circumstances beyond Publisher's control and if Publisher at any time thereafter receives written notice from Author demanding publication, Publisher shall within 90 days of Publisher's receipt of such written demand either publish the Work or revert to Author in writing all rights to the Work granted to Publisher in this Agreement, subject to any outstanding licenses, which shall be assigned to Author, and Author shall retain any advance payments made under this Agreement prior to such reversion as liquidated damages for Publisher's failure to publish the Work.

The Agency Clause

This is an almost-universal clause (see section 17.13 of form 5—Trade Publishing Agreement—in the appendix) requiring the publisher to send all royalties to your agent (if you have one), and for the agent to keep her commission before passing the money on to you.

Watch for the words "coupled with an interest" anywhere in this clause. This is a bit of legalese intended to make the agency relationship irrevocable. Ordinarily, a principal (you) may terminate your relationship with the agent at will (or at the end of a contract term), and the agency relationship terminates automatically on the death or disability of the principal. This clause, however, grants the agent the exclusive, irrevocable right to royalties from your work for the entire term of its copyright and the right to receive your royalty checks.

This means that even if you terminate your relationship with the agent, and the rights to your book revert to you from the publisher, you are obligated to pay the agent a commission forever for all future sales, even if the agent did nothing to cause that sale! If you get a new agent and sell the book to a new publisher, it could even mean you would be paying two agency commissions, which could amount to thirty percent or more. This also would apply to your heirs.

The benefit to the agent of this clause actually is negligible because once an agent has closed a deal for a publishing contract or the sale of other rights, the right to receive commissions is "vested" in the agent. That is, the agent is entitled to his commission for the life of the publishing agreement, even if you subsequently terminate your relationship with the agent. The apparent goal of the clause, to obtain royalties for the exploitation of the work after it goes out of print with this publisher, seems rather pointless, as usually there is little such value.

So why fight it? Besides the fact that you shouldn't have to pay an agent for work he hasn't done, the clause means that you can't terminate the agent relationship, and your royalty checks will always be routed through him. If he dies, or his corporation or LLC goes under, or he/it goes bankrupt, your royalties could be tied up for a long time in probate or bankruptcy court. You must have the right to direct the publisher to send royalty checks directly to you in the event you terminate your agency agreement or in the event of the agent's death or bankruptcy.

Subsidiary Rights

The only obvious right you must confer to a publisher is the book rights. Of course you're giving the publisher the right to print and sell your book. But there are lots of other rights involved with your work, too.

The only obvious right you must confer to a publisher is the book rights.

These are called "subsidiary" rights because they are subsidiary to your primary grant of print rights. For example, if your book is being published in hardcover, these would include motion picture and television rights, paperback and book club rights, rights to make various kinds of adaptations and sequels, sound recording rights, foreign publication rights, etc. If you grant these rights to the publisher, it usually will not exercise them directly but will administer them for you.

Most publishing agreements split subsidiary rights equally between the author and publisher. The primary exception is first serial rights (serial rights are the rights that magazines, newspapers, and e-zines take if they want to run an excerpt of your book), which generally are 90 percent to the author, 10 percent to the publisher.

Unless there is a specific reason not to do so, always try to retain as many subsidiary rights as you can. They're worth money, and chances are good that the publisher will not actively pursue selling most of them. The most important subsidiary rights for most authors are film, foreign, and translation rights.

Most publishing agreements split subsidiary rights equally between the author and publisher.

Film rights allow your book to be made into a movie. This is a right I'd almost always advise authors to keep for themselves. This can be a sizeable chunk of money, and if the publisher is not involved in selling or making the movie, why should it get all (or any) of the money from the sale? An agent can exploit these rights better than most publishers: Most literary agents have film sub-agents, which means that the agent can give your book to another agent who specializes in dealing with film producers. If you've kept the rights and the producer bites, you have to share a commission with your agent, but you don't owe the publisher any money. If the publisher shares a fifty-fifty split with you, not only does your agent get a commission, but you have to share the sale money with the publisher, even if the publisher wasn't at all involved in making the deal. And again, if they control the rights, they make all the decisions; you don't get to negotiate the terms.

Foreign rights give the publisher the right to market your book to non-U.S. publishers. **Translation rights** give the publisher the right to have the book translated into other languages; often these two rights are grouped together as "foreign and translation." Should you give them to the publisher? Some publishers do aggressively pitch their books to foreign publishers (and many now are part of the same multinational corporation), so they may be in a position to make more sales than you or your agent could. In that case, it's not bad to split the money—they do the work, and you just collect extra checks. But in most cases, it's better for you to retain the foreign rights yourself.

If you have an agent, the agent can pitch your book either herself or through sub-agents, so you keep all the money aside from agency commissions. If you don't, you have to do the legwork and contact foreign agents or foreign publishers yourself. In some cases, the publishers will come to you: If your book does very well in the United States, chances are good that "scouts" will be watching to offer you a deal to print the book abroad (in English or translated into other languages).

The main problem is that it's hard to determine how aggressive the publisher may be with exploiting foreign rights. Twice, I've asked for an honest assessment before I signed over those rights: I wanted to know if the publishers really would use them. They both assured me that they worked with foreign houses all the time and would pitch the book like crazy. Never happened. Not once did I hear a peep about their pitching my book to any overseas publishers. Be smarter than I was: If you're considering letting them keep foreign rights (with a percentage of the money to you, of course), ask for details: How many of their books have been published overseas? Do most of their books have multiple overseas deals? Where will they pitch your book and who will be responsible for it?

> If you've written a book that pertains to a very
> American way of doing things (in a nonfiction book,
> for example), no amount of salesmanship is going to
> make the book right for a foreign market,
> so it's a less crucial issue.

The secondary problem is that if you let them keep foreign rights, they're the ones who get to negotiate and determine the deals, and you have to agree to them. They could agree to sell French rights to your book for $100, and you couldn't turn it down.

All of this supposes that you have a book with international appeal. If you've written a book that pertains to a very American way of doing things (in a nonfiction book, for example), no amount of salesmanship is going to make the book right for a foreign market, so it's a less crucial issue.

Publishers usually retain **book club rights**, which is the right to sell to book clubs, who print their own run of your book, again with a fifty-fifty split of the proceeds. They'll typically also ask for **audio rights** and **electronic rights** (the right to turn your book into an audio recording and an e-book). The larger publishing houses often publish audio and e-books themselves.

Merchandising rights cover the right to sell things like T-shirts, mugs, stuffed animals, board games, and tote bags related to your book. In most cases, these rights have little value and the publisher will allow you to keep them. On the other hand, if the potential for exploitation of such rights are obvious, it is a rare publisher that will let them go.

Front and Back Matter

For nonfiction books, publishers often require authors, at their cost, to provide "front matter" and "back matter" such as tables of contents and illustrations, indices, and the like, even though the publisher is much better equipped to generate these. This can be negotiated. Be sure you understand your responsibilities and the cost to you (such as paying an indexer) before you sign on the dotted line.

Most publishers can't even have the author do the index without holding up the book—it has to be done at the very last minute. So what many publishers mean is that they want the right to ask the author for a list of indexing terms, and they'll build the index from it.

Some clauses say that the publisher will hire an indexer and take the money out of the author's advance or royalties. Before agreeing to that, spell out the cost (or upper limit of the cost). None of the publishers I've dealt with made me prepare an index or pay for its preparation. The truth is, that for most publishers, the "indexing charge" is simply a profit center that generates additional income. Don't be reluctant to negotiate this point if it's in your contract.

Corrections

Some contracts call for the author to pay for corrections to the manuscript that need to be made after the typesetting stage. In other words, after the manuscript has been copyedited, it goes to a typesetter for final layout. At this point, there should be very few corrections still to be made. Perhaps a few typos slipped through. Perhaps someone you thanked in the acknowledgments got married and changed her name. Perhaps a URL is no longer valid. You should never have to pay for small changes like this.

When there are significant errors in the typesetting stage (especially when the error(s) cause lines to be added or removed and alter the layout of all the following pages), the publisher has to pay the typesetter again for the next pass. So they want to ensure that you're being vigilant about checking for errors before it gets to that point.

However, there are things beyond your control. What if you finished the manuscript in January and it didn't go to typesetting until November, by which time some of the information in your book became outdated, some of the web sites disappeared, or new information needed to be added? If there is a clause that holds you responsible for the cost of corrections, make sure it's extremely restricted: It can include only corrections to mistakes that you made and were in your control and must be beyond a definable percentage or number of corrections.

Revised Editions

This clause applies to nonfiction books only, but in this case it can become paramount. Make sure the clause has a mechanism to determine when the revisions have become so extensive it is essentially a new book subject to a new contract (and more money!), and that the clause puts a cap on the number of revisions in any one time period. You might add a sentence that says revisions will not be requested more than once every two years.

To give an example of how this clause comes into play, let's say you wrote a book about taxes. Three years later, tax laws had changed significantly and a revised edition was in order. If your contract calls for it, you're obligated to rewrite the book in a timely manner for no extra pay. Negotiate for what you consider reasonable: If less than 10 percent of the text needs to be rewritten, maybe that's fine by you and you don't expect extra payment for it (especially if you're earning decent royalties). But what if 30 or 50 percent of the book needs an overhaul? That can be a lot of time and work for you, and you may see no payment for your efforts. The time to negotiate is not three years from now; you must make sure the protocol is laid out in your original contract.

Generally, a publisher will not call for a revised edition of a book that isn't selling well. They'd rather let the book go out of print than to pulp the books left and pay for new editing, proofreading, typesetting, and printing. They will do it only if they believe the book will go on to sell many more copies in the revised edition. But it may or may not feel worth it to you.

If you cannot execute the revisions or choose not to do them, what happens?

Many contracts specify that the publisher can hire someone else to revise the book, and to cut down your royalties to pay for that expense. Here's the clause I agreed to for this book: "If the Author does not agree to prepare the Revised Edition, the Publisher shall have the right to arrange with others for the preparation of the Revised Edition and charge the reasonable cost of doing so against sums accruing to the Author under this Agreement. In such case, in the Publisher's reasonable discretion, this charge may be in the form of a fee and/or a percentage of the Author's royalty for this Revised Edition or percentages for this Revised Edition and future editions, but in no event shall Author's royalties be reduced below 75 percent for the amount due for the previous edition for the second edition, 50 percent for the third, and 25 percent for all subsequent editions in which the Author's work appears. The Revised Edition may be published under the same title and may refer to the Author by name, but credit may be given to the reviser(s) in the Revised Edition(s) and in advertising and promotional material."

Always be on the lookout for vague terms that state simply that the publisher will hire a writer to revise and deduct the cost from your royalties; there should be specific caps on the amount of money the publisher may deduct from your checks.

Also, be sure that the revised editions don't start you at zero again in terms of sales numbers. Let's say your contract says you receive 11 percent royalties on the first 5,000 copies sold, 12.5 percent on the next 5,000, and 15 percent thereafter. You've already sold 12,000 books, which puts you in the 12.5 percent royalty bracket. If the publisher tries to consider the revised edition a separate book, you may go back to the 11 percent bracket.

```
Always be on the lookout for vague terms that state
simply that the publisher will hire a writer to revise
       and deduct the cost from your royalties.
```

For a model revised edition clause, see section 15 of form 5—Trade Publishing Agreement—in the appendix.

Right of Approval

Some new authors expect that the title they choose will be the title on the book. Surprise! This is often—maybe even usually—not the case. The publisher will want the right to change your title. Marketing teams often study successful books in your category to determine what kinds of titles work best—short, straightforward, artsy? They may also want to get certain kewords into the title. If possible, you'll want to have the right to refuse a title they've chosen.

Same with your cover art. With many of my books, I didn't even see the cover art until it was already up on Amazon.com, so I certainly didn't have any input.

Most contracts do not include a provision allowing the author any involvement in the course of choosing a title or approving cover art.

Of course you should trust your publisher, but you should also be included in this process and have the right to make suggestions. Most contracts do not include a provision allowing the author any involvement in the course of choosing a title or approving cover art. If you can negotiate it, try to include a statement to this effect: "Publisher agrees to consult with Author in the design and creation of cover art and titles."

Statements

Some of the contracts I've been offered have stipulated that if no royalties are due in a certain period, the publisher doesn't have to send me anything. That is, they don't even have to send me a statement to let me know how my book is doing. Not good.

Make sure that even if you're not owed a check, you still get a statement to tell you exactly how many books were sold and how much you earned toward recouping your advance.

There also should be a specified time limit on sending royalties and statements. Typically, publishers send royalty statements twice a year. In the contract, it should tell you which months the royalties are accounted; payments and statements should be rendered within thirty days of the end of those months, as most publishers do hold onto those checks until the last minute.

Audit Clause

Not all publishing contracts contain an audit clause, but they all should.

Rarely should you need to invoke one, but if you have reason to suspect that you've sold more books than the publisher has paid you for, you should have the right to have a certified public accountant examine the publisher's records as they relate to the sales and inventory of your book to certify the accuracy of the publisher's accounting.

Be very aware of clauses that give *you* the right to audit, but not an accountant.

Further, if the accountant does find errors and it turns out that the publisher owes you money, the publisher should pay for the cost of the examination. As a secondary option, if you don't want to pay for an accountant to visit the publisher's offices, the publisher should agree to mail photocopies or send faxes of records for the accountant to view.

Be very aware of clauses that give *you* the right to audit, but not an accountant. You, as an author, probably have no idea what to look for in the publisher's records. PublishAmerica has used this clause to block author's accountants from inspecting their records; they've insisted that the author is the only one allowed to see the records. What good would that do you?

MODEL AUDIT CLAUSE

Upon written request and reasonable notice to Publisher, Author's certified public accountant may, within one year of any royalty statement, examine Publisher's records of accounts as they relate to the sales and inventory of the Work for the purpose of certifying the accuracy of Publisher's accounting to Author. The audit shall be during regular business hours and Publisher shall reasonably assist in the audit. Author shall pay for all costs in connection with such an examination unless errors of accounting amounting to 5 percent or more of the total sum paid to Author shall be found to Author's disadvantage, in which case the cost shall be borne by Publisher. At Author's option, the records of account may be performed through examination of photocopies or facsimiles of Publisher's applicable records.

Out of Print

Your grant of rights to the publisher is generally limited only by this clause (in addition, since 1976, any author may terminate his or her grant of exclusive or nonexclusive rights after thirty-five years for post-1978 works). It therefore is critical that "out of print" be defined reasonably, especially now that digital and on-demand publishing can make the literal meaning of the clause obsolete. Ideally, the definition should be pegged to the publisher's marketing efforts—when the book no longer is in the publisher's catalog and/or available through major chains, it should be considered "out of print," regardless of whether it can be bought online. When a publisher sells a book for remaindering (deeply discounted), it should automatically be declared out of print because the publisher has no more copies to sell.

> ## MODEL OUT OF PRINT DEFINITION
>
> The Work shall be considered "out of print" if it is not available in the U.S. through regular retail channels in an English language book form edition (not print-on-demand, digital, or other mechanical means of reproduction) and not listed in Publisher's catalog.

Many "out of print" clauses are far too vague, suggesting only that when a book is no longer available, the author can ask for it to be declared out of print, and a publisher has to respond within a certain timeframe. But what does "available" mean? If there are no copies in bookstores anywhere, but the book can still be ordered on the publisher's web site or from its catalog, it's technically available. If there are no books left, but if the publisher still lists an e-book version, it's technically available, which means you're stuck with the same publisher.

Other contracts may state that the book is declared out of print if there are fewer than a certain number of books left in circulation, or if your royalties fall below a certain amount for one or more accounting periods.

It's not in your best interest to have your rights tied up by a publisher who's no longer doing anything with them. Once they're no longer actively marketing your book and it has stopped selling in decent quantities, your best bet is to get the rights back and either resell them to a new publisher (difficult, but not impossible), self-publish the book, cut it up and sell the serial rights to magazines or anthologies, or so on.

It's not in your best interest to have
your rights tied up by a publisher who's
no longer doing anything with them.

The publisher may well take the initiative, declare it out of print when demand has dried up, and return all rights to you; however, you can't count on this. A writer-friend of mine encountered the vastly frustrating situation of a publisher who let six months elapse between printings twice after print runs had already sold out. The publisher apparently had cash-flow problems, so his big idea was to wait until there were at least five hundred back-orders before ordering a new print run. The problem, of course, was that few people back-order a title that's not on bookstore shelves and not readily available at the major online bookstores. Each time he built up momentum, the print run sold out and his efforts were lost because no one could get the book while the publisher sat around waiting to see if at least five hundred people would order the book before going back to the printer.

This friend of mine would have been much better off if he could have invoked an "out of print" clause and had the book republished by another publisher who wouldn't have kept letting it go out of stock!

Also, what happens to the leftover books when the contract terminates? You'll want a provision here that allows you to buy the remaining stock at a significantly reduced rate; this way, you can still sell the books yourself through your web site, at public speaking engagements, and so on. Generally, you can negotiate to buy remaining stock at the rate of the publisher's cost. If you might ever want to self-publish the book, you can also negotiate a low price for the printing plates, which will save you an expense down the line.

Getting Past the Wall

Especially when you're a first-time author, negotiating can feel scary. Even if you get up the nerve to ask for changes, you may be afraid to push the issue if a publisher says no to any of them.

Here's a response you're bound to get sooner or later: "That's a standard clause." The implication, of course, is that you're too green to know the difference, and that you don't have the stature to warrant special treatment. But "standard" doesn't have to mean "acceptable."

Remember that once you've been offered a contract, you're the one with power. They want your book. Now it's up to you to tell them what you want. It's highly unlikely that a publisher would take back an offer because you want to fix the wording of an out-of-print clause, cross out the "first option" clause, retain film rights, or add an audit clause.

Sometimes contracts will go through several passes. You should never feel intimidated or pressured into signing something you're not comfortable with just because you feel pushy, or you're worried the publisher will see you as disagreeable. Even if they don't say so, publishers respect authors who know their worth.

Of course, it is possible to go too far. Remember that it's a friendly negotiation, not a war, and that both sides will need to compromise. There's a happy medium between being a pushover and being a pain.

Prioritize your requested changes; you can use the less-important changes as bargaining chips. You'll agree to let go of some of the less important changes if they'll make the important ones.

You should never feel intimidated or pressured into
signing something you're not comfortable with just
because you feel pushy, or you're worried the publisher
will see you as disagreeable.

Many authors look no further than the numbers on the advance and royalty rates. Of course those are important numbers, but you have to think long-term and imagine what your interests will be not only next year, but five or ten years from now, too. If you wrote *Harry Potter and the Sorcerer's Stone* and were so delighted that a publisher accepted it that you didn't pay attention to who controlled the film rights or merchandising rights, wouldn't you be furious with yourself?

Likewise, what if you wrote the first *Chicken Soup for the Soul* book and agreed to offer the publisher your next work on the same terms as the first?

Or if you were waiting for your first big royalty check and found out that the publisher decided that 80 percent was a "reasonable" reserve against returns, meaning that you'd be paid only 20 percent of what you earned that accounting period?

Just like you should never "settle" on a spouse, neither should you settle on a publishing agreement that doesn't make you happy.

It's okay to take it slow with negotiations and go back and forth several times until you're completely satisfied with the contract. Neither one of you wants to walk away from the deal at this point, so you'll both have reason to compromise on suitable terms. If you find that the publisher will not agree on a point you think is important, it may be better for you to walk away and find a publisher who will agree. Just like you should never "settle" on a spouse, neither should you settle on a publishing agreement that doesn't make you happy.

Chapter 6

After-Publication Rip-Offs for Book Authors

Dishonest Reviewers

Worthless Publicity Services

Lying Publicists

Sell Your Book, Keep Your Money

```
You might think that as long as you get through the
     publication stage unharmed, you're home free.
                  I wish it were so.
```

Once your book is published (or about to be published), though, you get the joy of being a target for other sorts of rip-offs and problems.

Paying for Reviews

As recently as 2002, I would have told you that there are no legitimate book review publications that charge for a review. Unfortunately, now I can't make it quite that black and white, because two high-profile trade magazines in the book industry now have an optional "paid review" service: *ForeWord* and *Kirkus*.

Yes, it bothers me that they crossed the line. And it brings up all sorts of ethical issues. And if people realize you paid for a review, they're less likely to take it (or your book) seriously.

The way it usually works is this: A publisher sends out review copies to all the book's major media targets. They may also send press releases to a book's less-influential or less-likely-to-feature-it media targets, along with instructions for obtaining a free review copy. Then, anyone else who catches wind of the book and is interested in reviewing it can also contact the publisher to request a copy.

Money isn't exchanged in either direction: Reviewers aren't expected to buy the book, and authors aren't expected to pay for reviews. Publications are supposed to review books as a service to their readers, to help point them to worthy books and steer them away from stinkers.

But as vanity presses rose, newspapers devoted less space to reviews, and desperate authors had more and more trouble getting their books reviewed, some people got an idea: "Hey! I'll review people's books . . . as long as they pay me to do it."

Some of these outfits (or individual reviewers) actually bought or rented email lists and spammed all the authors they could find to offer them this "great deal." For only $99 (or however much money), they'd read your book and write a review.

Sometimes they'd post the review on their own site, sometimes on Amazon and BN.com, and sometimes they'd just give the review to the author to deal with its publicity.

Then some people decided they just weren't exploiting writers' pocketbooks quite enough, and they added onto their services. "Hey! For more money, we'll put an interview of you on our site! We'll send our review to other publications for you! We'll put up your picture and ordering information on our site! Pay some more and we'll even make you this week's 'Featured Author!'"

Why, just two days ago, I got an unsolicited email offering me the wonderful chance to have my own author's page with an interview and a press release for "only" $250! It told me I could join bestselling authors Stephen King, Jonathan Kellerman, Alice Sebold, Jerry Seinfeld, and others. Are you telling me that those bestsellers paid $250 for their "author pages" on this little-known site, too? Please. (This same outfit, BooksAndAuthors.net, spammed me six times in three weeks, even after I asked them to remove me from their list. I finally blocked the email address.)

> Even if a publication has a small
> circulation, you can still feel safe about
> quoting from the review in your media kit,
> press release, web site, or book cover without ever
> worrying that someone's going to "out" you.

You might as well ask your cousin to interview you, then set up your own web site for about $50 and email your own press release out. You won't have to share space with any other authors, and you never have to worry about the site going out of business.

If you find one of these offers that appears too good to be true, write to other authors who appear on the web site or whose books were reviewed and ask about their experiences. Ask them what kind of results they got.

You can't use a review from a service like this in your media kit, because if an editor or journalist looks up the name of the reviewer and finds out it's a paid service, it automatically discredits the review and makes you look desperate or dishonest. You couldn't get anyone legitimate to review your book, so you had to pay someone to say it was good?

It's far better to keep plugging away and trying to get legitimate reviews. Even if a publication has a small circulation, you can still feel safe about quoting from the review in your media kit, press release, web site, or book cover without ever worrying that someone's going to "out" you. And if it's a small publication but well-respected in your niche, the review may carry more weight than one from a bigger publication that doesn't target your audience.

I'm not yet sure how *ForeWord's* and *Kirkus's* paid review service will affect their credibility, or if other legitimate publications will follow suit. Right now, both of these publications still offer free reviews to any books they deem to be noteworthy, but authors whose books aren't chosen have the option to pay for a guaranteed review. The review, mind you, is not guaranteed to be positive. They claim that all of their reviews, paid or not, are unbiased.

This is not the case with the enterprising schemers who solicit new authors, of course. You pay, they praise. That's how it works, or no one would pay again.

But before you spend all that money on a review or interview that will likely have no effect on sales, invest it in postage and send the book (or review copy ordering instructions) to all the real reviewers you can find.

Reviewers Who Don't Review

Then, of course, there's the problem of reviewers who request a book and don't actually have any intention of reviewing it (or have anywhere to place the review even if they mean well).

Depending on your or your publisher's budget, you may decide to just eat the cost of these few deadbeat reviewers, or you may do a little questioning before sending out your limited review copies.

```
If the person is (or claims to be) a freelance writer,
  however, ask where he's placed reviews before. If you
have any doubts, look up the person's name in Google to
     see if you can find any previous reviews.
```

Ask, of course, where the person intends to place the review. If you're dealing with a staff writer at a newspaper, magazine, or somewhat popular e-zine that seems appropriate for your topic, relax and send it. If the person is (or claims to be) a freelance writer, however, ask where he's placed reviews before. If you have any doubts, look up the person's name in Google to see if you can find any previous reviews.

If the person has no past credits or has placed reviews in only small e-zines or web sites, consider offering an alternative: an electronic copy of the manuscript. Ask your publisher to convert your manuscript into PDF format or do it yourself using one of the many free programs available for download on the Web or the converter at https://createpdf.adobe.com. (As of this printing, you can convert five files free before you have to pay a subscription fee.) This will significantly cut back on costs, and you won't have to turn down reviewers who may surprise you and end up placing great reviews.

If your publicity budget is low, you can offer the electronic file to book review web sites and sites related to your topic and see how many bite; then, if someone writes back to say, "I'd be interested in reviewing it, but only in hard copy," you can make a decision about whether or not to send it.

Just because an author sends something does not mean the reviewer is now indebted and required to pay back this "favor" with a review, especially if the book isn't a good match for the publication's audience.

Even if a person has requested a book, he's under no obligation to actually review it, and there's no point in trying to force it (you'll probably end up with a hostile review if you succeed, anyway). Even at small newspapers, book review staffs receive far more books than they could ever have space to review. They try to pick the books they feel deserve attention or will interest their readers the most, but even worthy books sometimes don't catch on with reviewers.

Keep that in mind, especially if you've sent a book to someone who didn't specifically request it. Once or twice, I've been amazed by an author's angry reaction when I didn't review a book that was sent to me unsolicited. Just because an author sends something does not mean the reviewer is now indebted and required to pay back this "favor" with a review, especially if the book isn't a good match for the publication's audience. Be realistic and make sure you're targeting the right kinds of publications. *The New York Times* is unlikely to review your book about how to become a stenographer, and Salon.com is unlikely to review your parenting title. Niche books aren't usually right for national publications, and general interest books aren't usually right for niche publications.

You'll stand a better chance of getting a review placed if you follow up politely once or twice; first (after about two weeks), you can write to make sure the book arrived and reached its intended recipient, and the second time (after about six to eight weeks), you can write to ask if the reviewer has had a chance to read it.

Reviewers Who Sell or Return Books

You will encounter reviewers every now and then who will capitalize on the free book and offer it for resale on Amazon, eBay, or at used bookstores. Or worse, there are some who try to return it for cash or credit at a bookstore—which means that not only did you spend the money to send the book to these idiots, but you've also just lost royalties. It's just not worth it to fret about this too much, and unless you're sending out thousands of review copies, it's unlikely to have an impact on your own sales potential. It's a nuisance, but not a cause for massive paranoia.

It's acceptable for a reviewer to donate the book to a library or charity or give it to a friend, but a reviewer should not profit from the sale of the book.

As a measure against these problems, many publishers stamp the words "Review Copy: Not For Resale" on the book's top surface, inside the cover, or over the bar code. This won't necessarily stop unscrupulous reviewers from selling it online, but it should stop them from being able to sell it or return it to a bookstore. Another potential solution is to autograph the books you send with the reviewer's name—this looks like special treatment and is a nice touch, but also makes it harder for a reviewer to return or resell a book on the sly.

It's acceptable for a reviewer to donate the book to a library or charity or give it to a friend, but a reviewer should not profit from the sale of the book. If you happen to see a book of yours that you know was a review copy on Amazon's Marketplace or on eBay, alert their abuse departments and they can end the listing. Beyond that, try not to lose sleep over it.

Advertise and We'll Review

Some magazines and newspapers pressure authors to place paid advertisements. "We can't guarantee a review," they may say, "unless you reserve a display ad." Then they'll tell you how an ad combined with a review will increase your response.

Don't do it. Don't advertise in a newspaper or magazine unless you get co-op dollars from your distributor or small press group, or your publisher does, and don't let the ad appear in the same issue as your review. It's expensive, it cheapens your review, and it's just not worth it—most booksellers aren't looking at ads, they are reading the editorial.

Commercial publishers spend very little money on advertising in magazines and newspapers (or even on TV or radio). Typically, the only advertising dollars they'll spend are in targeted book review journals; for example, romance publishers may advertise a hot new book in *Romantic Times BOOKclub*. This isn't because publishers are cheap; it's because conventional advertising is typically ineffective for books. Readers pay more attention to reviews, word of mouth, how much they liked the author's last book, bookstore displays, and author interviews or profiles than they do to advertisements.

Paying for advertising in exchange for a guaranteed review is really just a slightly less-obvious form of paying for a review. You still have no way of knowing if the review will be positive, negative, or lukewarm; and if it is positive, readers may assume it's biased because you're a paid advertiser.

Publications sometimes use a different approach and tell you that your review is scheduled to appear . . . then they pressure you to advertise in conjunction with it. Do not feel obligated, and consider the probable payoff carefully.

> Commercial publishers spend very little money on advertising in magazines and newspapers (or even on TV or radio).

Sad Marketing Stories

"I've actually heard of people mortgaging their homes to pay for ads in *The New York Times Book Review*, which won't sell a single copy of a subsidy-published book from an unknown," says author and self-publisher Morris Rosenthal (www.fonerbooks.com).

Diana Hignutt would agree with that. She's a former PublishAmerica author who's now published with a small, legitimate press, so she can compare the difference between the two. Diana was a poster girl for publicity efforts. With her first book, she spent a tremendous amount of money and time on promotion. She bought custom-made bookmarks, fliers, and posters. She took out ads in *Radio-TV Interview Report* (RTIR), and because of that, she appeared on hundreds of radio shows across the country. She also appeared on three national television shows, including *The O'Reilly Factor*.

Diana did book signings, was interviewed in virtually every major newspaper in the Philadelphia area, and landed dozens of reviews. She even bought her own books and sold them at cost to bookstores (sometimes at a loss). The grand total for her efforts? About seven hundred books sold.

Her Herculean efforts didn't pay off because the distribution wasn't in place. In other words, no matter how much work she did to publicize the book, people weren't able to find it in bookstores, so it didn't take off.

Not that there would be any guarantees even if the book were available in stores. If you have money to blow, I'm not going to stop you from blowing it, but I will warn you that most of the authors I know who've spent more than about $500 on their own publicity budgets have been sorely disappointed.

Morris has spent ad dollars to learn his lessons the hard way. A cooperative mailing to three thousand libraries sold only three of his books—and cost him $750. Over time, he learned that paid advertising was a waste for him, and that the most effective ways to draw in customers were to get reviews and to place significant excerpts of his books on his web site.

He says that many vanity presses offer worthless publicity services at high prices, and that they target vulnerable people in the same way telemarketers do—hoping that for every one hundred savvy authors, they'll find one or two who will buy into their hype. "The truth is, if you want to spend $10,000 to sell books, it would be much easier to give strangers on the street $10 and tell them to go buy a copy of your book," he says.

"Be a Guest" Services

Some fee-based web sites and newsletters focus on helping authors and experts land interviews on radio and television. I haven't personally used any of these services, but the only one I've heard mostly good things about is *Radio-TV Interview Report*.

What you need to examine is who visits the site, who reads the newsletter, and the success rate of the site's efforts. It's not good enough for a site to have a big, impressive list of the people who receive their newsletter or have at one time visited their site; they may have spammed lots of big companies (they can then say Oprah's staff receives their newsletter), and just because a radio producer visited the site once or twice doesn't mean he's actually booking guests who are listed there.

Be skeptical and play detective. Again, contact the authors who are listed and ask what their results have been. Their contact information should be readily available because they want show producers to contact them.

You might be shocked by what you learn. I contacted author Bill Sardi, who writes anti-aging books and reports, and asked him how many bookings he's landed by being listed on GuestFinder.com. "Zero," he told me. Another author and syndicated columnist, Isadora Alman of "Ask Isadora" fame, says, "A couple of years ago Guest Finder was great, resulting in several calls a month. It went on hiatus. Since its return, I haven't gotten one call that I know for sure came from there." The company currently charges $249 for a regular one-year membership.

It's not good enough for a site to have a big, impressive list of the people who receive their newsletter or have at one time visited their site.

This contrasts with the responses I got when I asked about the *Radio-TV Interview Report*. On average, respondents said they got five to six interviews a month from their ads, and most said they would continue advertising. One said his publisher paid for the ads, and he wasn't sure it was enough of a payoff to justify the price tag.

Author KayLee Parker says the timing counts. She's been advertising on and off in RTIR for two years, and says, "My best results were in my January ads when shows were looking for professional organizers for the beginning of the year to talk about getting organized. My ads at other times of the year were non-producers and not worth the money, so you need to understand when your book topic is hot or there will be no interest in having you on a program."

One site where you can pitch yourself or get listed by a show host without spending money is www.radioonline.com. "I did one interview a couple of years ago, and the producers put out a notice on the site and I had forty more interviews in two weeks," says Lauri Berkenkamp, author of several books in the *Go Parents!* series. "I still get calls from stations because of that."

Tim Bete, author of *In the Beginning . . . There Were No Diapers,* says most of his TV and radio interviews have come from his own direct pitches to producers. "If you can afford it, access to an online media directory such as Bacon's is wonderful. You can target your pitches and do a lot of ongoing publicity yourself." He also recommends ProfNet, where appropriate leads have come in almost daily, resulting in his appearance in magazines as popular as *Parenting*. If you're not represented by a publicist, you can instead join ProfNet's PR Leads at www.prleads.com, which is meant for authors and speakers.

Much of Tim's self-directed publicity efforts were online; before his book was published, he had already lined up about 125 book reviews on web sites. "Not all were huge sites, but the repetition is critical to get people to buy your book," he says. "You want prospective buyers to keep stumbling over your book until they buy it."

Pay to Be on the Radio?

No! Don't do it! There are even some internet radio stations now charging authors for the "privilege" of appearing on their shows. Show producers are supposed to choose guests based on merit and audience appeal. Once a show starts charging guests, it becomes a series of paid infomercials, and you tell me: how likely are you to tune in to a station where anyone who can pay their way in gets to appear so they can hawk their products to you? In much the same way as publishers are supposed to make their money from readers, not authors, radio shows are supposed to make their money from advertisers, not guests!

Inexperienced Publicists

You may decide that you want to hire an independent publicist to help you promote your book. A savvy publicist can, indeed, do a lot to help your career, but this isn't a cheap gamble. A good publicist can cost you several thousand dollars per month, and most book campaigns run for at least three months.

This is an area where referrals are important. Write to authors you respect and ask them who they've worked with and who they recommend. Really ask around.

The greatest publicist can't do a thing about an author who comes across as dull or inarticulate in interviews.

When you've narrowed the field, scrutinize the publicist's track record. Has she worked as an in-house publicist for a major publisher? How long has she been a publicist? Has she represented best-selling authors? Has she represented books like yours before? Did the books like yours get national media attention? How did they sell?

One way to get an idea of sales is to find the book's ISBN (check on Amazon), then call Ingram's automated hotline at (615) 213-6803. Listen in for the sales figures. Keep in mind that Ingram's numbers usually don't represent all sales for a title, so don't use this alone as a bellwether for sales; it doesn't count sales the publisher made directly, book club sales, most library sales, or sales by other wholesalers, for example; but it does give you a point of comparison. Check the book's sales against similar books and see which fares better.

A publicist is not solely responsible for sales numbers, mind you. It's the publicist's job to get the book media attention and to give the author opportunities to appear on radio, television, and in print . . . but then the author has to do a good job with those appearances. The greatest publicist can't do a thing about an author who comes across as dull or inarticulate in interviews, nor can she ensure that the reviews will be positive!

Because of this, don't expect a publicist to work on commission. My publicist, Marsha Friedman of Event Management Services, says she frequently gets "offers" from authors who don't want to pay her up front, but instead say they'll "cut her in on the action" by giving her a percentage of sales. Forget it—publicists have heard this line before, and they know better. The publicist may do her job beautifully and your book could still tank. What if she manages to get you on *Good Morning America* and then you freeze up, stutter, and do an all-around lousy job of plugging your book? Or what if you do beautifully, but your distributor isn't prepared for the demand or your publisher is a POD press that can't get books stocked in stores? Neither is her fault.

Some publicists, however, offer a "pay as you go" plan where you pay based on how many bookings they get you. Don't be too quick to jump on this option—it's not necessarily cheaper than hiring a publicist on a monthly basis, and you'll likely get fewer bookings than you would if you hired a publicist outright.

The quality of the bookings is more important than the quantity, as well. One national talk show appearance will probably do a lot more for you than a dozen local news appearances. Pay attention to radio stations' wattage and Arbitron ratings to get an idea of the station's popularity and reach.

Arbitron ratings for radio work like the Nielsen ratings for TV; they take a random sampling of the population on an ongoing basis and ask them to record their radio listening habits to determine how many people listen to each station. In general, you want publicists who book their guests on stations with at least 50,000 watts and high Arbitron ratings.

Pre-Publication Publicists

I put the information about publicists in the "after-publication" chapter because that's where it belongs. If you decide to hire a publicist, it should be done after you have a book contract. I've run across articles, however, grossly misinforming writers about the desirability of hiring a publicist before the book is even sold. What a colossal waste of money!

One such article ("Hire the publicist to get the Publishing Deal"), written by publicist R. Scott Penza and posted on several web sites for writers, tries to convince writers that they should hire publicists to shop their manuscripts to agents and publishers. According to his logic, "When an agent gets the call from the PR guy or PR gal, s/he is more likely to take a look at your book because, after all, there's a PR firm behind it. There must be something here worth looking at."

According to my logic, the agent is more likely thinking, "This is a clueless writer with money to burn." Especially considering that this publicist charged $2,000 to $3,000 per month for his "services."

Having a publicist is not any sign of the merit of your writing. It's a sign that you know how to sign a check. Agents and publishers are not fools, and you can't bribe them into publishing your book by showing them that you have bucks to burn.

Victoria Strauss of WriterBeware.com had this to say on Absolute Write's message boards, about Penza's firm, Creative Hive: "If the company is asked questions about success stories—books placed and agents secured for clients—they are simply ignored. Our own independent research hasn't turned up any books sold to publishers by Creative Hive. Creative Hive is just one of a number of companies that promotes a 'pre-publication' publicity service for authors—supposedly to raise your profile so that a publisher will be more interested in you. In addition to being quite costly, this is a worthless service . . . publicity isn't useful until you actually have something to promote: i.e., a published book."

> If you decide to hire a publicist, it should be done after you have a book contract.

Penza showed up on the message board to offer such mind-boggling rationalizations as, "Other professionals—agents and publishers, alike—take our calls. There's probably a good reason, there's probably a lot of good reasons. But to list those here, we'd be potentially accused of flaunting our credits and successes."

Ignoring the poor grammar, we're left with a pretty lame excuse. Penza never did come back to live up to the challenge to name one client whose work he successfully placed with an agent or publisher.

Luckily, the web site for Penza's publicity firm is now gone, and it's assumed that he's out of business. But of course, he won't be the last to try such a scheme.

Agents act as intermediaries for publishers. They don't need their own intermediaries. All they need is a solid pitch. Deliver that, and you won't need any extra help from a paid shill to find representation. A publicist does not carry any more clout during the manuscript-shopping stage than the author does; if anything, it just makes the author look foolish.

PUBLICIST RED FLAGS

- Spams you by email
- Spams writers' message boards or email groups
- Writes poorly (you don't want someone who doesn't understand basic grammar rules representing you!)
- Provides vague credentials like, "Our clients have appeared on the *Today Show, Good Morning America,* and in *The Wall Street Journal,*" but doesn't give details you can verify
- Mostly represents authors with vanity presses
- Doesn't provide full names and contact information (a street address and phone number, not just a PO box and email)

Web Site Services

"Beware search engine optimization (SEO) firms," says Steve O'Keefe, author of *Complete Guide to Internet Publicity*. "Most authors don't need SEO and most likely will not benefit from it enough to cover the cost. It's far more important for authors to get mentioned on high-traffic web sites than it is to pull traffic to their own web sites."

While it's a good idea for an author to have a web site, it shouldn't cost much money to build or maintain it, especially when you're a new author. It's a convenient place to put all the information about you and your book (ordering links, synopsis, reviews, endorsements, your bio, and so on), and you can use the link in your signature line for email and online postings. However, don't expect that many people will just happen to find your site and buy your book because they looked up "mystery novels" on a search engine.

A web site's value increases for many authors as they amass a body of work. If a reader has read one book by an author and enjoyed it, the reader may visit the author's web site to see what else he's written. But you don't need to spend a bundle on design, hosting, or site promotion. Far better ways to attract people to your site are to write articles for high-traffic sites or newsletters and include your site link in your bio, become an active participant on message boards and post your link in your signature line, offer freebies (like free e-books or reports), and ask for reciprocal links from sites that attract your book's audience.

Content is king in the internet world, and the prettiest site in the world won't draw traffic if it's merely an advertisement. Make sure you have articles, excerpts, short stories, or other writing of yours online to encourage people to sample your work before buying.

Far better ways to attract people to your site are to write articles for high-traffic sites or newsletters and include your site link in your bio.

Sell to Hollywood Listings

"Pay us, and we'll make sure all the big Hollywood executives hear about your book!"

Hardly. There are several catalogs and web sites that purport to pitch books to film producers and agents. Don't do it. Hollywood executives don't read catalogs or web sites looking for books to option. They find out about books that might make good film candidates by reading *Publishers Weekly* and *PublishersLunch,* by taking calls from agents they trust, and by following industry gossip to find out which best-selling author is about to come out with a new film-worthy title.

Hollywood executives don't read catalogs or web sites looking for books to option.

They don't have time to read a catalog full of descriptions of unknown books, many of which are self-published and of poor quality (or not even published yet), then request all the books that sound interesting and read them. Trust me, Hollywood has no shortage of submissions.

One of the sad things about con artists is that they feed off each other. It's not unusual to find a writer who paid to publish with a "subsidy" publisher on the advice of a fee-charging "agent," then spent all kinds of money on dodgy publicity services, put an ad in a "sell to Hollywood" catalogue, then got a call from a fee-charging film agent and paid an up-front fee for representation.

If you want to pitch your book to Hollywood, first try to find a repu-table agent who can handle film projects. Most literary agents work with sub-agents who fulfill this role. Without an agent, you can still use the *Hollywood Creative Directory* (www.hcdonline.com) and contact production companies yourself. Don't bother doing this until you at least have galleys of your soon-to-be-published book ready. Few film scouts want to read an unpublished manuscript from an unknown writer. Get the book deal first.

Chapter 7

Vanity Poetry Contests

The Most Notorious Poetry Scheme

Poetry's Hall of Shame

Spotting Lame Contests

Finding Legitimate Contests

Remember how I mentioned that poetry contest I entered back when I was ten years old? That was the National Library of Poetry, which has gone through a few name incarnations: Later it became the International Library of Poetry and the International Society of Poets, and now you probably know it best as Poetry.com.

I had seen the contest advertised in the back of a magazine. I bet you've seen the ad, too: "Free amateur poetry contest! Win $10,000 and publication!" What did I have to lose? I submitted my poem, which had to be twenty lines or less, and a few weeks later, I excitedly tore open the envelope bearing the National Library of Poetry's return address.

"After carefully reading and discussing your poem, our Selection Committee has certified your poem as a semi-finalist," the letter began, and I could hardly believe my eyes. I, little Jenna Glatzer, was a semi-finalist in a prestigious poetry contest!

But it just got better from there. Next, they told me my poem would be published in what promised to be one of their most popular collections ever! It said, "Your poem was selected for publication, and as a contest semi-finalist, on the basis of your unique talent and artistic vision."

The letter was personalized—and by that, I mean it had my name inserted in strategic spots throughout. This was all the proof I needed that they had indeed read my poem and thought it was fantastic. It was also all the encouragement I needed to ask my mom to fork over the money—about $40 at the time, which is now $49.95—so I could buy a copy of this gorgeous hardcover book. Then, if I wanted to pay extra (which, of course, I did), I could also have my biography printed in this book so editors and publishers could contact me!

Soon thereafter, they sent me a tiny silver medal that said "Editor's Choice." I won an Editor's Choice award! My career as a poet was starting with a real bang. Boy, I couldn't wait to see that gorgeous hardcover book with my very own poem in it.

Then it arrived.

My elation was slightly dampened by the fact that there were thousands and thousands of poems all crammed into this book and I had a really hard time finding my own. My elation got soggier as I read through the other poems in the book . . . even as a ten-year-old, I had a good sense of spelling and grammar, and the poems in this collection were full of egregious mistakes.

The Better Business Bureau of Maryland has a report on the International Library of Poetry. Amazingly, it states that the company has a satisfactory rating with the Bureau and is, in fact, a member in good standing.

I say "amazingly" because I know full well that many people have sent complaints to the BBB, myself included. I got back a response to tell me that "the number and type of complaints are not unusual for a company in this industry." I translate this to mean that out of the millions of people this company has swindled, even several thousand complaints aren't enough to change the Bureau's official rating.

However, if you read to the bottom of the Bureau's listing, you'll find this note:

> The [International Library of Poetry] is a vanity publisher of hardbound anthologies, which feature amateur poets, of paper-

back volumes of poetry by single authors, and of a magazine for amateur poets. The books are not distributed and cannot be found in bookstores. They are only distributed to those who pay to have their work included. The quality of the poetry does not appear to be a significant consideration for selection for publication. However, according to the company, poems containing obscenities or offensive language are rejected.

For a cost of about $49.95, the amateur poets are given the opportunity to purchase the book in which their poem(s) will be featured. The company also sells other products that feature the poem(s), which are priced separately.

So the BBB does know just what's going on—but for some reason, they find it satisfactory that writers are misled. The BBB lists the International Library of Poetry as a "vanity publisher," a point that is not made clear at all in the literature the company sends to writers. I fail to see how they can get away with making statements such as "after carefully reading and discussing your poem . . ." and "selected on the basis of your unique talent and artistic vision," while admitting elsewhere that they accept anything sent their way (as long as it doesn't contain profanities), and I can personally prove that they do not read the poems sent their way.

How can I prove this?

It's all Wergle Flomp's fault. Many years after the truth had finally sunk in with me, I made it a point to let other writers know about the Poetry.com racket (by that point, the company was best known for its web site, where amateur poets could now submit their work online for the world to see). Along the way, someone pointed me to a new contest seeking parody poems that had been sent to vanity poetry contests as a joke.

The Wergle Flomp Poetry Contest, sponsored by WinningWriters. com, earned its namesake from poet and journalist David Taub. David was experimenting to find out just how bad a poem had to be before Poetry.com's "Selection Committee" would reject it. He was on a mission to earn a rejection letter.

After a few remarkably bad attempts, he finally threw in the towel after the company failed to reject the poem "Flubblebop," which he had submitted under the pen name Wergle Flomp. The poem's longest line reads, "yibberdy yobberdy hif twizzum moshlap." That's right—the whole poem is gibberish.

In celebration of Wergle's unique talent and artistic vision, the Selection Committee decided to make "Flubblebop" a semi-finalist and publish it in what promised to be one of their most highly sought after collections of poetry ever.

And in celebration of that same unique talent and artistic vision, WinningWriters.com decided to start a contest in Wergle's name. I entered the contest by submitting a fake poem to Poetry.com. My poem opened by plagiarizing several lines from Martin Luther King Jr.'s world-famous "I Have a Dream" speech. It went on to insult the entire Poetry.com operation and chastise them for charging writers for their "honors." The poem was declared a semi-finalist, and I was sorely tempted to pay to have them read it on cassette tape for me, but just couldn't stand the idea of adding to their coffers.

HALL OF SHAME

Poetry.com's "International Library of Poets Convention and Symposium" costs $595 in registration fees alone, and was the subject of a heartbreaking testimonial here:

http://windpub.com/literary.scams/bigmoney.htm

The author says there were about four thousand people in attendance, many who flew from overseas, all of whom were told they were nominated for "Poet of the Year" or "Young Poet of the Year," or were paying guests of the hopeful poets. The attendees read their poetry to each other in small rooms and were told to vote for one another. Winner Teedie Richardson-Tremble's poem in the "past winners" section on Poetry.com is well beyond the required twenty-line limit.

A second testimonial tells the story of a woman who attended the 2004 convention. "They draw you in by making you think your poetry is special," she says. Find it at:

www.winningwriters.com/wergleflomp/silverbowls.htm

The convention is obviously flourishing despite warnings like these; in 2005, they've raked in enough money to hire Tony Orlando and The Drifters to perform.

> It's amazing to me how many times this company has been "outed," yet they still have no problem sucking in millions of new writers.

The Wergle Flomp annual contest (free to enter) awarded $1,609 in prizes in 2005. The award amounts, which differ from year to year, represent the cost of various Poetry.com offers, such as the opportunity for poets to purchase their award-winning poems read on cassette, mounted on a plaque, laminated in a wallet card, or printed on a mousepad or sweatshirt; to buy an engraved silver cup commemorating their achievement; or to send a loved one a poem as a message in a "deep azure blue glass" bottle. Poets may also join the International Society of Poets if they pay dues of about $100 a year.

It's amazing to me how many times this company has been "outed," yet they still have no problem sucking in millions of new writers. ABC's *20/20* investigated by doing an experiment: An entire class of second graders submitted poems and all got identical acceptance letters informing them of their semi-finalist statuses and impending publication. Who else has exposed this company? *Consumer Reports,* humor columnist Dave Barry, the *Philadelphia Enquirer,* and NBC's *Channel 4 News,* among others.

Wind Publications tried to estimate how much money the International Library of Poetry rakes in, and came up with this: "The Greater Maryland Better Business Bureau reports that the ILP has 500,000 customers each year. If only half purchase a single $50 book, that's $12.5 million each year." That doesn't even count sales of all the ancillary products—the plaques, symposiums, keychains, silver cups, and so on.

But That's Not All!

Unfortunately, Poetry.com isn't the only crooked game in town . . . not even close. After my experience with them at age ten, I decided to try different contests. Like Iliad Press's free poetry contest. Once again, I got an acceptance letter, but this time, my mom wouldn't spring for the book. Thanks, Mom.

Advertisements for vanity poetry contests litter the classifieds sections of newspapers and magazines, and have sprung up all over the Internet. Others that fall into this category include The Poetry Guild, The Famous

Poets Society, The Amherst Society, Sparrowgrass Poetry Forum, and American Poets Society. This is just a small sampling, and by the time this book is in your hands, it's likely that there will be many more.

Kira Cleo and the Circle of Poets

While researching for this book, I came across a site that was new to me, www.circleofpoets.com. Its web site begins:

"Our mission is to promote poetry and poets through technical workshops, improvisation cessions [sic] and contests. An independent panel of experts reviews poems on the following criteria: technical quality, flow and use of imagery. Winners compete for publication and for a prize of $5000. This is a free contest, open to all and based on merit."

Hmm. It smelled fishy to me, but I decided to test it out by allowing my cat, Kira Cleo, to submit a poem to their contest.

The following day, Kira got this by return email:

Dear Kira Cleo,

As a contest winner, your poem I have a ceramic worm No, it's not ceramic It's clay of some sort, I think And I bought it at Target Or Michael's Craft Store, maybe. It is in the soil of my office plant Which is not a fern But I don't remember the name for what it is And it turns from red to brown (The worm, I mean, Not the plant) When it's time to water my plant, The one that's not a fern. Good thing for the worm Else my plant would have died long ago Of thirst (If thirst is what you call it when plants need water) For I am forgetty And mostly irresponsible. is indeed being published in the 2004 edition of our manuscript and, as such, you have been accepted within the Circle of Poets community.

We are offering you the following three options as we finalize our 2004 year. Our next publishing event will only be in one year (October 2005), so do not miss these specials!

1) Special offer on the best of 2004 manuscript

As we are finalizing orders, benefit from a heavily discounted last minute price of only $29 (instead of $49). Please note that this offer expires soon . . .

2) Your own personal manuscript: 100 top poems

As we are finalizing orders, benefit from a heavily discounted last minute price of only $69 (instead of $89). Please note that this offer expires soon and all orders are over on November 7th 2004.

The cover will read Kira Cleo's book of poetry in golden letters.

Need I mention how tempted I was to have a book of Kira Cleo's inspired ceramic worm poetry? Somehow, though, I resisted. Maybe it was the $8 shipping that pushed it over the edge for me.

I wonder if Kira would be delighted to know she's officially a poetry contest winner, and that she's been offered the opportunity to have her best one hundred poems published with her name in golden letters on the cover.

I wonder if she'd be angry with me if she knew I took her out of the running for the grand prize:

"Please note that only finalists who order our manuscript qualify for the $5,000 prize (in order to support our team, fund the grand prize, assemble/print the manuscript - thank you for your understanding)," the letter finished.

Circleofpoets.com boasts more than 4,000 members. Sadly, this doesn't surprise me.

Spot the Signs

So how does one figure out which contests are scams and which aren't? There are several tip-offs:

- Huge prizes. Nearly all legitimate poetry contests offer modest prize money and publication of winners. A big, enticing number ($10,000, $48,000, etc.) is a bad sign. It means the company is raking in enough money to be able to offer these kinds of prizes and still make a profit. The truth is that real poetry isn't exactly big business. Literary organizations aren't swimming in excess cash; rip-off contests are.

- Where do they advertise? When you see "free poetry contest" ads on Google or in newspaper classifieds, consider that a bad sign. When you see poetry contest ads in mass-market magazines that are not meant for writers—particularly celebrity tabloids—run. If you get unsolicited email inviting you to enter a contest, laugh and delete it. Legitimate contests don't spam you! Unfortunately, even reputable magazines do accept ads from these lame contests, so don't take inclusion as a sign that a contest is legitimate.

- Will you get a copy of the work free of charge? If your poem is selected to be included in an anthology, chapbook, or magazine, at the very least, you should get a free copy of the publication. Many literary magazines and organizations operate on shoestring budgets, so it's possible that they can't offer to pay you for your poem. However, you should not have to pay them to see your work in print! If they've deemed it good enough to publish, they can certainly afford to mail you a copy.

A big, enticing number ($10,000, $48,000, etc.) is a bad sign. It means the company is raking in enough money to be able to offer these kinds of prizes and still make a profit.

- How selective are they? If the contest has a web site where entrants' poetry is posted, take a good look around. What's the quality of poetry on the site? As a more objective measure, investigate how many anthologies the company publishes each year. If they're cranking out book after book, they're making a profit somehow . . . do you really think people are just rushing out to buy these in-demand anthologies by unknown poets? (Even known poets have trouble selling their collections to the public!) How many contests do they run per year?

- They attach Post-it Notes. Twice, when I sent poems to vanity contests, I got back typewritten acceptance letters with Post-it Notes attached. The notes said something like, "Compelling poem!" and "Very touching!" They sure looked handwritten to me, though I later realized (while my heart broke into pieces) that it was just a good computer job. Just because your name and the title of your poem are mentioned in the letter, or you receive one of these seemingly handwritten notes, do not assume there's anything personal about it: There are plenty of computer fonts designed to look like handwriting, and it's easy to plug a person's name or poem's title into a form letter.

- They're trying to sell you something. Anything. Your poem on a plaque, membership in an "exclusive" poetry society, a book, a certificate, whatever. Or they give you the "chance" to pay extra to have your photo or biography included. Your acceptance letter should be unconditional and not mixed up with solicitations to buy anything!

- They have short length limits. "What got me to discard [the International Library of Poetry] out of hand was their requirement that the poems be 20 lines or less," says James D. Macdonald. "I figured that if they wouldn't have accepted 'Xanadu' by Samuel Taylor Coleridge, they weren't interested in poetry."

- You can't find their past winners. Either you literally can't find the past winning entries to judge them for yourself, or you look up the names of winners and find nothing about them online.

- Lack of contact information. If the organization running the contest has a post office box and an email address, and that's all the information you can find, bad sign. There should be a phone number and a real live street address. Post office boxes are great for companies who have something to hide or don't want to be tracked down by hordes of unhappy poets.

- They just run contests. What else does the organization do, besides running poetry contests? Do they publish a magazine, participate in charity events, sponsor visiting writer chats or workshops, publicize grants for writers, campaign for funding for the arts, publish calls for submissions for poets? If the organization has a web site, is its main focus the contest and things you can buy, or does the site show that there's more going on behind the scenes?

If the organization running the contest has a post office box and an email address, and that's all the information you can find, bad sign.

- No anonymity in judging. One site, www.foetry.com, is dedicated to exposing poetry contests in which the site owner believes judges have selected a friend, former student, or "sycophant" to win the contest. For example, the site declares that one judge selected a winner who had edited a book about him, and another judge picked a winner whose manuscript she worked on. The odds of judges' bias are greatly reduced when entries are submitted anonymously; that is, the entrant submits a cover sheet separate from the poem, and the poem does not contain the entrant's name. In this case, poems are generally assigned numbers that judges use to identify them, and matched up with the entrants' names after judging is complete.

- Play online detective. Let's say you just got an email from Noble House Publishers. The email offers you the chance to have your unbelievably fabulous poetry published in the U.K. It looks like a personalized email and it praises your talent. What do you do now? You go to Google and type in the words "'Noble House' scam." As of this writing, more than five hundred links will appear. Many of them are posts on message boards where writers have compared notes and realized that, indeed, Noble House is another vanity press associated with the International Library of Poetry, and has already duped thousands of writers into submitting work and buying over-priced and unedited anthologies that will never be seen inside a bookstore or library. The International Library of Poetry has openly admitted to sharing their mailing list with Noble House. You must perform this simple check before entering a contest or forking over your credit card number.

DO YOUR HOMEWORK

Always type the name of the contest or the name of the organization (in quotation marks) into a search engine and see what pops up. If the results are overwhelming, add the word "scam" or "complaints" to the search and you'll get more targeted results.

What About Entry Fees?

You may be surprised by the fact that I didn't mention entry fees as a warning sign. In fact, plenty of legitimate contests have entry fees, and I don't find this unethical in itself. Even major awards like the National Book Awards and the Pulitzer Prize charge fees.

Literary magazines often sponsor contests where the price of the entry fee (usually about $15) includes a subscription to the magazine. It can certainly be worth it as a budding poet to read the works of other poets whose work is chosen for publication. Even if you don't win the contest, you get something of value out of the deal.

Plenty of legitimate contests have entry fees,
and I don't find this unethical in itself.
Even major awards like the National Book Awards
and the Pulitzer Prize charge fees.

Entry fees may go toward the prize money, judges' fees, and administrative costs. The fee should be reasonable compared to the prize money; for example, I wouldn't enter a contest that charged a $15 entry fee and offered only a $50 prize. The company stands to make far too much of a profit off the entry fees for my taste. However, if the entry fee were $15 and the prize were $500, I might not balk.

I would also warn you against paying an entry fee where the "prize" is publication only. This is really just a reading fee; you can submit your work to thousands of magazines and journals for consideration without paying any sort of fee to have it read and considered for publication. If any money is to change hands, the publication should be paying you, not the other way around.

I would also warn you against paying an entry
fee where the "prize" is publication only.

The only potential exception I'd make to this is when the prize is publication of a poet's own chapbook. It's extremely difficult to get mainstream publishers interested in poetry collections, so many poets self-publish. If a small press or literary organization offers an entry-fee contest where the winner's chapbook is published and distributed with a standard royalty contract, I'd consider it. Especially if the entry fee included a copy of the winner's book.

If you prefer not to pay entry fees, there are still plenty of reputable contests for you to enter. They just don't tend to advertise all over the place.

WHERE TO FIND LEGITIMATE CONTESTS

- Winning Writers (www.winningwriters.com): This site publishes a free monthly newsletter as well as the quarterly Poetry Contest Insider (less than $20 a year for a subscription, and you can sample it free). The Poetry Contest Insider ranks and profiles more than 650 contests, giving important information such as the average number of entrants, who sponsors the contest, links to past winners' work, and interviews with judges.

- *Poet's Market*: Published annually by Writer's Digest Books, this massive directory provides information about places to submit your poetry (book publishers, magazines, and competitions) as well as informative articles and interviews for poets. Inclusion here does not guarantee that the contest is reputable, but the editors do try to vet the listings appropriately.

- Absolute Markets (www.absolutemarkets.com): In the free version of Absolute Markets, columnist Moira Richards provides a monthly listing of writing contests that have guidelines available online.

- *Poets & Writers* magazine: There's a "Grants and Awards" section in each issue. See their web site at www.pw.org.

- *Academy of American Poets*: provides links to well-established contests in their "On Writing" section: www.poets.org.

Other Avenues for Poets

On the Absolute Write message board, author James D. Macdonald wrote, "Every magazine out there that accepts poetry has a contest every month. The entry fee is postage; the prize is publication."

Finding publications that accept poetry submissions isn't hard at all. Finding ones that pay well is another matter.

Finding publications that accept poetry submissions isn't hard at all. Finding ones that pay well is another matter, but if you're looking to build up your reputation and credits as a poet, you'd do well to start with literary magazines and e-zines. Editors do pay attention to credits, and writers with a strong history of publication in literary magazines have a much better chance of getting a poetry book published.

In addition to the *Poet's Market,* there are a few other solid resources for finding markets for poetry:

- *The International Directory of Little Magazines & Small Presses:* Not all markets listed here pay for accepted submissions; in many cases, the only payment is in copies of the magazines. Listings are also not very detailed in most cases, but it is a superb place to find new markets. You can then do more research on the ones that interest you.

- *The CLMP Literary Magazine and Press Directory:* Guidelines and contact information for almost six hundred publications, from the Council of Literary Magazines and Presses. Order at https://www.clmp.org/about/order_publications.html.

- *The Absolute Markets Premium Edition* (www.absolutemarkets.com): Each issue lists at least two paying markets for poetry and short fiction. There aren't any nonpaying markets listed in this biweekly newsletter, and it costs $15 for an annual subscription.

- *Poets & Writers:* This magazine lists calls for submissions in their classifieds section at www.pw.org, but writers should note that they do not investigate these ads and can't vouch for their legitimacy. From what I can tell, most of the publications advertising here are nonpaying markets.

Be wary of any contest targeting amateurs, offering big prizes, and sending praise mixed with order forms.

Do Your Own Hunting

You can also simply look up "literary magazines" online and wade through the links until you find several you want to submit your work to. Try these lists for starters:

- http://dir.yahoo.com/Arts/Humanities/Literature/Poetry/Magazines

- www.fglaysher.com/LitLinks.htm

- www.clmp.org/directory/index.html

Last Thought

Be wary of any contest targeting amateurs, offering big prizes, and sending praise mixed with order forms. If you really want the publication of your work to be an accomplishment, there are no shortcuts and rarely any engraved silver cups or medals along the way. You just write, keep improving, keep sending out your work to reputable publications, and celebrate in earnest when those genuine acceptances come your way.

Chapter 8

Deceptive Contests for Novelists, Short Story Writers, Screenwriters, and Others

Lies About Prizes

What Happens When a Contest is Canceled?

Bogus Entry Fees

Contests Claiming Your Rights

Signs of a Good Contest

```
Look at the Beautiful Prizes . . . That We May Not Award
```

My Sob Story

I won the third People's Picture Show screenwriting contest. Wahoo, right? Except that the entirety of my grand prize ended up being a copy of Final Draft screenwriting software, which I did not need, and a subscription to an email group that I found useless.

The contest, sponsored by TVWriter.com, was for writers who had written scripts appropriate for made-for-television movies (sometimes known as movies-of-the-week, or MOWs). I paid $45 to enter a script of mine because I believed it had a good chance of winning. I checked out the prize package and recognized that I didn't need (or couldn't use) most of the things on the list—enrollment in workshops, for example, that I couldn't go to; software that I already had; representation by an agent I didn't believe was credible . . . but the main prize was cold, hard cash for an option agreement with a legitimate television production company. Yep, I could use that.

To be more specific, Cosgrove-Meurer (producers of *Unsolved Mysteries* and several TV movies) would option the script at WGA (Writers Guild of America) standard rates. According to the rules, "The original option price shall be that designated as 'minimum' for an option of a 'Teleplay' for a 90 to 120 minute Low Budget television show per the Minimum Basic Agreement of the Writers Guild of America, west. Should the Teleplay be picked up for production at a budget defined by the WGA as High Budget the fee will be adjusted accordingly per the WGA MBA."

Wearing my "realist" hat, I decided to find out the minimal amount of money the winner would get. I checked the WGA Schedule of Minimums and found out that the Guild requires writers to be paid at least $19,935 for a teleplay for a 90 to 120-minute low-budget, non-prime-time network television show. For a 180-day option, they'd have to pay the writer at least 5 percent of that price, or $996.75, to be exact. For an additional 180 days, they'd have to pay 10 percent of the purchase price ($1,993.50).

There would also be a "Reader's Choice" award, the winner of which would get $500. This was to go to a writer whose "creative merit" the judges enjoyed best, regardless of commercial considerations.

So, for my $45, I figured I had a good chance of earning back $500–$1,000, an option with a television producer, a nice little honor to add to my résumé, and some prizes I could give to friends as gifts.

Now, I did notice this ugly little disclaimer in the small print:

> If in the judgment of the PEOPLE'S PICTURE SHOW, TV WRITER.COM, WRITESAFE.COM, Cosgrove-Meurer Productions, Brody Productions, or Larry Brody the winning entry does not meet minimum standards of acceptibility [sic] for network and cable channel motion picture submission, as defined by their years of experience in television development, then Cosgrove-Meurer Productions is not required to purchase the original option and a suitable prize of lesser value may be awarded.

But I looked at past contests and noticed they had never not declared a winner, this site was run by a television producer with an impressive list of credits, and they seemed to have an active list of happy members on the site's bulletin boards. I figured they put in the disclaimer in case every entry they got was total garbage, and I didn't think too deeply about it.

Until I got the letter.

The letter was from Larry Brody, the producer who runs TVWriter.com and all its contests. He was writing to inform me that they had decided not to pick a winner of the third People's Picture Show, after all. But! To comfort me, he wanted me to know that my script was Cosgrove-Meurer's favorite, and if they were going to pick a winner, mine would have been it. They just decided it would be hard to sell it to a TV network—it wasn't "commercial" enough, they thought.

I was utterly perplexed and went back to check the rules. Nowhere did it say they had a right not to pick a winner, but indeed, that's what TVWriter had just announced in their newsletter. They let the entrants know that they had decided not to option any of the scripts or name a winner. (But hey, thanks for your money anyway. We won't be refunding any of it.)

I wrote to Mr. Brody with a copy of his own rules, pointing out that it never said they could avoid picking a winner; all it said was that a "suitable prize of lesser value" could be awarded in place of the option.

He agreed with me and promptly posted an announcement that let anyone who wandered onto his web site know that I, Jenna Glatzer, had won the contest even though Cosgrove-Meurer thought the script didn't have commercial potential and would therefore not option it. They also included a synopsis someone had written about my script that was entirely, utterly wrong and made my script sound really clichéd.

This was humiliating. I explained to him that he was actually hurting my chances of selling this script by posting such an announcement—now any producer who looked up my name or script's name could see that another producer deemed it unmarketable. I don't remember his exact rationale, but he denied my request to remove the announcement or the insulting explanation.

The "alternate prize" he offered was admittance to a summer workshop he was teaching that I couldn't attend. I asked if I could send a friend in my place, and he said no (you know, because then every winner would want to do that and that would be . . . well, what exactly would be bad about that?). He also wouldn't allow me to take a raincheck for a future workshop. Although I was also supposed to have won admission to a different seminar as well, despite asking about it twice, I never got an invitation or further information about it. Like I said, I ended up with a copy of Final Draft. That was it.

Other People's Sob Stories

Sadly, I'm not alone. In an editorial in the *Missouri Review* online, writer Scott Kaukonen expressed his outrage upon receiving an email from Zoo Press telling him that they were canceling their first-ever book-length short fiction contest in 2004. He was livid because of a few lines in Zoo Press's email, starting with this one:

"We still love fiction, but we admit that we cannot publish it as well as others (FSG, for example). The experiment did not unfold the way we had hoped, as, I guess, is the nature of experiments."

The email went on to let entrants know that they would not get their entry fees returned. The explanation? "Unfortunately, the entry fees for the relatively few number of submissions we received went toward promoting the prizes; (specifically we received approximately 350 submissions for two prizes totaling less than $10,000, which we put into a full page ad in the *Atlantic Monthly* and two other smaller email campaigns, to our financial loss)."

The company even had the gall to suggest that they'd be happy to send entrants two books of poetry they'd published . . . if the entrants would pay for shipping and handling.

What's utterly outrageous to Scott, to me, and I'm betting to you, too, is that Zoo Press never informed entrants that they were paying for an experiment. That they were unwittingly donating funding to the contest's advertising campaign and would not be reimbursed if the company decided to call off the "experiment" for whatever reasons they rationalized. Galling.

Scott had spent nearly $40 to copy the manuscript, pay for the entry fee, and pay for postage. He was not doing this in the name of charity. He was doing it because the judge was *Atlantic Monthly's* fiction editor (sounds legit!) and the contest offered a prize of $5,000 and the publication of the winner's book of short fiction.

Similarly, Chuck Bowers sent a letter to *Poets & Writers* to complain about a contest they announced: the Bakeless Literary Prizes sponsored by Bread Loaf Writers' Conference of Middlebury College. Seems that Chuck entered in the creative nonfiction category in the hopes of landing the prize (a publishing deal with Houghton Mifflin and a fellowship to the Bread Loaf conference), only to get an announcement later that no winner was selected. No explanation. No refund.

As *Poets & Writers* pointed out, the contest retained the right not to choose winners. It says on the contest web site, "No judge is mandated to pick a winner if he or she does not deem the finalist manuscripts ready for publication." Incidentally, there was no creative nonfiction winner in 2002 or 2004, either. They're legally covered, but ethically? You tell me.

Anthology Contests

It infuriates me when publishers have "contests" (with entry fees) to fill an anthology. For example, you pay a $10 entry fee, and if you're one of the "winners" or "finalists," your short story or essay gets published in an anthology. Maybe they'll send you a copy of the book if they publish your work, maybe they won't even do that much. And maybe the "grand prize winner" (whose work is chosen to start the book) will get a small cash award.

The thing is, there's no reason to pay anyone to consider your work for publication. There are so many anthologies today hunting for stories and essays; most don't pay extraordinarily well (*Chicken Soup* pays $200–$300 and *A Cup of Comfort* pays about $100), but they certainly don't expect you to pay them to consider your work! Remember, when an anthology puts out a call for submissions, you're doing them the favor of responding. They need stories or they won't have a book to publish. An anthology "contest" isn't really a contest. It's a call for submissions and should be treated just like any other.

When an anthology puts out a call for submissions, you're doing them the favor of responding. They need stories or they won't have a book to publish.

Book Contract Contests

Similar to the anthology contests, some publishers run entry-fee contests where the prize is book publication—almost always for novels. Again, how can this be a contest? Every day, writers send manuscripts to publishers for consideration. Considering manuscripts for publication is part of the publisher's job, and it's up to them to absorb the cost of having readers and editors evaluate each query, proposal, or manuscript to determine if they want to publish it.

Charging entry fees for consideration in this type of "contest" is like asking job candidates to pay an entry fee to be interviewed. And, hey, the winner will get the job!

You know how I mentioned early on in the book that there are some people who don't mean to be sharks? That, I believe, is the case with Eraserhead Press and their misguided book contest.

"Books by new authors do not sell very well," they explain on their web site. "In fact, it is very tough just to break even on a book by a new author. This is true 9 out of 10 times. So we had to make a decision: either stop publishing new authors entirely and concentrate on established authors, or obtain funds somehow. We have chosen to do this contest, which helps us get more titles out and leaves doors open to unknown writers."

Now, I don't know where they get their stats, but I don't argue with the fact that it's challenging to market the work of an unknown novelist. However, that's the challenge they've chosen to undertake by virtue of becoming a small fiction publisher. Why should writers subsidize their fledgling—and unprofitable—business?

Charging entry fees for consideration in this type of "contest" is like asking job candidates to pay an entry fee to be interviewed.

They no longer accept submissions unless they come with a $20 "entry fee" for this "contest," which is really just a reading fee for publication consideration. The check is to be written out to Rose O'Keefe, the publisher. If you want her to critique your entry, that's an extra $30. The winner of the contest does not get any money. There is no book advance. And there is no guarantee that this publisher will be around next year, will know how to market and distribute the book, will hire a decent cover artist, and so on. In fact, there are pleas on the web site for volunteers to help out with publicity and other matters.

Then there's the last answer on their "frequently asked questions" page, which is the one that made me smack my forehead in amazement: "We are very busy and hope this contest scares a lot of authors away. That way we only get the very serious authors who truly believe in their manuscripts."

Oh. So the logic is that very serious authors who believe in their manuscripts will fork over $20 to submit to small presses on free-hosting web sites that have already admitted they don't know how to make money any other way than by charging writers. And if you don't enter that contest, you're probably a lousy writer who doesn't believe in your work, anyway. Puh-leease.

To be fair, I do know a writer who won a contest like this sponsored by a reputable publishing house, and she was thrilled. Even though I'm against the concept no matter who runs it, I do recognize that a few well-established publishing houses sponsor contests like this to enable unagented writers to submit unsolicited novels. The writer I'm referring to told me that she couldn't convince publishers to read her mystery novel until she entered the contest; she wound up with a modest book contract as a result of it.

So if the publisher is well-known and if you can't seem to get read any other way and if you have a little extra money to spend, I won't fault you for entering a contest like this. But I'll still tell you to exhaust your other options first: perfect your query letter, make sure you've written a compelling synopsis and opening chapter, and ensure that the manuscript itself is well-edited and as strong as you think it can be. If you can accomplish that, it would surprise me if you still can't get agents and publishers to read it . . . without your having to send them a check.

But also stay on the lookout for contests with no entry fees. For example, Mysterious Press/Warner Books held their first Sara Ann Freed Memorial Award in 2004, and authors did not have to pay to enter. Alas, it, too, had one problem. Here's part of the entry form writers had to sign: "If chosen for this award I agree to accept the $10,000 contract for the below mentioned work and allow Mysterious Press to publish my book in hardcover and soft-cover. I will sign and accept the standard Mysterious Press author agreement for publication of my work."

The problem? Entrants are not allowed to see the "standard" contract before they enter. How do they know if the contract is fair? How do they know if they're giving up the right to their next book, or agreeing to a 2 percent royalty on net, or . . . ? Even reputable publishers often have author-unfriendly boilerplate contracts. I've never signed a book contract exactly as is; there's always some negotiating and rewording involved. Now, again, you may be willing to take this risk just to get a foot in the door, see your first novel published, and get a $10,000 advance, but be aware that it is, indeed, a risk.

Even though I'm against the concept no matter who runs it, I do recognize that a few well-established publishing houses sponsor contests like this to enable unagented writers to submit unsolicited novels.

Another contest making the rounds on writers' warnings sites is Woman's Day/Scholastic Book Clubs' "I Want to Be a Children's Book Writer" contest. The winner of this contest has to sign over all rights to Scholastic. Phenomenally, there is no advance or royalties for the winner—just the "delight" of having the book published and ten free copies (or, if Scholastic decides to publish it only as an e-book, the writer gets a flat fee of $40), plus five autographed picture books. Seriously, that's it. You give up every right to ever make any money from your book.

Compare these contests to the Milkweed Prize for Children's Literature, where the entrants have to agree only that the advance will be $10,000, but do not have to agree on a particular royalty rate or agree to sign a contract sight-unseen: The contract terms are negotiable. All children's manuscripts sent to Milkweed are eligible for the prize.

The Big Prize Money*

Every now and then, you'll come across a contest offering really big prize money and a low entry fee . . . with a tiny asterisk that leads to fine print that explains the prize money is actually dependent on a percentage of entry fees.

To use an extreme example, let's say the contest offers a first prize of $10,000, a second prize of $5,000, and a third prize of $3,000. In the fine print, you'll find out that those amounts are actually ceilings; the contest may award up to those figures if, let's say, twenty thousand or more people enter the contest. Otherwise, it's a percentage of entry fees. In other words, the contest may award the first-place winner 30 percent of the total entry fee money, the second-place winner 20 percent, and the third-place winner 10 percent. Will it ever come close to that $10,000 figure for the top winner? It's about as likely as my cat learning to touch-type.

Unspecified Prizes

There are also some contests that don't commit to prize amounts or even formulas for determining prize amounts. This is what I found at http://traditionalcountrymusicfoundation.com: "Prize money will vary according to number of entrants per category." Well, okay. And on first glance, I thought the division of prize money sounded good:

"50% of prize money will be awarded to first place winner . . . 30% of prize money will be awarded to second place winner . . . 20% of prize money will be awarded to third place winner." I added that up and thought, wow! They're giving all 100 percent of the entry fees to the winners.

But that's not what they said.

They said 100 percent of the prize money would be awarded; they never said 100 percent of the entry fees would go toward prize money. So how much of the entry fees would go toward prize money? No idea. They repeat a few times that the prize money will vary according to the number of entrants, but nowhere on this page do they give any idea of how that prize money will be calculated. If they decide that only one percent of entry fees will go toward prize money, and you win first place in a category with few entrants, you could wind up "winning" less than your entry fee.

A screenwriting contest appearing at www.thescreenwriterdig.com shows this on its main page: "Pitch & Script Contest 2005. First Prize Scripts $30,000. First Prize Pitches $15,000. And see your idea turned into a feature film or TV series." Nifty, except that when you dig further into the rules, you find out that they're not cash prizes: They're "prize packages" valued at approximately $30,000 and $15,000, respectively. This could mean anything—30,000 boxes of spaghetti would fulfill the first prize requirement, or the contest sponsor could award you with "editing services" or "publicity services" and say they're worth the amounts listed.

> They're "prize packages" valued at approximately
> $30,000 and $15,000, respectively. This could
> mean anything—30,000 boxes of spaghetti would fulfill
> the first prize requirement.

And the "see your idea turned into a feature film or TV series" part? In the rules, that morphs into the opportunity to work with the host and his team to develop and possibly make a film or TV series. Possibly.

Among the other questionable points in this contest's rules are the sponsor's right to change the deadline and notification dates without restriction (what if he decides to extend the deadline until the year 2030 and not announce winners until 2050?) and the rights-grabbing clause that automatically grants the sponsor "the sole and exclusive option to acquire all right, title, and interest in and to the Submission throughout the universe and in perpetuity."

In the "are they really serious" department, this contest's grammatically challenged press release on Business Wire included this tidbit: "Designed to generate significant revenues for XRAYMEDIA, the Company is very excited about the launch of this exciting, high profile competition. Projected contest submissions are over 150,000 for the first year of the competition with 25% increases speculated for each subsequent year . . ."

One hundred and fifty thousand entries? Perhaps the most prestigious screenwriting contest in existence, The Nicholl Fellowships in Screenwriting, received 6,073 entries in 2004. It's a huge leap of logic to surmise that a new contest with unspecified prize packages will get at least 143,952 more entries than the industry's best-known competition, which has been running annually since 1986.

Perhaps more telling is the first part of the sentence, though: The contest is designed to generate significant revenue for the company. Compare that to this explanation on the Nicholl Fellowships' "Frequently Asked Questions" page: "In 2003 the Nicholl Fellowships program received approximately $170,000 in entry fees. By the end of each fellowship year, we will have distributed $150,000 to the Fellows. Add in the various costs that I just mentioned [administration, mailings, printing, advertising, first round reading costs] and you'll quickly realize that the Nicholl program is not remotely close to being a moneymaking operation."

Contests Claiming Rights to Submissions

One of the most frightening bits of language you can find in contest guidelines is this: "All submissions become the sole property of Company XYZ and may be published and reproduced in any and all forms and media throughout the world, without further obligation."

Say what?

Indeed, many contests claim all rights to all entries—winners and losers alike—with no compensation required.

What does this mean? If effective, you could conceivably win nothing in the contest, but the company would have the right to sell your writing to magazines, newspapers, anthologies, etc., use it in their promotional campaigns, publish it on their web site . . . all with no payment to you.

Under U.S. copyright law, however, transfers of exclusive copyright ownership are not valid unless an "instrument of conveyance, or a note or memorandum of the transfer, is in writing and signed by the owner of the rights conveyed or such owner's duly authorized agent." (17 U.S.C. 204(a)). This means that unless there is an assignment of rights in your signed contest application (or a specific reference to contest rules containing the assignment), you retain copyright, regardless of what the contest sponsors may say on their web site.

I have, on occasion, written to contest organizers to protest this clause. One contest organizer wasn't even aware that the language (which had been inserted by the parent company's legal department) was on the contest web site, and she was as appalled by it as I was. She promptly had it removed, as she had no intention of ever using or reselling contest entries without writers' consent.

Many contests claim all rights to all entries—winners and losers alike—with no compensation required.

Some contests ask for limited rights, such as the right to print winners' and finalists' entries on their web site or in their publication and in publicity materials. Keep in mind that even this limited right will prevent your ability to sell first rights to the piece; even if your short story has been published online on a small contest web site only, you cannot legally sell first rights to the story anywhere else. You are free, however, to sell reprint rights or one-time rights anywhere else you like as long as you haven't agreed to any sort of exclusivity or given up all rights by entering the contest and signing a transfer of copyright.

It's always best to clarify exactly what rights you are assigning before you decide whether or not to enter and before signing any documents, including the contest application, that contain the grant of rights. The contest sponsor should be seeking only limited rights at most, such as the right to publish in a book of contest winners; if the contest wants exclusive rights, you should require compensation. Even if you don't see how you would reuse the entry right now, you never know what will come up in the future. Maybe one day you'll want to include it in your own book, sell it to a magazine, enter it into another contest, or sell it to an anthology.

> It's always best to clarify exactly what rights you are assigning before you decide whether or not to enter and before signing any documents.

Win A House Essay Contests

If you saw the movie *The Spitfire Grill,* you know the concept behind this one. Instead of selling a house (or business, car, or any other high-ticket item) the usual way, the owner runs an essay contest to determine who will win the prize.

Unfortunately, if you did see *The Spitfire Grill,* your view of this scenario may be a bit rose-colored. In the movie, the restaurant's owner got tons of entries, awarded the place to a young mom, and all was well. That's not how it usually works.

First, understand that there's a reason most of these places aren't sold the usual way—often, the owner has tried and hasn't gotten good offers.

The contests call for short entries (the topic is often "Why I Should Win This House") accompanied by a $100–$200 entry fee, or thereabout. The owner plans to get lots of mentions in the media and lots of entries, therefore making more money from entry fees than he would have by selling it on the real estate market. But in truth, most of these contests don't get enough entries, so the contests are canceled.

"I don't know of any houses that have actually been given away in Washington," says Jon McCoy, an assistant attorney general who represents the Washington State Gambling Commission. "Usually there aren't enough contestants to pay for the house, so the contest is canceled or postponed to allow for more entries."

In truth, most of these contests don't get enough
entries, so the contests are canceled.

Usually, the contests have a minimum number of entries listed in their guidelines. The owner can always decide to accept fewer entries and still run the contest, but he can't change his mind and increase the minimum number because contest expenses cost more than he expected.

A canceled contest is not terrible for the entrants as long as the money gets refunded. But you must read the fine print: In many cases, you must agree that only part of your money will be refunded if the contest is canceled. The rest of it will be used to offset contest expenses (like advertising, attorney fees, and web site hosting). Some want to keep a dollar or two just for postage expenses, while others expect to keep 15 percent or more of your entry fee.

Further, it's hard to guarantee that the winner isn't a "plant." Maybe the owner wants to give this house to his nephew, so he's already decided that the winning "entry" will be his nephew's. Check to see who certifies the contest, and if an independent panel is judging entries. No identifying information should appear on the essays; they should be marked with numbers or codes once the sponsor receives them, but names should not appear on the essays themselves. The sponsor's friends and family should be excluded.

The state's attorney general or secretary of state should consent to the contest, which means checking to make sure everything is being done legally, in their opinion. They can't actually approve or endorse the contests. A few states outlaw these kinds of contests altogether. All states require that the contest be a judgment of skill and not a random sweepstakes.

A canceled contest is not terrible for the entrants
as long as the money gets refunded.

"Although the Attorney General's Office and the Gambling Commission are often asked whether these contests are legal, we do not approve or license them," McCoy said. "If the contest sponsor is implying that we do, they are not being honest."

Be extra careful not to send a check to a person at a post office box, which is virtually untraceable. The guidelines should mention where the funds will be held: The money should stay in an escrow or trust account until the contest ends, and the bank's name and address should be listed. Ideally, entrants should send payment directly to the escrow agent.

Check to see if the contest is bonded, too. According to the Washington State Gambling Commission, bonding is a form of insurance that is one way to guarantee that the prize will be actually awarded, or that refunds can be made if the contest is not completed.

There should be a time limit for extensions and refunds. In most cases, the sponsor will reserve the right to extend the deadline. But is it an open-ended right? If so, the sponsor may just keep delaying and delaying, just to avoid sending refunds. A specific time frame for refunds (e.g., within three weeks of contest cancellation) should be listed up front.

There's also the danger that the sponsor is in debt and doesn't have the right to sell the property. The Washington State Gambling Commission states, "In one contest to give away a service station, it turned out that the gas tanks and pumps were about to be repossessed." Ask if the sponsor has proof of ownership and be sure there are no liens on the property (besides the mortgage).

Save a hard copy of the rules and contest description. Keep any paper-work (ads, articles, etc.) about the contest handy just in case something goes wrong. This will give you evidence to show if the contest sponsor disappears, if refunds are not made, if the property is misrepresented, or if any rules are broken.

Even if you win, the tax liability may be too much to bear. The IRS expects you to report the "fair market value" of any contest prizes on your income taxes in the "miscellaneous earnings" category (Form 1099-MISC). There may be other fees to think about as well, like licensing and insurance fees for a car, and sales tax.

There are, of course, happy tales from contests like these. Guinness held several "Win Your Own Pub" essay contests where winners received their own pubs in Ireland, and some privately run contests actually do attract thousands of entrants and the homes or businesses are awarded. If you're careful about which contests you enter, the risks should be minimal, and it could be fun. The odds of getting enough entries increase if the sponsor works hard at publicity, so the best-publicized contests are your best bets for seeing a prize awarded.

You can call the sponsor's state's attorney general's office if you want to report suspected fraud or ask whether a particular contest is legal. The attorney general's office can act if they believe a contest sponsor is being deceptive or unfair.

Editing Tests

This is one I wouldn't have believed if I hadn't seen it myself.

One of the regulars on the Absolute Write message boards posted this request for advice:

> "I just received my first "real" rejection from an agent who said she loved the strong story concept but that my writing contained "many common writing errors."

> "She recommended using an editor to polish the manuscript into shape, then resubmitting to her at a later date. She didn't recommend a specific person or company.

> "Any advice anyone? I really have no clue how to find a legitimate 'book doctor.'"

She got plenty of good advice from our members, including author advocate Victoria Strauss. Victoria told her what to look out for in book doctors and provided a link to a page where the writer could read about various editing scams. One of the scams included an editing "test," where a victim had written a story about how she'd been suckered into editing a chapter of someone's manuscript as a test for future work. After she completed the "test," the supposed employer sent her a link to a web site where his future book would be sold, and she never heard from him again. The victim contacted other people who had responded to the ad, and they all discovered that they had each edited different chapters of this person's manuscript. No one was hired for the job. In other words, he got his whole book edited for free, under the guise of an "editing test."

A few hours later, the writer registered a new screen name and posted this:

> Editor needed by May 1, 2005. Freelance/Work from home. Manuscripts sent by PDF or regular mail from client.
>
> Pay rate: $5 per double-spaced page. Sample: For a 300 page book pay rate is $1200. A four-week turnaround time per manuscript is asked for.
>
> Send resume to: [the writer's email address].

It raised a red flag or two; why did she need to create a new fake screen name for this? It read a lot like the ad from the story Victoria posted, where the would-be editor had to take a "test" to get the job. One of our members wrote to the address to ask more about the position and got a response saying the job had already been filled. But that wasn't enough. The writer registered another new screen name and posted this:

> First annual Book Editing competition. Edit one chapter of a book (sample will be sent to you along with competition details).
>
> Closes April 30, 2005
> Entry fee: $5 (payable by paypal)
> ALL entry fees are to be used to offset prize money!
> First place: $150
> Second place: $75
> Third place: $25
> Entries are strictly limited to 50 places.
>
> Entries will be judged according to adherence to general editing guidelines, including the correction of:
>
> ___ Telling narrative instead of showing characters feelings.
>
> ___ Heavy use of adverbs and adjectives.
>
> ___ Lacks effective background development.
>
> ___ Heavy description that stops/interferes with story.

Full competition details available upon request, please email for full details.

You don't have to be a genius to decipher that this writer was actually trying to entice people to pay $5 to enter her "contest" to edit her novel. Most likely, the guidelines were the critiques she'd gotten when her work was rejected ("Your story is telling instead of showing, using too many adverbs and adjectives, lacks effective background development, and has too much description that interferes with the flow of the story").

I have no idea if she'd have paid that prize money to anyone, but in essence, she would have actually convinced other people to pay for the privilege of editing her unsold novel.

You don't have to be a genius to decipher that this writer was actually trying to entice people to pay $5 to enter her "contest" to edit her novel.

What amazes me more than anything is that she had the gall to post this on the same forum where just about every noted writers' advocate and scam hunter hangs out—the very same place she came to ask for advice about questionable agents and book doctors. That's brazen, but it shows you just how clueless many would-be scammers are.

What Does a Good Contest Look Like?

Here's one I feel safe in using as a model: The L. Ron Hubbard "Writers of the Future" contest. The first line of the rules? "No entry fee is required, and all rights in the story remain the property of the author." On the issue of anonymity in judging: "Each entry must have a cover page with the title of the work, the author's name, address, telephone number, email address and an approximate word count. Every subsequent page must carry the title and a page number, but the author's name must be deleted to facilitate fair judging."

On their web site (www.writersofthefuture.com), you can find past winners' names and story titles dating back to 1985, and you'll notice that many winners have gone on to have successful science fiction writing careers.

> Entering smaller contests can have many benefits: encouragement, the motivation to meet a deadline, an incentive to improve, an honor to add to a resume, and possible recognition and prize money for outstanding work.

Another? Try the Don and Gee Nicholl Fellowships in Screenwriting (www.oscars.org/nicholl), which I mentioned earlier. Sponsored by the Academy of Motion Picture Arts and Sciences (yes, that Academy), this competition truly has the power to launch a screenwriter's career. That's easy to tell from the web site: Just look at the list of past winners and what they've done since then. Mike Rich *(Finding Forrester)*, Susannah Grant *(Erin Brockovich)*, and Andrew W. Marlowe *(Air Force One)* are among them.

The entry fees are low compared to other screenwriting contests ($20–$30), names are disallowed on scripts, all entrants receive acknowledgments, the web site is professional. Better yet, if you make it as far as the quarterfinals, your script title and genre and your contact information will be sent to producers and agents—and I know from friends that this results in script requests.

One year (1988), when the competition was open only to college students, no fellowships were awarded. Since then, at least four fellowships have been awarded every year, and names and titles are easily verified.

The odds of winning contests like these are slim, of course. In 2004, the Nicholl competition received 6,073 entries and awarded five fellowships of $30,000 apiece. The upshot, of course, is that winning or placing well in such a prestigious contest can truly start a writer's career, whereas many smaller contests can't.

Entering smaller contests, though, can have many other benefits: encouragement, the motivation to meet a deadline, an incentive to improve, an honor to add to a resume, and possible recognition and prize money for outstanding work. Whether you win or not, as long as the contest hasn't claimed rights to your entry, you can always submit it elsewhere for publication or production, too.

Chapter 9

Crash Course in Copyright

Is Registration Necessary?

How to Protect Your Rights

Public Donain and Fair Use

Copyright Myths

```
Let's start with the basics:
what the heck IS copyright?
```

Simply put, copyright is legal protection against others using your work. This protection is given to authors of original works, including literary, dramatic, musical, artistic, and certain other intellectual works, both published and unpublished.

Contrary to what many people believe, you can't copyright an idea—only the expression of an idea. You also can't copyright book or movie titles, names, short phrases, and slogans. There are other exceptions, but they generally don't apply to writers.

All the economic value of your work comes from copyright. In the United States, this protection means that you, as an author, have the exclusive right to do and to authorize (license) others to do the following:

- reproduce the work in copies or electronic form;

- prepare derivative works based upon the work;

- distribute copies (electronic or paper) of the work to the public by sale or other transfer of ownership, or by rental, lease, or lending;

- perform the work publicly, in the case of literary, musical, dramatic, and choreographic works, pantomimes, and motion pictures and other audiovisual works;

- display the copyrighted work publicly, in the case of literary, musical, dramatic, and choreographic works, pantomimes, and pictorial, graphic, or sculptural works, including the individual images of a motion picture or other audiovisual work; and

- in the case of sound recordings, perform the work publicly by means of a digital audio transmission.

Contrary to what many people believe, you can't copyright an idea—only the expression of an idea.

How Do I Claim Copyright Protection?

You don't have to do a thing—no publication or registration is necessary. In the United States and most Western countries, copyright protection attaches automatically from the time the work is created in fixed form. For example, if you're writing an article or book, the instant you lift your pen from paper or save your word processing file, you have copyright protection in the document created. (Before 1978, U.S. federal copyright was generally secured by the act of publication with notice of copyright.) If a work is prepared over a period of time, the part of the work that is fixed on a particular date constitutes the created work as of that date.

In the United States and most Western countries, copyright protection attaches automatically from the time the work is created in fixed form.

Copyright automatically belongs to the person who created the work (except for "made for hire" work: see explanation to follow). The authors of a joint work are co-owners of the copyright in the work, unless there is an agreement to the contrary. Copyright in each separate contribution to a periodical or other collective work is distinct from copyright in the collective work as a whole and belongs to the author of the contribution.

Do I Need a Notice of Copyright?

No, the use of a copyright notice is no longer required under U.S. law. Nevertheless, it is advisable to use it (and because the previous copyright law required notice, its use may still be relevant to the copyright status of older works).

Using a copyright notice informs the public that your work is protected by copyright, identifies the copyright owner, and shows the year of first publication. Furthermore, in the event that a work is infringed, if a proper notice of copyright appears on the published copy or copies to which a defendant in a copyright infringement suit had access, the defendant may not claim "innocent infringement" to reduce actual or statutory damages.

The use of the copyright notice is the responsibility of the copyright owner and does not require advance permission from, or registration with, the Copyright Office. The copyright notice on "visually perceptible copies" (i.e., print, web pages, computer text files) should contain all the following three elements:

- the symbol © (the letter C in a circle), or the word "Copyright," or the abbreviation "Copr."; and

- the year of first publication of the work; and

- the name of the owner of copyright in the work, or an abbreviation by which the name can be recognized, or a generally known alternative designation of the owner.

Example: © 2005 John Doe

How Long Does My Copyright Last?

For works originally created on or after January 1, 1978, the work is automatically protected from the moment of its creation for your life plus an additional 70 years after your death. In the case of "a joint work prepared by two or more authors who did not work for hire," the term lasts for 70 years after the last surviving author's death. For works made for hire and for anonymous and pseudonymous works (unless the author's identity is revealed in Copyright Office records), the duration of copyright will be 95 years from publication or 120 years from creation, whichever is shorter.

Can I Transfer or License My Copyright?

Yes, that's precisely what you do when you sign a publishing contract or authorize publication of an article (see chapter 5). A copyright is personal property and may be transferred or licensed for a fee, and may be bequeathed by will or otherwise pass to your heirs under state law.

The Copyright Act, however, requires that any transfer of exclusive rights must be in writing, signed by the copyright owner. Mere assent is not enough—there must be a written transfer. This means, for instance, that if you are giving exclusive audio rights to an audio book publisher, there must be a publishing agreement signed by you, just as with exclusive print rights. If you have not signed an agreement, you have not given up exclusive rights.

A copyright is personal property and may be transferred or licensed for a fee, and may be bequeathed by will or otherwise pass to your heirs under state law.

On the other hand, nonexclusive rights need not be in writing. You can offer one-time or reprint rights to a magazine verbally, but it still always is better to have a written agreement spelling out precisely what rights you are giving.

Should I Register My Copyright?

Yes. As noted above, registration is not necessary to obtain copyright protection, although registration is necessary as a prerequisite to filing a copyright infringement suit in the United States. In addition, the law confers certain benefits to copyright owners who formally register. They are as follows:

- Registration establishes a public record of your copyright.

- If made before or within five years of publication, registration makes it more difficult for anyone to legally challenge your ownership.

- If registration is made within three months after publication of the work or before an infringement of the work, statutory damages

(damages without proof of loss) and attorneys' fees will be available to the copyright owner in court actions (see following explanation) Otherwise, only an award of actual damages (lost profits you can prove) is available to the copyright owner.

• Registration allows the owner of the copyright to record the registration with the U. S. Customs Service for protection against the importation of infringing copies.

The most important of these benefits is your right to statutory damages and attorneys' fees. Without registration, you can recover only the money you lost as a direct result of the infringement (what you might have charged for the work) plus any profits that the infringer made by selling your work. In many cases, you may be unable to prove any such loss or damages.

If you have registered in a timely manner, however, the Copyright Act gives you the right to sue for damages without actual proof of loss by you, or actual profits by the infringer. Statutory damages for "innocent" (non-willful) infringement currently range from $750 to $30,000. If any infringement was committed willfully, you can obtain up to $150,000 for each infringement.

Just as important is the right to attorney's fees. If you have "timely registered" and win your case, you are entitled to recover your attorney's fees—even if the award of damages is small. Practically speaking, unless you are independently wealthy, you won't be able to hire a lawyer without this benefit.

When Can I Register?

Registration may be made at any time within the life of the copyright. Unlike the law before 1978, currently, when a work has been registered in unpublished form, it is not necessary to make another registration when the work becomes published, although the copyright owner may register the published edition, if desired. Usually this is done only if the work is substantially altered in its published form.

Generally, if you've written a book, it is advisable to register just before or at the time of publication, when it is in its final form. The publisher usually does this on your behalf. And no, you don't have to register your work before you submit it to a publisher unless you are unusually paranoid (see chapter 17).

How Do I Register?

To register a work, go to www.copyright.gov, where you will find a complete set of instructions and forms. You can also call (202) 707-9100 to request forms. The filing fee is $30. It usually takes four to five months for the Copyright Office to send you a certificate, but the registration becomes effective on the day they receive your application, payment, and copy(ies) in acceptable form.

Can I Register Multiple Works at Once?

Yes. If you write for magazines, e-zines, newspapers, and so on, you can copyright several pieces at one time, for one fee. The Copyright Office permits you to file a single copyright registration for a group of works if all of the following conditions are met:

- all of the works are by the same author, who is an individual (not an employer for hire); and

- all of the works were first published as contributions to periodicals (including newspapers) within a twelve-month period;

- all of the works have the same copyright claimant; and

- the application identifies each contribution separately, including the periodical containing it and the date of its first publication.

Keep in mind that if you are a professional freelance writer, your livelihood is based entirely on the articles and columns you produce. Your work is your property, just as much as your computer or car or bank account. You wouldn't allow your other property to sit around unlocked or unguarded. Without registration, your intellectual property effectively is "unlocked" because it would not be practical for you to file an infringement lawsuit. Therefore, every ninety days, you should file a group registration (Form TX with Form GR) of your articles published in the previous ninety days, paying a single $30 fee. Just make sure that the Copyright Office receives your registration within the ninety-day period.

This is cheap insurance: For $120/year, you can rest assured that if you must bring a copyright lawsuit, you will be able to hire a lawyer, collect attorneys' fees, and obtain statutory damages.

What Is Work "Made for Hire?"

Under the "work-for-hire" doctrine, the author of a work for copyright purposes may be a publisher or employer rather than the actual creator. Section 101 of the copyright law defines a "work made for hire" as a work prepared by an employee within the scope of his or her employment or a work specially ordered or commissioned for use as: a contribution to a collective work, a part of a motion picture or other audiovisual work, a translation, a supplementary work, a compilation, an instructional text, answer material for a test, a sound recording, or an atlas.

For example, everything written by New York Times reporters is under the copyright of the Times, not the individual reporter. The Times is the author for copyright purposes. Under recent court decisions, however, there can be no "implied" work for hire between publishers and freelance writers or artists—"made for hire" must be specified in a written contract signed by you.

In general, you should try to avoid writing anything as work for hire—it means you are giving up your rights in the work forever.

For book authors, work for hire is sometimes the norm in the case of series work (i.e., if you're going to write a book in an already-established young adult series, or a television tie-in line, the publisher will almost certainly require work-for-hire rights). Often, when you work with a book packager (also known as a book producer) who has developed an idea in-house and sold it to a publisher, you'll also be expected to sign a work-for-hire agreement. In general, you should try to avoid writing anything as work for hire—it means you are giving up your rights in the work forever.

Is My Copyright Protected in Other Countries?

Probably, but not necessarily. Although there is no such thing as an "international copyright" that will automatically protect an author's writings throughout the entire world, most countries do offer protection to foreign works under certain conditions, and these conditions have been greatly simplified by international copyright treaties and conventions.

Other Copyright Issues

As a writer, you also should be familiar with two other important concepts of copyright law: "public domain" works and "fair use."

"Public Domain" works are anything not protected by copyright. Such works can be used freely by anyone without permission. The numerous changes Congress has made in the term of copyright duration, however, has made it difficult to determine whether a work currently is in the public domain. Some general rules: Any work created since January 1, 1978, is still protected. Any unpublished works from authors who died before 1935 is in the public domain. Any work that was published before 1923 is in the public domain. Any work published between 1923 and 1977 without a copyright notice is in the public domain. Any work published with notice between 1923 and 1963, but copyright was not renewed, is in the public domain.

Works in the public domain also include U.S. federal government documents and publications (but not those authored by private contractors on behalf of the federal government, even though published by the federal government) and many state government documents and publications. In addition, copyright owners can voluntarily donate their works to the public domain.

"Fair use" is the doctrine stating that you can use small portions of copyrighted material without obtaining permission from the author. It is a frequently abused concept in copyright law. Section 107 of the Copyright Act provides that "the fair use of a copyrighted work . . . for purposes such as criticism, comment, news reporting, teaching (including multiple copies for classroom use), scholarship, or research, is not an infringement of copyright."

Legitimate fair use generally is a short excerpt, usually attributed, used in connection with genuine criticism, parody, or teaching. In my experience, most of what people label as fair use isn't.

Four factors are to be considered in order to determine whether a specific action is to be considered a "fair use." These factors are as follows:

- the purpose and character of the use, including whether such use is of commercial nature or is for nonprofit educational purposes (non-profit uses are more likely to be considered fair use);

- the nature of the copyrighted work (an "informational" work—a work of facts or reporting, as opposed to a more "creative" work such as a novel—is more likely to be considered fair use and an unpublished work is less likely to be considered fair use than a published work because the right of the author to determine how a work is first published is paramount)

- the amount and substantiality of the portion used in relation to the copyrighted work as a whole (is it a small fraction of the work or a major portion?); and

- the effect of the use upon the potential market for or value of the copyrighted work (how much will the market for the work be diminished by its use?)

Some people believe that when they use other's work, they are giving the copyright owner free advertising, and the owner should be grateful. But it is up to the owners, not the reusers, whether they wish their work displayed or published—and in what context.

Just remember this: Simply giving credit or attribution, without having permission, is the same as stealing Joe's wallet and then saying, while using Joe's money, "This came from Joe." It's still theft, and it's still infringement.

So when in doubt, don't use material without permission.

Copyright Myths

Myth #1: "Anything on the Internet is in the public domain."

Wrong. The Internet is just another medium of publication. All the rules of copyright apply as much as they do to print publication, unless the copyright owner specifically and explicitly places the work in the public domain.

Myth #2: "I may use characters from other writers as long as my story is original."

NO! The making of "derivative works" belongs exclusively to the copyright owner. If you use characters, scenes, or settings from another author's work, you need permission—unless your work falls under the parody or criticism exception of "fair use." Therefore, you may make fun of Jessica Fletcher in a parody or satire, but you can't use her in your novel without a license from David Bain, her creator. And yes, it is true that a lot of fan fiction web sites and zines violate copyright—but that's because the owners tolerate such violations, for their own reasons. They could decide not to tolerate it at any time.

Myth #3: "Anything mailed or emailed to me becomes my property."

Well, yes, you do own the physical print copy of the letter or email print-out. But no, you do not own the copyright for the content, and you may not publish the letter without the consent of the person who wrote the letter, although you may report on what it says, and perhaps even quote from a portion of it to make a point (fair use).

Myth #4: "Song lyrics aren't protected by copyright."

Song lyrics are like any other creative work, and are protected by copyright. Yes, this means that generally you must get permission from the copyright owner if you wish to use even just a line or two of song lyrics in your novel. And no, it's not fair use unless you are reviewing the song or making a parody.

Myth #5: "If the copyright holder didn't register the copyright, I can't be sued."

Yes and no. Registration is a prerequisite to filing a copyright infringement suit, but registration may be made at any time within the life of the copyright (for works created after 1978, author's life plus 70 years). If the registration is made within three months of first publication, the law confers certain additional benefits, such as statutory damages and attorney's fees. Thus, the fact that the owner has not yet registered the copyright will not prevent you from being sued.

Chapter 10

Special Screw-Overs for Screenwriters

Why Producers are Paranoid

Free Options

It's Called "Back-End" Payment for a Reason

Script Submission Services

In recent years, producers have shifted further and further into "cover your butt" mode, thanks to lawsuits from screenwriters and wannabe screenwriters. While I have no doubt that some of these lawsuits have been legitimate, a great portion of them are from writers who believe they can collect some cash because a producer "stole" their idea.

The first issue here is that "ideas" can't be copyrighted, which means you can't seek damages for an idea unless it is uniquely expressed in written or recorded form. Although people can and do start lawsuits over potential copyright infringement—sometimes on amazingly tenuous grounds—these kinds of lawsuits are more infrequent than you might think. Copyright lawsuits must be filed in federal court, and federal rules provide stiff penalties against both clients and lawyers for unjustified lawsuits. On the other hand, when the book or movie in question was a big hit, lawsuits have been common.

Take *E.T.,* for example. Playwright Lisa Litchfield filed a $750 million lawsuit because she alleged Steven Spielberg had stolen the idea for *E.T.* from her play *Lokey From Maldemar.* Spielberg has also been sued over *Raiders of the Lost Ark, Jurassic Park, Amistad, Small Soldiers* . . . and probably every other film he's ever made. In each case, the writer (or cartoonist or filmmaker) believed Spielberg had stolen something from his or her work. In each case, a judge decided in favor of Spielberg.

An author who wrote *The Legend of RAH* and the *Muggle*s sued Time-Warner over trademark infringement for the Harry Potter movies. Director Orson Welles was sued for allegedly plagiarizing a biography of William Randolph Hearst to make *Citizen Kane.*

I chose to break off contact with an aspiring writer I was mentoring because of his constant paranoia about people stealing his ideas. He had written spec episodes of *The Simpsons,* and watched the show vigilantly. A week or two after sending the producers one of his specs, he was positive they used one of his jokes on the air. The next week, he was sure they based a plot on an idea in another of his scripts. I tried and tried to tell him there was no way they read and incorporated his ideas into a show that aired a week or two after he mailed the script, but he wouldn't hear of it. He hired a lawyer, and I gave up on him.

So, you see, producers are a little gun-shy about reading work from writers. If a writer sends in a script about bunnies, and ten years from now, the company produces a movie about bunnies, that writer could very well think, "Hey! They stole my idea!" and start up a lawsuit. It doesn't matter if the reader who was assigned to the script couldn't get past page five of the writer's script because it was awful. It doesn't matter if the produced script has almost nothing in common with the writer's script. Anyone can sue over anything, although usually such lawsuits make news only when they are filed, not when they are summarily dismissed for lack of merit. Unfortunately, some writers genuinely believe their ideas are so original that no one else in the world could have thought of anything similar.

Producers, then, had a choice: Either they could quit reading the work of unrepresented writers altogether, or they could get writers to agree up-front not to sue the producers. Many chose the latter, and release forms were born.

Scripts that come from agents or attorneys are not subject to these release forms, not for any legal reason, but simply because the producer is willing to trust the source as being professional. Professional writers don't make it a practice to file frivolous copyright lawsuits because it would kill their future careers, and legitimate agents and attorneys represent professional writers.

Unfortunately, some writers genuinely believe their ideas are so original that no one else in the world could have thought of anything similar.

Free Options

"I love your script, and I'd like to option it."

Well, ain't that just the cream cheese on my bagel? Them's exciting words. In the olden days, words like those were enough to get me to crack open my best bottle of ginger ale and begin picking out Academy Award dresses. Now I know a little better. Now I know how to respond:

"Great! What are you offering?"

Really, no point in pussyfooting around the issue. Unfortunately, at this point, many producers and wannabe producers stammer and eventually say, "Well, I can't pay you to option it, but it'll be WGA rates when I sell it!"

The "when I sell it" part is, of course, the big shiny carrot at the end of the stick. I'm asking you to pay attention to the other end: the splintery stick end.

A producer who asks for a free option is asking to tie up your rights without giving you anything in return. Many producers ask for a twelve-month option; some will ask for six months.

What it means for you is that for six months to a year, you can't market that script, and even if someone comes to you with an offer, you can't take it without involving that producer.

The best scenario is that the producer really does have good contacts and really can get it seen at places where you can't.

Believe it or not, the worst scenario isn't that the producer sits on your script and doesn't show it anywhere; the worst is if the producer is a hack wannabe and shows it all over town. Then the producer has severely handicapped you from selling it on your own later.

A producer who asks for a free option is asking to tie up your rights without giving you anything in return.

I know of one situation where a free option paid off. My screenwriting professor at Hofstra University, Charles Purpura, sold his first script as a result of a free option. A young wannabe producer loved the script and thought he could sell it; Charles didn't have anything else going on at the moment, so he went for it—and it worked. *Heaven Help Us* was produced in 1985, and Charles went on to write two more produced movies.

Knowing that, I gladly allowed producers to option my scripts without paying me. It didn't pan out the first time, but I was hopeful. Then it didn't pan out the second, third, fourth, or seventh time, either.

Most of the time, the producers who wanted my scripts were inexperienced. A few had produced television movies and independent films; none had produced major studio hits. Of all of them, only one made a concerted effort to sell my script. She really did have some good television connections and tried her best to get it sold, but the timing was off—a movie similar to my story aired just as she was shopping mine.

My general policy now is not to accept free options. I came around to an important thought: If a "producer" is unable to pony up even a few hundred dollars for a token option payment, how would that producer ever raise the funds to make the movie?

Movie-making is expensive—theatrical releases typically have budgets in the millions of dollars. Even independent filmmakers need to spend tens of thousands of dollars to shoot an ultra-low-budget flick. If the producer can't pay a dime for the option rights, it either means he doesn't have any money or he doesn't believe in the script enough to take the gamble. Neither is a good sign.

Keep in mind that a producer needs scripts to find work for himself. A producer who is looking to work with studios will use your script as his calling card. He's showing your script—with himself attached—in the hopes of securing work for himself. It's not a favor he's doing for you; it's a favor you're doing for him. He's going to have to get a script somehow if the studios aren't handing them to him. If he can't get one for free, he'll have to start paying for them or writing them himself.

If a "producer" is unable to pony up even a few hundred
  dollars for a token option payment, how would that
    producer ever raise the funds to make the movie?

Producers who want to entice you to hand over your rights for a free option will often dangle their connections. They'll tell you about all the people they know in the industry and all the places they can bring your script. Be aware that name-dropping is practically a competitive sport in Hollywood.

There are many, many people who have worked in the industry in some small capacity before (sound engineer, key grip, production assistant) and now hope to produce or direct. They think they made "connections" on the set when they were positioning the boom microphones. Maybe they did. Who knows?

So much of your decision here must rely on your gut. If a producer wants a free option, you have to decide whether you want to gamble on the producer. You won't be allowed to show the script around elsewhere while the producer has the option, so your gamble is time: Do you want to trust this person to be your script's sole "salesperson?" Do you think this person is capable of getting your movie made?

As I got wiser, I learned to negotiate my time limits. When I absolutely couldn't get producers to pay me a dime for an option, I limited the option to three months. At the end of any option, you have the ability to renew, and often the contract is automatically renewable if the producer is in the middle of a deal (or seemingly close to it).

Or, if I had little faith in the producer's ability to make a deal, I might offer a nonexclusive option; that is, I give the producer the right to show the script to his contacts, but I retain the right to keep shopping it on my own at the same time.

> When you're dealing with major companies,
> options can be very well-paid.

Keep in mind that there are some screenwriters who've made full-time livings without ever actually having a script produced. They just get paid well to have their scripts optioned. Some wind up in what's affectionately termed "development hell," others just get dropped. But when you're dealing with major companies, options can be very well-paid.

Free Rewrites

If you do decide to take the free option, be sure it doesn't come with an obligation to do any rewriting at the producer's behest. If the producer expects you to go back to the keyboard, he should pay you for that.

You may find that the producer makes good suggestions and you decide to add them into your script—on your own time and because you want to, not because the producer demands it.

What's In an Option Contract?

First, the term of the option usually will be six to eighteen months, during which time the producer has the exclusive right to purchase your screenplay, book, or article's story rights (yes, even magazine articles often are optioned—the movie *Top Gun* was developed from an article about the Miramar Naval Air Station). Second, the contract will specify both the compensation paid for the option and the purchase of your work. How much for the option? For a hot property, this amount will be about ten percent of the purchase price if the option is exercised. In many deals, however, the option money is nominal. The range is wide—from as little as $500 to about $50,000, with the average around $10,000.

Third, there is the purchase price to be paid when the option is exercised and the story rights are purchased. This is critical; it's also complicated. Generally the purchase price will be either a minimum payment (floor) or a percentage of the budget of the production, with a maximum amount (cap). Television and movies will have different formulas based on the length of production and the type of production. A feature film might have a purchase price of the greater of $100,000 or 3 percent of the film's budget (but not more than $250,000). Often, however, the amount of the option payment will be subtracted from this price.

For example, suppose you optioned your screenplay to a producer under the following formula: $10,000 for the option, and a purchase price of 3 percent of the film's budget, with a cap of $250,000, and the option price to be charged against the purchase price. A movie is made with a budget of $15 million. Three percent of $15 million is $450,000, but this exceeds the cap of $250,000. You would receive $240,000: $250,000 minus the option payment of $10,000.

You'll also still have to deal with grant of rights in the option contract. Ideally, writers should grant only limited media rights, on an exclusive or non-exclusive basis. The producer will want all theatrical film, cable, television, pay-per-view, video, DVD, music, and all subsidiary rights including merchandising. You should try to reserve at least sequel, radio, and audio book rights (keep in mind that if your story is a published book or a screenplay adapted from a book, you may have previously granted some of these rights to the book's publisher and will not be able to offer them to the producer).

May the producer alter or adapt your story without your permission? Although this is negotiable, the answer usually is yes. Unlike some European countries, the United States does not generally recognize an author's "moral rights" to his or her work. Frequently, however, the author will be able to get a "consultation" clause in the contract, requiring the producer to consult with the writer before making major changes in plot or character.

If your work is a screenplay (rather than a book or article), don't count on it being the actual screenplay used for the film. Typically the producer will bring in a veteran to adapt it (it's tough to get established actors and directors for a film by an unknown screenwriter). In that case, credit generally will be allocated according to Writers Guild of America (WGA) rules. For instance, you might be given a "story by" credit while the person who rewrites the screenplay will be given the "screenplay by" credit. You may, however, be able to negotiate a clause giving you the first opportunity to be employed to do the rewrite, usually for the minimum fee specified by the WGA.

If your work is a book or magazine article, it is highly unlikely you will be given the chance to write the screenplay (unless, of course, you otherwise are a screenwriter). If you have a lot of leverage, you might get the producer to agree to let you write the first draft, again usually for the minimum fee specified by the WGA. If the producer likes your draft, great—otherwise, the producer will be free to hire someone else to rewrite or draft a new screenplay.

If your work is a screenplay (rather than a book or article), don't count on it being the actual screenplay used for the film.

As with all such agreements, you will have to give certain "warranties and indemnifications" stating that you own the rights to the work and have not defamed anyone or violated any person's right of privacy or publicity.

And last but not least, the agreement will specify what screen credit you will receive, subject to WGA guidelines. In general, unless you write the final screenplay, you will receive a "written by," "created by," "story idea" or "story by" credit.

Back-End Payment

An option or purchase contract also may include a "back-end" payment in the form of a net profits participation in the theatrical release of the film—a percentage of the producer's net (the amount earned by the film after payment of all expenses) or a royalty payment in the case of television movies (a fixed sum per hour of television time).

Beware, beware, of anyone offering you back-end payment; that is, payment based on the film's profits instead of up-front money (or in addition to nominal up-front money).

Hollywood is amazing on paper: If you believe producers' accounting departments, no movies ever make a profit. Yet they keep making them. Strange, isn't it? But there are a million funny little accounting tricks that help producers get away with making sure writers never see that back-end money. Sometimes you'll encounter inexperienced producers who don't mean to con you with this one, either. They'll advertise on places like Craigslist.com, saying they need a writer for a great script and they'll offer a credit, $500, and a big split of the proceeds! Maybe they really believe you'll both get rich. The problem is, there usually aren't any proceeds for independent films, and the big guys who actually do make money are great at concealing it.

Hollywood is amazing on paper: If you believe producers' accounting departments, no movies ever make a profit.

A writer needs to get paid in real, green money up front. If a producer wants to throw in some back-end percentage points on top of your already-tidy sum, hey, no reason to stop him. But steer clear of deals where this is the main payment plan.

WHAT IS CRAIGSLIST?

Craigslist.org is a huge, international web site that resembles a turbo-charged newspaper classified section. There, you can find housing, community events, and jobs—lots of writing jobs both in the "jobs" sections and the "gigs" sections. It's usually free to post ads, and the ads are not vetted before they're posted. (They count on viewers to flag inappropriate ads.) Therefore, while there's plenty of legitimate work to be found here, you need to be cautious. Visit www.absolutewrite.com/freelance_writing/craigslist.htm for tips.

Short Films Wanted!

Again, these ads abound on Craigslist and sites for screenwriters. Read between the lines, and you'll often realize that the people asking for scripts (no payment offered, of course) are film students who need a little help with their homework. They'll usually tell you that they want to shoot a film for the festival circuit and you'll get a credit and a copy of the tape.

Now, maybe that's okay with you. The market for shorts isn't exactly dazzling anyway, and maybe you have a short script you wrote for practice, or could adapt an excerpt of one of your feature scripts into a self-contained quickie. I won't deny that it's exciting to see your words transformed by actors and directors and come to life on your TV screen or at a film screening. I donated a script to a film-school friend and got a kick out of seeing the result at a student festival.

Just understand that the likelihood of its being seen at Cannes is slim. Student films are not usually seen by any real decision makers and rarely launch careers for writers. But you never know—that USC film student may wind up being a prominent filmmaker in five or ten years, and you may have made yourself a good connection.

Attachments

Be careful not to attach yourself out of a deal. You may notice that many agents and producers say they want "packaged" scripts—that is, scripts that already have actors and/or directors attached. This means that actors or directors have committed to doing the movie no matter who makes it.

Now, it's not likely for a new writer to get any meaningful attachments. That is, you probably won't get Julia Roberts or Tom Hanks to sign a contract saying they want to star in your movie. So some new writers think the next best thing is to get someone attached, no matter how obscure. Maybe it's a TV actor who had a series in the '80s, or someone who once had a supporting role in a cult horror film. Maybe it's someone who directed an episode of *The Love Boat*.

```
        Be careful not to attach
        yourself out of a deal.
```

Not a good idea. A sub-par attachment can actually kill a deal. Maybe the producer loved the script, but refuses to work with the washed-up actor you attached to it. Or maybe, because you mentioned that washed-up actor in your query letter, the producer won't even read your script.

Worse yet, many writers try to attach themselves as directors or actors. This is a huge handicap.

As a new writer, you're already an unproven talent; you can't add to that by demanding to direct or act in your own film, too. You earn that right over time, by proving yourself in the industry. As your success grows, you'll be able to make demands, but not in the beginning stages. Attaching yourself only makes you look like you're going to be egotistical and difficult to work with, and it can sabotage your script's chances.

Paid Packagers

Don't ever pay anyone to package your script. A few of these con men hang around on the Internet, usually trolling message boards and script-listing services to find targets. They spam unproduced screenwriters and offer to do all sorts of tasks that are useless to you: finding talent, scouting locations, writing out a budget. All an agent or producer wants to see is your great script. He'll handle everything after that point.

Script Submission Services

Over the years—and especially in the last four or five years—there's been a rise in the number of paid services meant to help screenwriters connect with agents and producers.

Most of these services are web-based. For a set fee, they'll list your script's title, genre, logline, and synopsis on their web site. You may even upload the whole script.

I've tried many of these services. Only one had any results for me: Inktip.com. I'd heard that they were having success getting scripts optioned and sold, so I spoke with the proprietors to find out what they were doing differently. It turned out that they were not just web-based—they sent out regular mailings to producers—and they made frequent contact with producers and agents to get to know their needs and remind them to visit the site. They pre-screen the industry pros who use the site; few stinkers get through. To pass muster, the pros must have verifiable credits or experience and pass a short interview process. I was elated to see that agents from ICM (International Creative Management) read my scripts on Inktip—I had been unable to get them to look at my scripts on my own.

Although I didn't make a sale from my listings on the site, they did lead me to my manager and a producer who wound up optioning one of my scripts, and I was able to look at my stats page to find out who had read my synopsis or full script. Some of my works drew more attention than others, but I felt the service was worthwhile. None of the other paid services I tried had any measurable results—and most went out of business quickly.

Agents and producers don't often troll the Internet looking for the next great script. They get plenty of submissions by mail; they don't need to go looking for more. It's a rare company that can convince industry pros to come search for talent online.

> Agents and producers don't often troll the
> Internet looking for the next great script.

If you're considering using a paid service like this, check references. Ask about their success stories and their stats; if they boast of two sales, great—but in what period of time and out of how many scripts? Then track down the writers of those scripts and verify the story. Did that sale really come through the submission service? If the service boasts of options, check with the writers and ask politely if the options were paid. Some may not want to divulge this information, but many will be candid with you. If all the service's big successes are free options, you may not want to invest your money with them. It is likely they are not attracting heavy-hitters in the industry.

Chapter 11

Monstrous Magazines and E-zines

"Exposure" Isn't Payment

Look Out for Non-Guaranteed Payments

Get It in Writing

What to Do if Your Work Gets Plagiarized

Dealing With Difficult Editors

When Good Articles Get Killed

Literally tens of thousands of magazines and e-zines hire freelance writers, and it's entirely possible to make a full-time living writing articles and essays. However, this market is fraught with its own trouble spots.

Problematic Payments

Exposure

Here's a line frequently seen in guidelines of magazines and e-zines: "At this time, we do not pay for articles, but we provide excellent exposure."

Well . . . yippee.

I'm not judgmental about writing without pay. I've done it, and no one can make me feel guilty about it. Nor can anyone make me feel guilty about writing for payment. If you want to write without pay, that's completely up to you. But it's extremely rare for any non-paying market to be able to deliver meaningful "exposure."

A little e-zine about adopting kittens or starting a home business is probably not being read by editors at major magazines. In other words, it's highly unlikely that an editor will read your article in a little e-zine and decide to hire you for a high-paying assignment.

MediaBistro.com doesn't pay for its "How to Pitch" articles, which many writers think is hypocritical and wrong, considering that they're a seemingly well-funded site for media professionals. But they are one of the very few places offering useful exposure; two people I know who've written for them have ended up with paying assignments from magazines as a result. That's because editors are in MediaBistro's target audience.

If you want to write without pay, that's completely up to you. But it's extremely rare for any non-paying market to be able to deliver meaningful "exposure."

But with few other exceptions, the e-zines and small magazines that boast of how many "hits" they get, how your work will be seen by a vast international audience, etc., will probably do nothing to influence your career directly.

Now, you can take those nonpaying articles you've had published and use them as clips when you send query letters to paying markets. That's probably the best value these nonpaying venues can offer you, unless you're also promoting a book or other business in your bio.

But consider that all the effort you expend writing for markets that pay in "exposure" could be directed toward writing for paying markets, too.

Pay-Per-Click

For quite some time, pay-per-click was a major online trend. In particular, Themestream.com and Epinions.com attracted many, many writers who hoped to make fortunes by writing whatever they wanted. The idea was that every time a person clicked on a particular article, the writer would get paid—up to ten cents a click at one point.

Themestream went out of business; Epinions is still around, but most writers have realized that any writing they do for Epinions is just for fun —it's not the path to fame and fortune. Rules for both venues changed many times over to add more and more obstacles so writers wouldn't make as much money as they expected. First, rates were lowered, then only the clicks from other registered site members would count toward payments, then there were minimum payment thresholds, and checks wouldn't be issued unless writers specifically requested them.

Lesser-known sites have similar offers: Write for us and we'll pay you based on traffic. In some cases, writers are promised payment each time someone clicks on a banner advertisement on the article's page, or each time someone buys a product from a link mentioned in the article, or each time someone subscribes to a service on the article's page.

> In the best-case scenario, writers
> I know have made ten or twenty dollars
> a month by writing dozens of articles for
> these pay-per-click sites and annoying
> their friends and family
> into clicking on the sites
> and reading all the articles.

For more than five years, I've run the most popular online magazine for writers and its corresponding bulletin board, so as you can imagine, I hear from an awful lot of writers every day. Not once have I ever heard of a situation like this working out for the writer. Most of the time, the writer never gets paid at all. Either there's tricky language to ensure the writer never earns enough money to meet the minimum threshold before payment is made, the site goes out of business before writers get paid, or there's no way to track traffic to ensure site owners are being honest.

In the best-case scenario, writers I know have made ten or twenty dollars a month by writing dozens of articles for these pay-per-click sites and annoying their friends and family into clicking on the sites and reading all the articles. If you want to do it for fun, to express an opinion about a product, to give yourself a goal and a deadline to meet, or to get a little feedback on your work, go right ahead. But be aware that your efforts are best spent elsewhere if you're looking for financial compensation.

Payment in Stock Options

Start-up companies love to tell you how you're getting in on the "ground floor" of a revolutionary new publication. Proliferating in the late 1990s, these companies offered payment in stock options or other such stake in the companies.

This has almost always proven to be useless; within a year or two, the revolutionary new publication is out of business and the stock certificates are worthless.

Consider that the companies that tend to actually make enough of a splash to pay off and stick around are typically well-funded to begin with. Writer payments (even if modest at first) should be written into the business plan.

Deferred Payment

Unfortunately, I know many writers who've devoted an awful lot of time to writing for start-up publications on the promise that the companies would reimburse them for their work at some undefined point in the future when the company made some money.

---

60 percent of start-up magazines fail in the first year and 80 percent are gone within four years.

Don't be so eager to be helpful unless you're just doing a good deed for a friend or family member. Keep in mind that most new print magazines fail within two years; University of Mississippi journalism professor Samir A. Husni (a leading expert about magazines) says that 60 percent of start-up magazines fail in the first year and 80 percent are gone within four years. I have yet to see a reliable statistic about e-zines, but I'd guess that the failure rate is even higher. Most of the people who start e-zines have no business plan and no particular publishing experience—and once they realize how hard it is to make money running an e-zine, they quit, leaving all those hopeful writers behind.

Mind you, some start-up proprietors are very convincing. Two writers I know spent almost a year writing for ShesGotItTogether.com, a site that looked professional and whose owners seemed to have a solid background in publishing. Finally, the writers got frustrated with all the broken promises about how long it would take to settle their invoices for thousands of dollars. The site has disappeared, and last time I checked, those two writers were still waiting for their payment.

It boggles my mind that anyone would be quite that patient and rack up so much time writing for a publication that's shown no sign of paying off their debts. But it's not the first time I've heard that story. Don't be so passive or understanding that you undervalue your work and become a human doormat. It's not worth it.

Writers want to believe that editors and publishers will make good on their word, so we sometimes act on faith longer than we should. If you intend to make a living as a writer—or even just supplemental income—then you're a small business owner, and you need to act as such. If you owned a store, how long would you let a customer run up a tab before you demanded payment or cut them off? Would you allow someone to come in and take anything he wanted from your store for a year before you finally said, "Hey, I can't let you take anything else until you pay me"?

Don't be so passive or understanding that you undervalue your work and become a human doormat. It's not worth it.

Contract Quandaries

Often—but not always—writers run into problems collecting their money because they never had a contract to begin with. Without any sort of written record of what's owed, what rights are conveyed, when payment is expected, etc., writers are usually out of luck if a publication decides not to pay up.

Unfortunately, new writers are often afraid to ask for a contract if none is offered. Don't be! When an editor offers an assignment, it's well within your right to ask for a signed agreement. If an editor doesn't send you one, write one up yourself and don't start your work until the editor signs it.

Among other things, the contract should spell out when payment is due—typically on acceptance or on publication. Then, if payment hasn't arrived within thirty days of acceptance or publication, it's time to complain—and to hold off writing anything else for this publication until your check clears.

> Quick turnaround time is no excuse for a
> lack of a contract.

"I got a call from an editor who was putting together custom publications for large companies," says freelancer Jena Ball. "He needed one of these publications edited ASAP. This was Friday morning. I asked for a contract and he said he'd send it first thing Monday morning, but was on the road. Could I get it done over the weekend? Dummy that I was, I agreed to do it, and spent most of my weekend rewriting and editing a 100-page text. This guy not only refused to pay me, but threatened to come to my home and 'teach me a lesson about hounding employers.' Very, very spooky."

Jena never did get paid for that work, deciding that her personal safety was more important than the $800 he owed her. But her story illustrates an important point: Quick turnaround time is no excuse for a lack of a contract. Editors can fax or email contracts within minutes, and it's not your fault that they're in a rush. Hold out.

"Obviously I've learned to do nothing without a contract in hand and have since hired a good lawyer," she says. "He's been able to collect from a couple of deadbeats since and is worth every penny I pay him!"

Fighting for Your Rights

First, a quick run-down of rights as they pertain to articles.

One-time rights contracts are the best scenario for writers. One-time rights means that the publication acquires the right to publish the article one time. They're not demanding that they be the first publication to run the article; you can sell the article to more than one publication at the same time if the publications ask for one-time rights.

First North American serial rights is the second best type of contract. It means the magazine or newspaper is buying the right to be the first print publication in North America to print the article. Sometimes the contract will specify a period of exclusivity (for example, First North American serial rights, exclusive for sixty days). Otherwise, after the article is in print, you're free to sell it again elsewhere.

Reprint rights (or second rights) are the rights conveyed every time you resell an article after it's already been published.

Electronic rights are for web sites, e-zines, and any other digital media.

Archive rights means the web site retains the right to keep your article in their online archives.

Anthology rights means the publication gets the right to use your article in a book.

Now for the two dastardly deals for freelancers: **all rights** and **work-for-hire.**

One of the more modern trouble spots for freelance writers is the newfangled dance called the "rights grab." As it became more common for newspapers and magazines to publish online counterparts, more publications began expecting electronic rights from freelancers . . . for no extra pay.

Early on, many publications just assumed they had this right, regardless of what writers' contracts said. Then came *Tasini vs. The New York Times,* a lawsuit initiated by then-president of the National Writers Union, Jonathan Tasini. The union fought for extra payment for electronic rights and won, but it was a Pyrrhic victory. Now, instead of buying First North American serial rights and paying extra for electronic rights, many publications responded to this lawsuit by requiring freelancers to assign electronic rights together with print rights (for the same money they once got paid for print rights alone).

Some publications ask for "all rights," that is, the transfer of exclusive rights, which would mean the writer may not resell it anywhere ever again, and the publication has the right to use it again and again in whatever formats it wishes (magazine, online, book, etc.). Even if the article becomes the basis for a movie, the writer has no claim to extra payment.

Obviously, all rights never should be granted unless you receive considerable compensation. Luckily for writers, as noted in chapters 8 and 9, under the Copyright Act a transfer of exclusive rights is not valid unless it is in writing and signed by the copyright owner. So unless you affirmatively signed a document giving the publisher all rights, such a grant is ineffective.

Similar to an assignment of "all rights" is the work-for-hire (or "work made for hire") described in chapter 9. Work for hire can apply in two situations: when work is created by an employee, or when work is commissioned under an independent contractor agreement. If a work was created for hire, the writer has no authorship in the work—you lose all rights.

Work for hire is legitimate when a writer is a full-time employee of the company. If the writer gets paid a regular salary and benefits, the company can expect to own whatever work the writer produces during working hours. But it becomes much more questionable when the worker is a freelancer.

Obviously, all rights never should be granted unless you receive considerable compensation.

The good news is that work created by a freelance writer under an independent contract may be considered as work for hire only if it falls within one of nine specific categories in the Copyright Act, was specially commissioned (not simply transferred after its creation); and both parties agree in writing before the work actually is created.

Still, some publications do demand work-for-hire rights from freelancers. In effect, this is the same as all-rights, but with one extra kick in the teeth: The publication is considered the author of the article, so they don't even have to give you credit when they use your article. They might list it under an editor or publisher's name or give it no byline at all.

By all means, you can and should negotiate rights-grabbing contracts. In many cases, an editor will first offer the "all-rights" contract, but when a writer balks, miraculously, the first North American serial rights contract appears. The only time a publication deserves all rights or work-for-hire rights is when they're paying you enough to compensate for the fact that you can never use that article again. Very few times in my life have I found that to be the case. About the only time I gave in easily was when an editor paid me $2 a word for a feature assignment on a topic I knew well . . . in that situation, I considered it fair compensation for all rights.

By all means, you can and should negotiate rights-grabbing contracts.

Some jokers really love to exploit inexperienced writers. Check this out:

> If we accept an article, we will become the copyright holder. This is essential, especially on the Web, to allow us to actively protect our publications from copyright infringement . . . If you submit an article to ZATZ and we choose to publish it, you are thereby releasing any and all copyright to us. This, by the way, is the usual practice among most major magazines.

> In general, we do not provide any payment for articles submitted.

What?!

Yeah, really, they're serious. They're going to claim your copyright and they're not going to pay you. But on the plus side, this claim is ineffective unless you both agreed to the transfer of exclusive rights in writing (see earlier explanation). And they're straight-out lying when they say that work-for-hire is the "usual practice" among major magazines.

Then comes one of the lamest excuses I've ever heard: "Honorariums are rare (the tax paperwork is a royal pain) and are at the sole discretion of the editorial staff."

Tax paperwork?! That's why they won't pay writers? Oh, come on.

In other sections, they tell writers that simultaneous submissions are not allowed, and that writers may not even post their articles on their own web sites. (Though, generously, Zatz will allow the writers to link to their own articles!)

But here's the kicker of it all:

"You can't run a published article in more than one publication. It's just not done and it's really, really bad," they write.

However, if you look on Zatz.com, you'll see that they advertise reprint articles for sale for $200–$400. What does this mean? If the author wants to resell his or her own articles, it's "just not done and it's really, really bad," but if Zatz wants to resell authors' articles and pocket the money, it's apparently just dandy. I questioned the vice president of the company about this and she wrote back, "We have sold two reprints in the entire history of the company. Whoo hoo. $400."

I don't find that valid justification. Just because they're not successful at their scheme doesn't mean that it's okay. On principle, how is it okay that they can profit from the authors' writing, but the writers can't?

"If your main priority is eeking [sic] out every bit of cash mileage from a piece of writing you can, than [sic] you are scarcity conscious and no kind of artist. This kind of thinking is very anti-creativity. You must not be very connected to yourself or to the great creative well if you don't trust that you can come up with another piece, that there's always more where that came from," wrote Vice President Denise Amrich.

```
There is a strange subset of the literary world that
espouses the notion that artists should starve—indeed,
   must starve—to prove their dedication to the arts.
```

Don't ever let anyone feed you a line of bull like this. The funny thing is that Denise gets paid.

Denise's statement is exactly where many writers get into trouble. They do think, "Well, I can always write more." But where does one draw the line? How many times does a writer give away her work and her rights before realizing it's time to get paid and retain her rights?

There is a strange subset of the literary world that espouses the notion that artists should starve—indeed, must starve—to prove their dedication to the arts. Nonsense. Early on in my career, I had written a post on a message board about fair payment, and a writer posted back, "Write for writing's sake." I don't remember the rest of her post word for word, but the gist of it was that I was somehow a traitor to the craft if I put a dollar value on my work, and that payment should be the furthest thing from my mind when I write. I should just feel compelled to write and do it for the sheer love of it, with no expectation of payment.

If that's the case, then Alice Sebold, Stephen King, James Patterson, Barbara Kingsolver, Wally Lamb, and probably every other writer you can name is a traitor, too, and "no kind of artist." Each of them gets paid. Each understands that the words "starving" and "artist" don't need to be inseparable.

My final email to the proprietors at Zatz contained the following points:

- Neither of you has found a single plausible reason to justify your embarrassingly poor policies.

- Why is it that you charge $200–$400 for article reprints and yet writers receive none of this money?

- Why is it that you demand to own writers' copyrights?

- Why is it that you charge advertisers up to $1,000 a pop, considering how gauche money is and how you're so creative and outside-the-box that you think money is evil and those who want it must be greedy?

- How do you face your own hypocrisy when you tell writers that printing the same piece in more than one publication is "just not done" and "bad," then happily sell reprint rights to the pieces yourself, keeping the writers' money?

- Writing a story for a nonprofit literary zine is an outlet for creativity.

- Writing a researched article for a for-profit computing magazine and letting others directly earn money for your hard work is masochistic.

- By the way, I will own the copyrights to anything further that you write to me. By writing back, you acknowledge that you understand this policy.

Yes, I know that, legally, merely writing back to me would not be a valid transfer of copyright, but the president of Zatz did not email me again, although he did manage to get himself lambasted on AbsoluteWrite.com's message boards.

Non-Compete Clauses

Some publications include a non-compete clause in contracts. This clause varies in its level of restriction, but the basic idea is that writers cannot write for the publication's competitors.

This is understandable for staff writers and editors. If they receive salaries from *American Baby*, it's rather rude for them to freelance on the side for *Parenting*, is it not? Some employers don't restrict moonlighting, but it's logical that many will not want employees to contribute to publications that share the same target market. But what about freelancers?

Signing a non-compete clause may be necessary if you become a columnist or contributing editor for a magazine. If you're receiving guaranteed income on an ongoing basis from a particular publication and they want your name to be associated with their publication, it's reasonable for editors to expect that you will not write for their direct competitors.

That's part of the bargain you strike at times. When I became a contributing editor at *Writer's Digest* magazine, the editor-in-chief asked me not to write for *The Writer* or *Poets & Writers*, their closest competitors. In exchange, they'd guarantee me a certain number of feature articles per year at their highest pay rates. This wasn't too restrictive for me; it stopped me from writing for only two other magazines, and those other two magazines didn't pay as well as *Writer's Digest* anyway.

Signing a non-compete clause may be necessary if you become a columnist or contributing editor for a magazine.

When you're faced with a decision like this, weigh it out: How restrictive is the clause, and is it likely to limit your income or increase your income? If a lower-paying magazine wants you to sign a non-compete clause that will stop you from writing for higher-paying magazines, unless they're promising you significant ongoing income, it's probably not in your best interest.

It becomes more problematic, though, when you're asked to sign a non-compete clause as a regular one-assignment-at-a-time freelancer.

I offered a reprint article to a regional parenting magazine a few years back. They wanted it, but only if I would sign a contract that included a non-compete clause stating that I would never write for any other parenting magazine in their state. This is much different than agreeing that I wouldn't sell that same article to another parenting magazine in the state; this meant that I would never be allowed to sell any article to another parenting magazine in the state!

Some publishers make silly excuses for clauses like this, saying that they invest so much in training and building up their writers that they don't want the writers to take that training elsewhere. Silliness. Their "training" is also known as editing, which is what every good publication does. If a publisher is not paying you a full-time income or at least a significant ongoing paycheck, it has no right to limit where else you can earn money. Imagine telling your hairdresser that she has to agree never to cut the hair of anyone else on your block.

These clauses can be negotiated, like any other part of the contract. Don't ever assume that you just have to "take or leave" a contract. Tell an editor that you'd love to work with her, but you're unwilling to sign a non-compete clause. You may not even get an argument.

If that doesn't work and you still want to sign the contract, make sure competitors are specified by name. The editor should list the names of the magazines they consider direct competitors, not just include a vague statement like "competing publications" or "health magazines." A national magazine may not mind if you write for a local magazine in the same category; a local magazine should not mind if you write for a magazine outside of their circulation area.

Be aware of the duration of the clause, too. Never, ever sign a non-compete clause that lasts "forever." For a high-paying assignment, I might be willing to sign a contract that says I will not write for specified competitors for up to six months, but not longer than that.

```
If a publisher is not paying you a full-time income or
at least a significant ongoing paycheck, it has no right
to limit where else you can earn money. Imagine telling
your hairdresser that she has to agree never to cut the
                hair of anyone else on your block.
```

None of Our Other Writers Complain

One of the most common comebacks editors give when a writer challenges a contractual clause is, "None of our other writers have complained."

First, who cares? Just because other writers may be willing to be treated like indentured servants doesn't mean that you have to. This is a particularly popular comeback from unscrupulous publishers, who will brag about all their "happy writers." The problem is, often the happy writers are hobbyists who are just so darn excited to be published that they don't care about the terms. And the unhappy writers are somehow erased from the publisher's memory.

Second, who says? In many cases, I've heard of editors saying this, when I know for a fact that it isn't true.

Third, they may not have heard the complaints because writers who know better never bothered to approach them in the first place, or simply said "No, thank you" when they saw the contract.

No matter the truth behind the statement "all the other kids are doing it," it never worked on Mom, so why should it work on you? An appropriate response might be, "Guess there's a first time for everything. So, how would you like to handle this?"

Term Paper Mills

Here's an ad recently posted by EduWriters.com:

> Are you a freelance writer seeking a substantial source of income while working at home? If so, we have great news for you! EduWriters.com is hiring 2–3 academic model term paper/ research paper freelance writers this month. The earning potential is unlimited and the positions need to be filled immediately! We are looking for freelance writers who can write on a variety of subjects. We write model academic papers on Accounting to Zoology. The more diverse you are the better!

"Model" term papers, you say?

Yes, your raised eyebrow is entirely appropriate. According to sites like this (which have cropped up all over the Internet), they provide term papers and research papers for students to use as models when the students write their own papers. Yeah . . . right. Sort of like the phallic-shaped neck massagers in catalogues . . . wink, wink.

Take a look at the come-ons on these sites. Read www.duenow.com and www.papermasters.com. You'll notice the "Plagiarism Report" on www.duenow.com, which states, in part, "The staff of many high-schools, universities and colleges have begun using online anti-plagiarism databases to ensure that all work that is handed in is 100% original and does not match any of the papers in their database . . ." It goes on to explain that the free term paper sites are easily searchable by teachers, but their site is a paid service and can't be searched. It concludes, "So, while we do charge a small fee for our papers (as low as $1.95 per page) please keep in mind that what you're paying for is both high quality and peace of mind."

Yep, peace of mind. No teacher will know that a freelance writer wrote that paper and the student will find out that money can buy grades.

Of course I could give you a hundred reasons why writing for services like these is wrong, but ask yourself how you'd feel if you found out your doctor, dentist, or president got through grad school by buying term papers from professional writers.

Syndicate Services

There are some syndicates that are reputable and can help you earn a solid income if you write a column on a regular basis (daily, weekly, or monthly, usually). However, there are also a number of article syndicates that are far more of a hassle than they're worth.

I've participated in three of these syndicate services, and regretted it each time. For one, I wrote a weekly column for a few months. The idea was that the syndicate would put it on their site and try to sell it to as many outlets as possible, and I would get a percentage of the fee. I believe that I earned a total of $10 from that company; two of my columns were picked up on a one-time basis at deeply discounted rates.

The second time, I spent two solid days reformatting my work to the syndicate's specifications to prepare it for database submission and search engine optimization. I signed contracts, spent a few hours setting up my account and learning how to submit my work, rewrote some of my older articles to fit their word counts . . . and I received precisely nothing for my efforts. The syndicate never really got off the ground. They realized too late how competitive the business is and how easy it is for web site owners to get free reprint articles from databases rather than buying them.

The third time was less of a hassle to set up, but still didn't earn me anything. Since that time, I've spoken with several writers who've signed up with syndicates, and none have reported particularly good results. A few have reported making small sales at www.constant-content.com. You set the price, Constant Content keeps half of it, and they pay by PayPal only after you reach the minimum payment threshold (currently $50). I don't find this a particularly good deal for original articles, but if you have many reprints to market and some free time, it may be worth it for you.

Help! I've Been Plagiarized!

I recommend that all writers with a few articles under their belts do a little "ego surfing." About once a month, go to Google and type your full name in quotation marks in the search box. See what pops up.

Then, if you have time, type some of your article titles (again, in quotation marks) in the search box, too.

You may find that your articles have been reprinted without your permission—and sometimes without your byline or under someone else's name! This is copyright infringement, and you have the power to do something about it.

If you find that your work has been reproduced with your name attached, it's time to approach the publication's editor or publisher to present the problem and ask for compensation.

Yes, ask for compensation. Many writers simply write to demand that the work be removed from the offender's web site, but you can go further than this.

If you find that your work has been reproduced with your name attached, it's time to approach the publication's editor or publisher to present the problem and ask for compensation.

Here's what I might write in an initial letter:

Dear Editor:

My article, "The Little Black Dress," is currently on your web site at the following URL: www.notarealurl.com. Please note that I have not given permission for my work to be reproduced on this web site. This is an infringement of my copyright.

Please cease and desist from infringing my copyright by removing this article immediately.

My reprint fee is $100; I will expect payment within thrity days for the use of my article. This represents my lost profit from your unauthorized use of my work.

Please understand that you may be liable for my attorney's fees and statutory damages if I seek legal action, which I will do if the article is not removed within five days and if my payment has not been received within thirty days. Thank you for your attention.

It's too easy for an offender to claim that an email didn't get through, so always send legal notices by postal mail or overnight delivery with some form of delivery confirmation, if possible.

If this letter doesn't work, your next step depends on your true goals: If you're mostly concerned with getting the material removed, you can accomplish your object quickly without going to court, using the provisions of the Digital Millennium Copyright Act (the DMCA). Under the DMCA, the owner of a work can notify the Internet service provider (ISP) of the web site of the copyright infringement. Once the ISP has been notified, the ISP is required to remove the material. In return, the ISP is granted complete immunity from liability for copyright infringement (for storing infringing material on a network that is controlled or operated by the ISP). However, to rely on this protection, the ISP must designate an agent to receive notification under the law. Not surprisingly, almost all ISPs have done so. The Register of Copyrights is required to maintain a directory of these agents available for inspection.

Step One: Finding the ISP's Designated Agent

First, you'll need to find out who hosts the offender's web site.

Try any of these sites to get the web site's registration information:

- www.internic.net/whois.html
- www.betterwhois.com
- www.allwhois.com

Let's use AbsoluteWrite.com as an example. On www.betterwhois.com, I see this:

Registrar: NETWORK SOLUTIONS, LLC.

Whois Server: whois.networksolutions.com

Referral URL: http://www.networksolutions.com

Name Server: NS1.HOSTEXCELLENCE.COM

Name Server: NS2.HOSTEXCELLENCE.COM

To translate, I registered the domain name AbsoluteWrite.com with Network Solutions, but that's not where it's hosted. The host is what's listed after the words "Name Server." In this case, both servers listed have the same root: hostexcellence.com. In many cases, that's the way to decode the host's url: just look for the extension (.com, .net, .org, etc.) and whatever precedes it, ignoring everything up to the first period.

So, knowing this, I'd go to the ISP's web site to see if they have listed a designated agent for DMCA notices, or I'd simply go to the Designated Agent directory on the Copyright web site at www.loc.gov/copyright/onlinesp/list/index.html.

Step Two: Send a Takedown Notice

Your next step is notifying the ISP of the infringement, using what the DMCA calls a "takedown notice." For your notice to be effective, you must:

- send a written notice to the ISP's designated agent;

- identify the copyrighted work claimed to have been infringed;

- identify the infringing material with specificity (i.e., the exact URL—vague statements that a network has infringing copies of content somewhere on their system are insufficient);

- provide sufficient information so that the service provider can contact you (address, phone number, and email address);

- include a statement that you have a good-faith belief the use of the material is not authorized by you, your agent, or the law.

- sign the notice with a statement that the notice is accurate under penalty of perjury.

Although these elements are a required part of the notification, the law does not require perfection, except with respect to the requirement that notification be in writing. "Substantial compliance" with the other requirements is adequate (this means that if you leave out one part, your notification may still be effective). The following form, however, meets all these requirements:

NOTICE OF TAKEDOWN REQUEST PURSUANT TO

TITLE II OF THE DIGITAL MILLENNIUM COPYRIGHT ACT

TO: [ISP's designated agent and address]

FROM: [you]

RE: [web site displaying your work]

1. Identification of Copyright Work Claimed to have been Infringed:

2. Identification of the Infringing Material:

3. Statement of Good-Faith Belief:

The undersigned hereby certifies its good faith belief that use of the material in the manner complained of is not authorized by the copyright owner, its agent, or the law.

I hereby certify under the penalties of perjury that the foregoing is true and accurate, and that I am authorized to act on behalf of the owner of the copyrighted material being infringed.

[your signature]

Now for the good part. Upon receiving your takedown notice, the DMCA requires the ISP to "expeditiously take down or block access to the material," and most ISPs will do so.

The web site posting your content, however, is entitled to respond with a counter notice stating that the content in question is not infringing. This rarely happens unless there is a genuine issue of ownership. The counter notification, like the initial notice, must be given pursuant to the DMCA's provisions. If the ISP receives an acceptable counter notice from the web site's subscriber, the ISP must give a copy of the counter notice to you. The ISP will replace the removed or disabled material within ten to fourteen business days following receipt of the counter notice unless it first receives a notice from you that an action seeking a court order to restrain the web site's subscriber from engaging in infringing activity has been filed.

Step Three: Calling in a Lawyer

If you can't get the ISP or offender to take down the material, or if you want to push for payment, it's time to consult a lawyer. You can't file a copyright infringement lawsuit, however, unless you've first registered the copyright with the U.S. Copyright Office. Keep in mind that although your article might have been published in a magazine issue that was registered for copyright, the article was not covered by that registration unless you assigned all rights to the publication or were work for hire. The magazine's registration generally only covers the editorial content, layout, and graphics created by the magazine's work-for-hire staff.

Registering your copyright before the infringement or within three months of its first publication also entitles you to receive attorneys' fees and statutory damages (see chapter 9). Your copyright registration date is the date your material and fee arrives at the Copyright Office, regardless of how long it takes them to process the paperwork (about four months). For a considerable additional fee ($580) you can request expedited service from the Copyright Office. Although technically you can't file suit until you have your registration certificate, attorneys often will do so, knowing that the paperwork will catch up before the defendant can move for dismissal.

Most of the time, copyright infringement cases are settled out of court.

By the way, this "within three months of publication" rule is a good reason for prolific freelance writers to systematically register their copyrights at least four times a year. If you file for copyright registration for your newly published work every ninety days, you'll always be covered.

Most of the time, copyright infringement cases are settled out of court. A publishing lawyer can advise you and send demand letters on your behalf.

Publishers Selling Rights They Don't Have

On occasion, you may find out that the publication that reprinted your article is not at fault—the original publication is.

If you've signed over all rights or work-for-hire rights, you can't complain if the original publisher uses or resells the rights to your article, in any format, at any time. If your contract doesn't give them this right, however, they're obviously not entitled to make extra uses of your work without talking to you first and reaching a new agreement.

Some contracts have extra-use fees built in. Contracts for *Physical* magazine and *Writer's Digest* both include clauses spelling out how much they'll pay you if they reuse your article in another form. It's delightful when I get an unexpected check; several times a year, I find out that *Writer's Digest* has decided to reprint an article of mine in one of their books, on their web site, or in a special publication of theirs. They don't need to contact me for each re-use because I've already agreed to the extra payments specified in the original contract.

If you've signed over all rights or work-for-hire rights, you can't complain if the original publisher uses or resells the rights to your article, in any format, at any time.

However, some publications fail to disclose that they share content with other publications. Note that the single benefit of having no contract is that, without a written contract, the legal system in the United States assumes that all you've sold is non-exclusive, one-time rights. So even if you have no contract, no publication has the right to re-sell or re-use your work without your consent.

It appears writers have recently won a major victory in this regard. In August 2000, The American Society of Journalists and Authors, the Authors Guild, the National Writers Union, and twenty-one freelance writers filed a class action lawsuit against twelve commercial electronic databases, alleging that these database companies had "infringed the copyrights of thousands of freelance contributors to newspapers, magazines and other print publications," according to a statement issued by the three writers' organizations.

"The lawsuit asserts that after the freelancers' works were legally published in the print publications (with the authors' permission), those publications then licensed the works to the commercial databases for electronic exploitation, without the authors' permission, and therefore infringed the authors' copyrights in their articles."

In March 2005, the group reached a proposed settlement with publishers including *The New York Times, Time Inc.,* and *The Wall Street Journal;* and database companies including Dow Jones Interactive, Knight-Ridder, Lexis-Nexis, Proquest, and West Group. The defendants agreed to pay a minimum of $10 million and a maximum of $18 million to settle the lawsuit, and a judge approved the settlement in September 2005. You can view the judgement at www.copyrightclassaction.com.

Even if you have no contract, no publication has the right to re-sell or re-use your work without your consent.

But these aren't the only problematic publishers. Freelancer Linda Wasmer Andrews ran into a double-whammy when she wrote an article for a start-up web publisher in Canada a couple of years ago. First, she didn't get paid. She tried asking nicely, then demanding, and waiting patiently. Nothing worked. Worse, when she went back to the publisher's site, she discovered that they had licensed their entire content package—including her one little article—to a number of larger organizations.

"I wrote the publisher an email saying that (big sigh) it was a shame, but I was going to have to spend my day off the next week contacting all those organizations, explaining the situation, and demanding that they cease using my article, since the rights to it had never been purchased," she says. "I received my check by FedEx within two days."

Changing Length

Let's say you have an assignment to write a five hundred-word article about bowling balls. You turn in the first draft, and the editor comes back with revision notes longer than the article itself. She wants you to add a lot of information to the piece. But you already have a contract for five hundred words at a set fee . . . what do you do?

Discuss. Tell the editor you're happy to make the changes, but that the piece will be longer than assigned. "I just want to make sure the contract will be amended to include my fee for the additional words," you might say.

Maybe you've turned in a great article, and now the editor wants you to add a sidebar. "I'd be happy to," you could write. "Will the sidebar be paid at the same per-word rate as the article?"

Often an editor will agree to pay you extra for your extra work. If not, you can refuse the extra work and probably lose the assignment (and the pay) and offer it elsewhere, or you can suck it up and do it for the sake of keeping the job. In most cases, I'd advise the latter: Unless the free work keeps growing, stick it out. You may choose not to work with the editor again, but you won't burn any bridges.

Changing Parameters

Don't be surprised if you encounter an editor who comes back to you with rewrite notes that are completely different from what she asked for in the original assignment letter. Sometimes this is the editor's fault for not being specific enough or for not really knowing what she wanted to begin with, and sometimes you can blame what veteran freelancers often call "editing by committee," where several editors all give notes on an article, sometimes in contrast with one another, and often in contrast with the original scope of the assignment.

> Unless the free work keeps growing, stick it out. You may choose not to work with the editor again, but you won't burn any bridges.

Now, you want a reputation as someone who's easy to work with, so if it's not going to be a big task for you to rewrite, just agree and do it. If, however, it will entail a lot of time on your part spent researching, interviewing, and rewriting, you shouldn't have to pay for the editor's changed whims, especially if it happens more than once in the same assignment.

Take a close look at the assignment letter or notes from your phone conversation with the editor. What did she ask for? Can you honestly say that you delivered—and that the editor is not complaining about quality, but significantly changing what she's asking of you?

If so, the best course of action is to remind the editor gently of the original assignment description and explain that you met those terms. Then say that you'd be happy to rewrite, but that you request an additional fee to make the changes.

If the editor will not agree to an additional fee, it's up to you if you're willing to break ties with that editor; if so, you may stand your ground and demand the agreed-upon payment for the agreed-upon article and let it stand at that; then the editor can make the changes or hire a different writer to make the changes. It's likely that the editor will offer just a kill fee (a percentage of what you're supposed to be paid), but hold out: Remind the editor that you completed the article as it was assigned to you and deserve payment in full.

You shouldn't have to pay for the editor's changed whims, especially if it happens more than once in the same assignment.

Consider, though, that doing this will likely sever your ties with the editor and possibly the whole magazine—and editors move from one magazine to another, carrying their tales with them. Don't let your temper stand in the way of your future earnings.

I don't mind being flexible for editors. Generally, I put up with any editorial requests they have of me, thank them for the check, and then decide whether or not to bother writing for a mind-changing editor again. For me, it usually feels better to simply complete my assignment and leave the editor with a good impression of me, even if I never plan to query that editor again. This way, I don't have to worry that the editor will talk to others about the "difficult" writer who refused to do rewrites.

There is a difference, however, between being flexible and being spineless. Only you can decide if you feel you're crossing the line and need to take a stand.

Getting "Killed"

Articles get "killed" (meaning that editors have decided not to publish them after the assignment has been made) for many reasons, but if you play your cards right, it can actually work to your advantage.

Some editors admit that they assign more articles than they could actually fit in the magazine. They do this in case a writer doesn't come through, or a story isn't acceptable. But even editors who have the best intentions may be forced to kill a story for reasons that have nothing to do with the writer's work. A story may become stale, a competing publication may run a similar story, another editor may have assigned something similar without the other one's knowledge, the editor-in-chief may have a change of heart, the magazine's format may change, and so on.

One of my best-paying stories was killed because of a "change in management." Apparently, a new editor came in and killed off most of the stories the old editor had commissioned. But all was not lost: I'd already been paid on acceptance, and my editor sent me a contract to verify that they would not use the piece and that its rights reverted to me. I was then able to sell the piece (as an original article) to a different national magazine, thus making more money than I would have if the original magazine had run it. Best still, I sold only first rights, so I can continue reselling that same article again and again.

Even editors who have the best intentions may be forced to kill a story for reasons that have nothing to do with the writer's work.

Leslie Limbo has a similar story with a slightly different moral. She wrote a short piece on mystery shopping for the "Navigator" section of the former *Modern Maturity* magazine (AARP) and got a check for $400—the most she'd ever made for an article. It was supposed to be in the July/August issue that year.

"Of course I had to be stupid and tell all my relatives about it," she says. "July and then August comes and no article. The family phone calls kept coming to me and my mom: 'Where is Leslie's article? We have an AARP membership and we didn't see her article in this month's issue. What happened?' This went on for several months, while I tried to explain that they had probably rescheduled it for a later issue. Finally I contacted the magazine again and asked politely when my article was coming out. They emailed me back that there had been a major editorial change and they had killed my article, but since they had already paid me the full amount for the piece just to go ahead and spend the check (which I'd already done) and I was free to resell the article somewhere else.

"While the money was nice I would have loved to have had that clip to add to my portfolio. I did learn my lesson about boasting. Now I never tell my family and friends what I've published until it actually comes out in print!"

The other lesson you can take from this is that it's okay to check in if your article hasn't appeared in the issue it was supposed to, or if you haven't heard from the editor about what issue it will appear in. Sometimes this can even jog an editor's memory if she forgot all about scheduling your article, but even if the news is bad, it's best for you to find out as soon as possible so you can shop the work elsewhere.

When the article's "death" is not your fault, you can and should negotiate to receive full payment. You fulfilled the terms of the assignment, and should not have to settle for a lower amount of money just because an editor changed her mind, waited too long to schedule it, or any other reason that doesn't involve the acceptability of your work.

It's okay to check in if your article hasn't appeared in the issue it was supposed to, or if you haven't heard from the editor about what issue it will appear in.

Check your contract carefully to make sure that if there is a kill fee built in, it is contingent on your work only; the publication should not be allowed to kill an article for reasons beyond your control, then pay you less than your complete fee (or, as some publications will attempt, not pay you at all). If you've signed a contract that allows them to pay you a reduced fee no matter why they decide to kill it, you can still try to reason with the editor, but it probably won't get you anywhere. If the contract doesn't have a kill fee built in, or the clause specifies that they can pay a reduced rate only if your work is unacceptable, you can often make the case that they owe you in full.

After Hours

Some editors love to play the "hurry up and wait" game. That is, they expect you to deliver an article with the speed of the Road Runner, but then the article will sit on their desks for the next month before it even gets read.

The frustrating thing about this is that, with any luck, you're not just sitting around waiting for this editor to get back to you. You're working on other assignments, other queries. And this procrastinating editor may well come back to you with rewrite notes—and another quick deadline—at the worst possible time.

One of my editors consistently called me long after I submitted my articles, then wanted me to turn around rewrites in 48 hours. This meant that I had to drop everything else and work on the article nonstop. I did it several times, which just taught the editor that she could keep doing it. Sure, she praised me and thanked me for always coming through, which felt nice. But eventually, I had to set limits with her: I wanted at least a week for rewrites. Only once did she break that "rule," and she apologized for it.

There is, of course, another way to get around these unfair deadlines: Don't make yourself so easily available. Don't feel pressured to respond to emails immediately, and don't pick up the phone after "business hours" or when you're on deadline. Let your answering machine screen calls for you. You should not be penalized for an editor's poor planning.

Payment Per Published Word

Typically, when you get an assignment for a magazine, an editor will assign you a word count. There's a little wiggle room; if the assignment calls for 1,500 words and you turn in 1,600, the editor probably won't complain. (In fact, most editors expect that writers will turn in articles that run a little long. This is okay with them because that gives them room to cut out information they think is unnecessary or too wordy.)

You'll get paid based on the assigned word count, most often, not on the number of words that are actually published or that you turn in. (So, no, if they ask for 1,500 words and you turn in 2,000, don't expect to get paid for that extra 500 words unless you renegotiated that with the editor.)

However! Every now and then, I come across a publication that pays based on the published word count, not on the assigned word count. This is something to watch out for because an editor could very well cut your article in half, thereby paying you half the amount you worked for.

Of course, there's the obvious conclusion in there that you're not getting paid until after publication, which is the first problem, but the bigger problem is that you may wind up getting cheated out of payment you deserved just based on an editor's whim or changed mind.

> Negotiate for payment on acceptance and for payment based on assigned word count, not based on published word count. Failing that, ask for a guaranteed minimum payment.

If she asked for a 2,000-word article about different types of phobias, then decides later that she shouldn't have devoted so much space to the topic and instead just uses the 300 words you wrote about arachnophobia, whose fault is that? But who do you think will get the short end of the stick?

Again, negotiate. Negotiate for payment on acceptance and for payment based on assigned word count, not based on published word count. Failing that, ask for a guaranteed minimum payment.

Expenses

Even if you're working for a low-paying or nonpaying market, do try to get your expenses covered, and never assume that specific expenses are covered unless they're spelled out in writing.

If you have to travel, make long-distance calls, buy books, pay for film or photo developing, or pay postage, discuss this with the editor beforehand and ask if these costs will be reimbursed. Many magazine and newspaper editors will meet reasonable expenses as long as you provide receipts.

Chapter 12

Dealing with Deadbeats

Invoicing

Late Payment Protocol

Getting Help and Warning Others

Taking Legal Action

Even experienced writers, and those who've done their research, sometimes run into bad deals, publishers who won't pay, ineffective agents, and companies that go bankrupt. So what happens if you find yourself in one of these nasty situations?

Late Payments

Waiting on payments can mean the difference between paying your rent and getting tossed out on the street. So who's to blame and what do you do when a publisher doesn't pay?

Did They Sign?

First, do you have a contract? Does it stipulate how much and when you'll be paid? Working without a contract is a lot like having reckless sex with

SAMPLE LETTER TO PERIODICAL PUBLISHER

[Editor's name]

[Publisher's name and address]

Dear _____ :

Thank you for giving me an assignment to write _____ for *Telephone Sanitizer Magazine,* a division of BigTime Publishers. I sincerely appreciate the opportunity. As discussed, I believe it important that we agree to the following terms:

1. The article will be appx. 1,500 words long and due in your office on _____ , 200_.

2. I grant BigTime Publishers exclusive Worldwide First Serial Rights (exclusive first publication of the Work in a print periodical) [or other rights]. If, however, BigTime does not publish the Work within twelve (12) months of acceptance, this right shall revert to me.

3. Within thirty (30) days of receipt of the article, you shall notify me whether you accept or reject the article for publication. If you accept, BigTime Publishers shall pay me the sum of $_____ (the "Payment"), within thirty (30) days of acceptance. If you do not find the article acceptable for publication, BigTime shall pay me a "kill fee" equal to 25 percent of the Payment within thirty (30) days of notice of such rejection. In that event, all rights shall revert to me.

4. You will give me byline credit in the article, and you may revise, edit, condense, or otherwise alter the article, but will make no substantive changes without my permission.

5. [any other terms you have negotiated]

If the above terms are agreeable, please sign this letter where indicated below and return to me. I look forward to working together.

Very truly yours,

Accepted by: _____

a stranger. I know that sometimes writers feel awkward asking about it if a contract isn't offered, but you can't afford to let awkwardness stand between you and your check.

> You must demand a contract for any kind
> of writing work you do.

Even if you think you can trust the editor, even if the publication is reputable, and even if you're a brand new writer who doesn't think she deserves anything, you must demand a contract for any kind of writing work you do—articles, books, scripts, copywriting, translating, essays . . . anything.

If the editor doesn't offer a contract, then you offer one. Write up a simple letter that explains the terms of the assignment—the topic, focus, word count, pay rate, due date, payment terms (when is their payment due?), rights sold, kill fee (if discussed), any extras you're providing (photos, sidebars), and any other agreements you've made (contributors' copies, whether a bio will be included, whether expenses will be covered). Fax, mail, or email it to the editor and ask her to sign it and send it back to you.

> And yes, as a writer, you absolutely do need to
> become a businessperson if you want to protect
> your rights and fill your bank account.

I must emphasize this: You can avoid many of the following dilemmas just by having a simple agreement in writing. Notes from a phone conversation and casual emails can help, but your position is much more powerful if you can point to a signed agreement.

So put your worries aside. You're not asking for a special favor or being distrustful. You're just being a smart businessperson. And yes, as a writer, you absolutely do need to become a businessperson if you want to protect your rights and fill your bank account.

Invoices

Next comes the very common business practice that also causes unwarranted worry among some new writers: the invoice.

When you submit your work, submit an invoice. It doesn't need to be anything fancy. You can create your own simple letterhead on just about any word-processing program, and then just write a short description of your work and the payment terms. Most U.S. publishers will also require your social security number or tax identification number; this is essential because they'll need to report your payments on their tax forms if you earn a minimal amount of money from them (currently, $600 in a calendar year).

It's the most preventable cause for late payments. Many editors need to have an invoice on your letterhead to get your payment authorized, and if you don't submit one, they may be too busy to think of it for you. So even if you've realized it a bit late, get that invoice in, and your payment may soon follow.

SAMPLE INVOICE

Your name _____

Your address _____

Phone _____

Email _____

Social Security Number_____

Date _____

"The Gym-Phobic's Exercise Guide," 1,500 words
Assigned by Louisa Kern
Submitted on [date]
Payable on acceptance: $1,500

Thank you!

The First Reminder

So let's say you did it right—you have a contract and you already submitted an invoice—but your payment date has come and gone, and your mailbox still contains nothing but bills.

It's time for a polite reminder to the editor. Just a simple email or call after about a week's grace period that says something like this: "Hi Louisa. Just wanted to check in with you—my payment for 'The Gym-Phobic's Guide to Exercise' hasn't arrived yet. Can you tell me if it's on its way? Thanks!" With any luck, the editor will talk to accounting and your check will be sent in the morning.

Sometimes, when it's an editor you like and have dealt with before, you want to send a light-hearted reminder. One freelancer reports that she sent a "my payment is overdue" email in limerick form! I've been known to send short emails that say things about how my cat is bugging me for food to one of my favorite editors, too. He tends to be a bit forgetful about putting payments through and needs reminders, but I prefer to keep things light because I know he's not going to stiff me.

Be aware that the editor may be completely in the dark about what goes on with writer payments, or of the financial situation at the publication. When I worked as the editor of one e-zine, I had no idea that the company was about to go bankrupt and that writers weren't being paid. I dutifully sent invoices to accounting, and when writers complained of late payments, I was assured that they would be "taken care of." So if contacting the editor doesn't work . . .

Send a Second Invoice

After another ten days, it's time to mail a second invoice, marked "overdue." On the outside of your envelope, write "Attn: Accounting Department," or "Attn: Accounts Payable." Note on your invoice that payment is expected within ten business days, and send it certified mail. (Keep track of all your correspondence!)

If you still don't get paid, call and ask to speak to someone in accounting, and again, politely but firmly state that you still haven't received payment. If this person tries to stall by saying you'll be paid in "the next cycle," or won't commit to a date, let him know that if you haven't received payment in one week, you will file a complaint. You don't have to be specific; many people cry wolf and threaten lawsuits, but those on the receiving end know how unlikely it is that writers will actually go through with it.

If the person says your check is in the mail, ask for the check number or a photocopy of the check to be faxed or emailed to you. Calling a bluff sometimes works.

> If you still don't get paid, call
> and ask to speak to someone in accounting,
> and again, politely but firmly state that
> you still haven't received payment.

Hold Further Articles

If you have a deadline coming up for another article for this publication, explain to the editor that you can't submit your next piece until you've been paid for the last one. And stick to that promise, even if editors assure you that checks are in the mail.

Investigate

At the same time, do some digging on the publication: Post your warning on writers' message boards and email lists. Ask if other writers have had trouble getting paid by this publisher. If so, did they eventually get paid? How? If not, what tactics have they tried and how long has payment been overdue?

Media Post (www.mediapost.com) is full of industry gossip and insider information about changes in the publishing world. You'll have to register (it's free), but then you can search their "Media-Knowledge" database to find out what's been written about the publisher lately.

Media Life Magazine (www.medialifemagazine.com) will also give you the dirt on popular magazines. When *Penthouse's* publisher declared bankruptcy, major women's magazines "took a beating," and *Biography* magazine was dramatically scaled back, Media Life splashed it on their web site for all to read.

Folio (www.foliomag.com) is the "magazine for magazine management," and it reports on magazines that are in trouble in the United States and abroad. If you were writing for U.K.-based Dennis Publishing's computer magazine division, you would have learned here that they were cutting the number of freelance writers in half.

Wooden Horse Publishing (www.woodenhorsepub.com) emails a weekly newsletter to subscribers announcing changes in the magazine world, including shutdowns, staff changes, and frequency changes.

Take It to the Top

If you discover that a magazine may be going out of business, your best shot is to go straight to the publisher—and fast. If the company declares bankruptcy, even though you may be listed as a creditor, chances are that you'll never be high enough on the list to get paid. You want to strike before the company gets bankruptcy protection.

If you discover that a magazine may be going out of business, your best shot is to go straight to the publisher—and fast.

Contact Writers' Associations

If you're a member of the National Writer's Union (www.nwu.org), you can take advantage of their free grievance assistance. Send an email to the grievance division at advice@nwu.org and a volunteer officer will review your case and possibly contact the deadbeat on your behalf. More than once, I've gotten paid after simply sending a final demand letter saying that I would be turning the matter over to the National Writer's Union's grievance department. If you're a member of other writers' associations, ask if they can do anything to intervene.

Contact Writer's Market Staff

If this publication is listed in the *Writer's Market,* alert the editors to the problem at writersmarket@fwpubs.com, and they will attempt to contact the publication to resolve the problem. (They may also omit this market from future editions to save other writers from this hassle.)

Visit in Person

If you live close to the publisher, consider dropping by . . . and refusing to leave without a check. Bring crying babies. Smile and park yourself in a seat and just continue staring at the receptionist until someone hands you a check.

If you're not close by, consider hiring someone who is close by to do this for you. Freelancer Linda Formichelli says, "I went onto an online forum I used to frequent and posted that I was seeking someone who lived near

Chicago to pick up a check for me. The company owed me $1,300, and I offered $300. I found someone right away. She emailed the publisher to let him know she was planning to stop by. When she got there, the secretary had three checks waiting for her, two of which were postdated, and one of which bounced. But I did end up getting $500, which is better than nothing!"

Consider Legal Action

It's rarely financially worth it to sue over an article; you'll wind up spending money on court fees, lawyers, and travel, and even if you win, it's unlikely that you'll ever get paid. But it's up to you if you feel the principle outweighs the financial gamble. Before running out to file your case, contact the Volunteer Lawyers for the Arts (www.vlany.org/res_dir.html). This is a network of lawyers who have agreed to answer legal questions and provide pro bono assistance to low-income artists (yes, that includes writers). If you've dug up other writers who've been stiffed, you might look into a class action lawsuit.

Even if you know you won't sue, that doesn't mean you can't have a lawyer send them a demand letter on your behalf. Some writers keep publishing lawyers on retainer for just this kind of purpose. You could also hire a collection agency, most of which don't charge you until they collect your debt (they'll take a percentage of the money).

It's rarely financially worth it to sue over an article; you'll wind up spending money on court fees, lawyers, and travel, and even if you win, it's unlikely that you'll ever get paid.

Get Creative

Freelancer Don Vaughn once called directory assistance to get an editor's home phone number after getting no responses to his invoices. At home, this editor was forthcoming about what was going on behind closed doors, cluing Don in on an important tidbit: The publisher was about to run for Congress. Well! Don headed straight for his fax machine and sent an invoice with a threat to tell the press about how this Congressional candidate was treating poor writers. "It was an extreme measure, but it worked," he says.

My all-time favorite creative measure to get paid comes from the Net Wits, a writing group I belonged to. When a member had trouble getting paid by a magazine, each member was asked to send a postcard every day for a month with four words on it: "Please pay Kim Lane."

> You can also threaten to alert the publication's advertisers of the situation . . . The last thing publishers want is for advertisers to smell a scandal.

Threaten Bad Publicity

If sweetly pestering doesn't work, use mild forms of blackmail: "I'd hate to have to post this on AbsoluteWrite.com's 'Bewares Board,'" you might write. "Seventy-five thousand writers subscribe to their newsletter, and if I don't receive payment within a week, I'll have to alert them." No magazine wants bad press.

You can also threaten to alert the publication's advertisers of the situation. The advertisers don't want to get caught up in bad press, either, and if they think the publication is in financial trouble, they'll be less likely to throw money at it. The last thing publishers want is for advertisers to smell a scandal.

Keep the Editor on Your Side

Remember that it's rarely an editor's fault when you don't get paid. Sure, every now and then an editor just forgets to submit an invoice or to clear an article for payment, but if you've already given her a reminder that you're waiting for payment, work with the assumption that she's not to blame. When the e-zine company I worked for quit paying writers, I got a series of nasty letters from writers. It made me feel awful, especially because they assumed that I was responsible. As soon as I found out what was going on, I stopped making assignments (I couldn't do it in good conscience until I knew writers were all being paid) and wrote entire issues myself under various bylines, free, just to keep the publication going in the hopes that they'd catch up and pay back the writers they'd stiffed. In the end, the company cheated me out of three months' salary and left many writers in the lurch.

> Remember that writing is your business, even if you're just getting started, and putting up with long payment delays is just bad business.

You don't want any editor to remember you as the nasty writer. Editors hop from one publication to another with surprising frequency, so even if you've already decided you'll never work for *Magazine X* again, don't burn bridges by telling off your editor. She may very well wind up at *Magazine Y* next month, and she'll remember. And beyond that, editors talk to other editors. Chandra Czape, deputy articles editor at *Ladies' Home Journal,* says that her seven best friends all work at women's magazines. Do they talk about writers? You bet. Think carefully about your correspondence and whether you'd be proud to have your editor talk about it.

Payment Up Front

Copywriters often get half their fees up front, or at minimum, require some kind of deposit. In general, this doesn't fly in the magazine world. However, it's worth a shot if you'd like to keep writing for a publication that's been late with payments in the past.

You might let the editor know that, while you'd love to continue writing for her, you can't accept the late payments, so you'll require payment up front for future work. If that doesn't work, you're back to deciding whether or not you can put up with payment delays.

Remember that writing is your business, even if you're just getting started, and putting up with long payment delays is just bad business. Too often writers feel like publications are doing them a favor by publishing, so they put up with a lot. But going from submissive to nasty isn't the answer, either. Practice being assertive and persistent without being hostile.

Getting Rid of an Ineffective Agent

Let's say you've signed with a fee-charging agent, and you've realized this is a bad idea. First, request a refund. Of course, it's not generally the modus operandi of the scammer to hand back money once it's in his grubby little hands, but some do offer refunds without much argument, just to keep the writers who've wised up from causing too much trouble. Usually, if they give writers back their money, the writers won't file complaints, hire lawyers, and crusade around the Internet warning others. Scammers much prefer to operate under the radar, and even one or two writers who refuse to back down can foil the scammers' dastardly plans.

Whether you've paid a fee or not, if you've realized you're with a useless agent (or at least one who can't help you), it's best to get out as soon as possible. Read your contract carefully. Most have a termination clause that explains what you must do; often, you just have to write a letter to the agent to say that you wish to end the contract. Sometimes you have to ride it out for a specified period of time, but make sure that if it says the contract automatically renews unless you cancel, you must cancel before the next term starts.

Usually, you're still tied to the agent for any deals already negotiated and any pending deals—meaning that even if you get a new agent, the old one still gets an ongoing commission from deals she worked on, or deals you made while under contract with her.

Don't Give Up

Working for a deadbeat publisher opened my eyes. Those who kept after them without losing their tempers often did get paid, while those who kicked and screamed or said nothing got left in the dust. Hang in there, and don't let anyone get away with breaking a promise to you.

While I was distressed at the time by the handful of writers who sent me angry letters, later, I was more distressed when I realized how many writers never got paid and never even told me. Payment is not a favor. So many writers never spoke up in any fashion, just politely got screwed over, and I had no reason to suspect that anything was amiss. Newer writers, especially, tend to think it's rude to "bother" a publisher for money. But remember that the publisher would have no publication without writers.

One publisher owed me a small amount of money—maybe $200—for almost a year. There were some points when I felt like it wasn't worth the effort to keep bothering anymore, but I decided not to be a doormat. Every few weeks, I emailed, called, or mailed another invoice. I started out polite, but once I realized the editor was lying to me and I never wanted to work for these people again, I became increasingly firm and short on chit-chat. They kept telling me stories about how my invoices didn't get through, and one day, I left an angry message saying that I didn't care whether they could find my invoice or not. They owed me $200, and if I didn't receive it within the week, I'd make sure the whole world found out about it. I got an apology and a check within days.

Newer writers, especially, tend to think it's rude to "bother" a publisher for money. But remember that the publisher would have no publication without writers.

Remember, too, that you're not just acting out of self-interest. Every time a writer lets a deadbeat get away with not paying up, this teaches the deadbeat that he can get away with it. In turn, that usually means a whole lot of other writers will get shafted, too. Standing up for yourself and demanding the payment you're owed helps all your fellow writers. It teaches deadbeats that writers are a force to be reckoned with, and may make them think twice about making false promises in the future.

If they have no money left, you may just force them out of business a bit sooner, which is still a victory, even if you don't claim your money. At least they can't keep pulling the stunt any longer.

Chapter 13

Costly Courses and Shady Seminars

Checking a Teacher's Credentials

Scrutinizing Big Promises

Warnings About Workshops

Reasonable Expectations About Conferences

"If it's in print, it must be true!"

That about sums up the whole reason unqualified "writing teachers" can still rake in big bucks. It makes me sick to see how many writers never bother to check on the credentials of those who teach others.

It bothers me even when the advice is free; if you've ever hung around a writers' message board, you've undoubtedly come across blowhards who issue advice as if it's factual insider knowledge when, in reality, it's bunk. Some of these advice-givers mean well and actually believe they know what they're talking about. Others just love feeling like authorities. Sometimes the loudest and most damaging advice comes from those who know a little and think they know it all.

I first noticed this trend on a screenwriters' board I frequented when I was very new to writing in general. Only one person on the board had ever had anything produced, and almost all of us (me included) bowed at her feet and happily lapped up any tips she cared to share with the unproduced masses.

Sometimes it was as if she were leaning in really close and saying, "Okay, now I'm going to share the big secrets that all the A-list screenwriters know. Don't tell anyone, because this is so powerful that it'll sneak you right over Hollywood's wall, and I wouldn't tell this to just anyone."

Then she'd tell us something like, "Make sure you use a bright green cover on your script so it stands out," or "Send your script by Fed-Ex to the president of the company."

Sometimes I scratched my head a bit, but I figured, "Well, she's the authority. She's the successful screenwriter."

But was she?

As it turns out, no. She had one television credit from the early 1980s. (I have no idea how she got it.) But since that time, she was just like the rest of us: unproduced and hoping. If her advice was so good, why didn't she have homes for any of her scripts in the last two decades?

I blame myself for not looking into this more closely from the beginning, but I do understand what happened: I fell into "groupthink." When I arrived at the board, she already had an obvious following of people who treated her like the greatest guru who ever lived. I subconsciously fell right into place, believing that if all these people respected her, she must be a real pro.

Then there was another board, where a member just happened to share a famous last name: Coppola. People assumed he was a relative of Francis Coppola's, and the fellow never corrected anyone. Again, just because some writers believed he was a member of this famous family, they hung on his every word and paid close attention to his critiques, no matter how off-base they might have been.

The reverse can happen, too, and in fact happened to me recently.

After I went on NBC and spoke out against PublishAmerica, some of their authors were eager to find a way to discredit me so they could ignore my warning about their publisher. One person got it in his head to look me up on Amazon and list some of my publishers on their message boards. He deliberately left out the bigger publishers and named the smaller and mid-sized houses. That led someone else to decide that since he'd never heard of these companies, they must all be vanity presses. Voila! A dozen authors congratulated him on his research and concluded that I was a vanity-published or self-published author and all of my advice about publishing could safely be ignored.

When weighing anyone's credentials to determine how seriously to listen to his or her advice, make sure you've done your own first-hand research, not relied on others to figure it out for you.

Unfortunately, all of this was done on a password-protected board where I couldn't chime in, but I figured for sure, someone among them would do a very simple search on Google and tell the rest of them the truth . . . right?

But days went on and they continued to congratulate themselves, even going so far as to write to the media to warn them about this "self-published author" parading as a publishing expert. It took a letter from my lawyer to make one of the ringleaders knock it off and begrudgingly admit the truth. But I have no idea how many people saw those postings and just assumed what the others said was true. All it took was one person to proclaim this lie, and no one else bothered to hunt down the facts.

When weighing anyone's credentials to determine how seriously to listen to his or her advice, make sure you've done your own first-hand research, not relied on others to figure it out for you. That applies whether you're deciding whether or not to follow advice you read in a writers' e-zine or whether you're considering investing in a $900 course. Speaking of courses . . .

Get Tough on Teachers

You don't get a choice when you're in high school. Whoever teaches English or creative writing is who you're going to get. You have to trust that the school hired someone who's qualified for the job. In college, you may have a little wiggle room to decide which professors you want to learn from, but probably not much. That's why, if you're planning to be a writer, you should take a close look at the faculty of any college before making your decision. Make sure there are some professors whose work excites you, or who specialize in areas you enjoy.

But once you're out in the real world, you'll still have an array of options if you want to continue your writing education.

Online courses are cropping up all over the place, and their quality varies. I've found perhaps too much skepticism from people when it comes to taking an online course. There's nothing inherently bad or sub-tier about teachers who've taken the leap to the electronic classroom. In the case of writing courses, the online media are a natural fit. Students can complete coursework on their own time, email it to the professor for critiques, interact with other students on bulletin boards or email discussion groups, and read coursework on the computer or print it out for future reference and less eyestrain.

Most of the writing sites that offer courses have prices in the $50–$300 range, depending on factors such as the length of the course (typically four to twelve weeks), the amount of feedback offered, and the materials (such as software or books) that are included. Compare that to a typical college course and you'll certainly see it's a more reasonable option.

But is it worth it?

Of course, the answer has to be "it depends." I've now taken six online courses. I was totally satisfied with four of them, reasonably satisfied with one, and let down by one.

The first one I ever took was "Writing Greeting Cards" with instructor Sandra Miller-Louden. Before taking her class, I was probably among the skeptics, too. I wasn't sure how an online course would "work" and why it would be any better than just reading a book on the topic. Sandra changed my perspective. Her course was more practical and in-depth than almost any of my college courses, and she offered ongoing feedback, up-to-date contact information for greeting card publishers, examples of verses she'd sold, exercises to help me brainstorm new ideas . . . in short, it was all anyone could ask for if hoping for a guide to greeting card writing.

The second course I took was the stinker. Luckily for the teacher, I don't even remember her name or what the course was called. What I do remember is that it was all based on someone else's book; the teacher herself had no practical knowledge on the subject, and though she was nice as pie, she had no writing or teaching skills. What should have tipped me off was the utter lack of a bio about the teacher on the course page. There was a great description of the course, making it sound like it would spark my imagination and set my creativity on fire.

Because it was inexpensive, I went ahead with it, figuring the teacher's writing credentials weren't so important—you don't have to be a multi-published author to have good ideas about writing exercises and ways to inspire someone. You do, however, need a basic command of the English language and a proven ability to show some imagination of your own. She had neither, and I never completed the course.

Some sites like mine have good vetting policies in place to ensure the teachers are qualified and the courses are worthwhile. Others don't. It's up to you to find out all you can before investing your money and time.

First, check to see what the cancellation policy is like. If you get your first week of reading materials and coursework and don't like it, can you get your money back? Is it issued as a refund or as a credit toward another class?

Closely scrutinize the teacher's credentials. If books are listed, check them on Amazon. (First, make sure they're there!) Look at the name of the publisher and the publication date. Check to see if the book is available immediately or if it's listed as a "special order" or will take more than a week to ship (if so, it's either out of print, self-published, vanity published, or published with a press that has no distributor in place—a bad sign). You can also look up the publishers on Google to make sure they're legit. Nearly all legitimate publishers have a web presence. If magazines are listed, check to make sure they're paying markets. Try looking up the teacher's name within quotation marks in Google to see if you can bring up any published articles, reviews, or other mentions of the person.

Anonymous or nearly anonymous testimonials ("Jean from Texas") could be legitimate, but they could also be completely fabricated. Ask for references. Ask for at least two people you can contact to verify that they were happy with the course. Even so, be aware that email references can be faked. I know of a person who supplied two email addresses of "clients" that were, in fact, free email addresses she had registered herself. Of course, the best verification is to find people who've taken the course and contact them on your own. You can try posting the question on a writers' message board (like the ones at AbsoluteWrite.com, Writers.net, or Write4Kids.com), or in an email discussion group for writers, or by tracking down people listed in the course's testimonials and emailing them individually.

Do this even if you trust the site or publication's editor. Sometimes the editor is not the same person who approves instructors, and sometimes they accept affiliate arrangements with others without reading all the coursework. I'm never offended if someone comes on our boards and asks for opinions on our courses; I respect that writers are taking the time to research.

Bestselling Author With Dozens of Books

In addition to online courses, there are also mail correspondence classes, teleclasses, seminars, audio courses . . . you name it, someone's probably teaching it. Regardless of the form a course takes, the research needs to be done similarly.

Many over-hyped courses feature statements to the effect of "I'm the best-selling author of dozens of books" or "You'll be taught by a world-renowned publishing expert" or "Our students have gone on to publish books with all the major houses!"

Read through the hype. Look for the proof. If a teacher claims to have written dozens of books, surely you can find them on Amazon, right? And a best-selling author can tell you which bestseller list his or her books have landed on *(New York Times? USA Today? Book Sense? Publishers Weekly?)* and when, and you can verify this by checking archives. All the books their students have gone on to publish—surely they can name a handful so you can do a little investigating, right?

Read through the hype. Look for the proof. If a teacher claims to have written dozens of books, surely you can find them on Amazon, right?

Promises, Promises

I'm really not a fan of the "we promise publication" guarantees. A few courses or programs come with a guarantee that looks something like this: "If you don't get a publishing contract within one year, we'll give you a full refund, no questions asked!"

Huh?

What a silly guarantee. Think about it: Would you ever believe that every total stranger who might visit your web page actually has the talent to write a publishable book? The statistics just don't work. Most publishers say they reject 98 percent or more of submissions, so how could anyone guarantee that every one of his students will beat the formidable odds?

No one can promise you that a particular course, book, or seminar will lead to a legitimate publication contract.

People who offer guarantees like this are often banking on a few human tendencies: First, the writers probably won't remember the guarantee a year from now. Even if they do, half of them will have misplaced the site address or the contact information. Others will have downloaded a virus at some point and their email receipts will have been wiped off their hard drives. Then there's another category: The ones who feel like such losers because they failed at the program when others obviously succeeded, so they're too embarrassed to ask for a refund. Then there are those who gave up on this whole writing "pipe dream" and took up marketing careers instead, those who don't feel justified in asking for a refund because they never found the time to complete the course, and those who realized they were suckered and decided to move on rather than upset themselves with the potential hassle of a refund.

All in all, it's a pretty safe bet that few people will ever ask for their money back. And the really dishonest instructors may plan to take down their sites before the year is up, anyway, thereby ensuring that no one can get a refund.

No one can promise you that a particular course, book, or seminar will lead to a legitimate publication contract. Not unless an editor from Simon & Schuster is teaching the class and she's agreed to buy every manuscript from every person who completes her course. (Oh, and that doesn't happen.)

About the only thing that should be promised is your satisfaction. If such policies are not posted openly, make sure to ask what happens if your instructor vanishes, if you have an emergency and need to postpone the course or turn in your homework late, if you're not happy with the course in the first week or two, or if the instructor doesn't deliver what's promised (e.g., timely feedback, coverage of topics on the outline, extra materials).

Several reputable sites for writers (such as AbsoluteWrite.com, FreelanceSuccess.com, and WritersDigest.com) offer classes, and are not fly-by-night operations out to take your money and run. Any organization that cares about its reputation will likely go out of its way to ensure your satisfaction.

Contact Info

If you're dealing with an organization that's strictly online or by-mail correspondence, do you have an alternate means of contact if the web site goes down, the email starts bouncing, or the letters come back "return to sender"? That is, do you have a phone number, fax number, mailing address (for a web-based company) or email address (for a postal correspondence company)?

You don't want to find out that the sole email address you had no longer works, so you have no way to contact the company after you've made your payment. If you discover this too late, you can try disputing the charge through your credit card company, putting a "stop payment" order on a check, or filing a complaint through PayPal. When in doubt, try not to pay by money order because you can't cancel it.

Workshop Warnings

Writers' workshops can be heaven for writers who crave camaraderie, in-person interaction, and even some possible one-on-one time with editors, agents, publishers, and producers. They can also be a colossal waste of time and money. Again, it pays to research up front and know what you're looking for.

First, determine your areas of interest. If you write children's picture books, it isn't going to do you much good to attend a workshop where all the presenters are magazine writers and editors and adult nonfiction authors. The first thing you should look for is compatibility between the type of writing that interests you and the types of workshops and faculty who will be there.

Now determine your motivation for attending. This is key: Although many (perhaps even most) writers attend workshops in the hopes that they'll walk out with a publication contract in hand, please understand that this is very unlikely to happen. Often, editors won't even accept manuscripts at a workshop or conference (how will they lug three hundred manuscripts home on an airplane?). If this is your expectation, you're setting yourself up for disappointment.

If you haven't even finished a manuscript yet, it might be in your best interest to look for conferences that focus more on the craft of writing than the business of writing.

That's not to say you can't meet editors, make contacts that you may be able to use later, and learn more about their needs. What often happens is that a writer will hear an editor speak about what she likes and doesn't like, or particular areas of interest, then the writer will go home and write a letter to say, "I met you at Conference X and I think I have what you're looking for."

What stage of the game are you in? If you haven't even finished a manuscript yet, it might be in your best interest to look for conferences that focus more on the craft of writing than the business of writing. Before you worry about how to sell your first novel or personal essay, you first must make sure it's in top shape! Too many writers want to skip quickly through the writing and get straight to the publishing. And believe me, I understand the temptation—I wanted my quick rewards, too. It took me a while to develop the humility to realize I still had a lot to learn before I could expect publishers, agents, and producers to invest in me.

Next, you'll want to find feedback on the workshop itself. How long has it been running? How many writers usually attend? As long as it's not in its first year, you should be able to find some kind of feedback from people who've attended before.

Occasionally, you may even encounter an all-out fake writers' conference. Elisabeth von Hullessem, also known by the names Lisa Hackney, Raswitha Elisabeth Meerscheidt-Hullessem, Melanie Mills (a fake literary agent), and Kat Baker (her fake assistant), set up two scam writers' conferences: first in South Carolina, then in Banff, Canada. Writers reportedly paid up to $1,600 to attend, and both conferences were canceled without refunds. Many of the presenters listed had no idea their names were being used to lure in writers—they'd never heard of the conference, much less agreed to attend. Von Hullessem also set up a fake autism benefit concert in Banff, claiming that celebrities such as Céline Dion, Elton John, and Barbra Streisand were going to perform.

The excuses were wild. First, Elisabeth faked her own death, sending out a note from her "assistant," Kat Baker, claiming she had died in a car accident in Germany. The Banff conference was "postponed" due to smoke from nearby forest fires, another note claimed. Police caught her twice while she was on the run, and as of this writing, she is being held on an extradition warrant in Canada, while the attorney general decides if she should be returned to Madison County to stand trial for a list of charges including assault, battery, and theft—among other things, she's charged with trying to run her mother over with a car. She was sentenced to "time served" (less than a month of incarceration while awaiting trial) for pleading guilty to charges related to the fake conference in Banff.

In the meantime, she tried to auction off a copy of her self-published book on eBay with a promise that the winning bidder would get to have lunch with the fugitive author. eBay canceled the auction. She had also run auctions for jewelry that she never sent.

I'm Never Leaving Home Again

Okay, hang on. That was an extreme example. It's not often that someone allegedly tries to run her own mother over with a car, sets up a fake literary agency, sells non-existent jewelry on eBay, then advertises two sham writing conferences and fakes her own death to get out of them.

But . . .

What happens more often is that conference organizers are a bit clueless. They mean well, but they don't do a careful job of scrutinizing potential workshop presenters, they don't have great organizational skills, they misjudge how much time or food or space they need, or they make promises they can't keep regarding who's going to be there, how much access attendees will have to publishing professionals, and so on.

Dr. Patricia Ferguson describes the first conference she attended as an organizational disaster. "We sort of wandered around from floor to floor, room to room, asking each other where we thought we might find someone connected to the conference," she writes on AbsoluteWrite.com. The hotel was in shambles, and the workshop rooms had beds and kitchen parts in them. She never did find one of the presentations she was supposed to attend.

That conference was in its first year (and perhaps its last), so there wasn't any way for Patricia to find reviews of its previous years. If you're looking for a safer bet, look for conferences that have been run at least once before and find out how they were handled. Did all the presenters show up? Did people enjoy it? Was it well-organized and in a comfortable space?

What happens more often is that conference organizers are a bit clueless.

A Real Live Editor

Some people get so excited when they see that editors, agents, or producers will be in attendance that they forget to look beyond the title. At the Wrangling With Writing conference in Arizona, for example, one of their presenters was the acquisitions supervisor from PublishAmerica. The workshop description read, "Michele will discuss what PublishAmerica looks for in its books, and how to craft writing into being more publishable."

The problem, if you read my discussion of PublishAmerica in chapter 3, is that PublishAmerica is not a mainstream publisher with . . . shall we say . . . high editorial standards. If you need further proof of this, look up *Atlanta Nights* by Travis Tea.

James Macdonald hatched the idea for this book on the Absolute Write message boards. In short, after PublishAmerica tried to discredit its detractors, many of them science fiction and fantasy writers, by calling them "plagiarists" and "parasites" on a vitriolic web page, the Science Fiction and Fantasy Writers of America struck back. They wrote the worst drivel they could possibly dream up and it was happily accepted by PublishAmerica.

The manuscript is utter nonsense. Parts of it were even run through a text randomizer, which created mind-blowing paragraphs such as:

I could only break us. I could. He paused for two weeks, how it felt to actually harm the saris sometimes had once dated the fridge.

He had his relationships simple, discreet, between the day . . . well, he was, pacing and pacing and driving Bubbles looked up. The smile broadened and quite dead husband Henry Archer, biggest nuisance when you get any clothes on. So how about One more noted his ears although he was rumored to watch the pool to get married by Elvis.

Characters changed sexes, died in one chapter and reappeared without fanfare in the next chapter, scenes were repeated, chapters were missing . . . it took real work to create a manuscript this bad. But PublishAmerica offered the writers a contract, vowing to give the book "the chance it deserves."

That said, would you want to pay to attend a workshop that will teach you how to write a "publishable" book for PublishAmerica?

Likewise, would you be happy if you made a five-hour drive to pitch an agent whose only credits are sales to vanity presses and who charges a $350 "marketing fee"?

Do your homework. Look up the presenters on Google. Find out what their real credits are, not just what puffery they've included in their bios.

It happens. Those who run conferences are not always experienced writers, and even when they are, they may have limited backgrounds and a lack of research skills. Sometimes even the conference organizers aren't aware that their presenters are less-than-stellar representatives of their profession. I've spoken with at least one organizer who was chagrined to learn that an agent she hired to speak was a fee-charger.

Do your homework. Look up the presenters on Google. Find out what their real credits are, not just what puffery they've included in their bios. An author claiming twelve published books may have self-published or vanity-published all of them, and they may be pure garbage. An agent is nothing without verifiable sales to legitimate presses. A "script doctor" is probably there just to drum up paid business. Don't let yourself get sucked in by hype; always check the facts.

Chapter 14

How to Know When They're Really Using You

"I'm Not a Writer. You Should Write My Story."

Bidding for Writing Jobs

Low Rates for All Rights

When Not to Write for Anthologies

There are some writing situations that can't properly
be termed "scams," but rather, lousy deals.
Let's examine some of these.

Ghostwriting on Spec

If you tell people you're a writer, eventually, someone is going to say to you, "Oh! I have a great idea for a story. I'll let you write it, and then we can share the profits."

These people can be divided into two groups: the clueless and the shysters. The clueless ones don't understand why that's not a fair deal. I mean, they came up with the great idea, right? All you have to do is write it down.

Whatever. It takes about five seconds to come up with an idea and six months or more to write a book. Who do you think deserves the bulk of the money?

That's not even the main point, though—the main point is that most of these people don't expect to pay you anything up front. They say, and they may very well naively believe it, that they'll cut you in on the profit when it sells. Maybe they have no idea how difficult it is to sell a book, script, or article. Maybe they do have an idea that it's difficult, but they believe they're the special ones who will overcome all the odds.

Either way, writing on spec about someone else's idea for half the potential profits is generally a terrible idea that won't pay off.

I say "generally," of course, because there are exceptions.

Soon after the show *The Bachelorette* ended, I got an email from Jamie Blyth, one of the contestants, telling me he wanted to write a book about his recovery from anxiety disorder, and would I be interested in co-writing it with him? There was no agent or publisher in place yet.

He didn't have up-front money to offer, and that didn't bother me too much. It was a nonfiction book, so all he really needed help with at that point was the book proposal, and I knew from my own industry experience that I could sell this book. It was a subject that really interested me because of my own experience with panic disorder, and I genuinely liked Jamie and what he had to say.

So I jumped in and trusted that there would be a payoff for my efforts—and there was. I helped with the proposal, sent it to an agent I knew, he agreed to represent it, and sold it to McGraw-Hill. Jamie and I split the advance money. It was a great experience for me and of course I don't regret my "deal."

Now, if Jamie hadn't been on a popular television show, would I have agreed to work on this project with no up-front payment? No. I would not have been convinced that there was enough of a platform to sell the proposal, and even if it did sell, it probably would have been for a small amount of money (memoirs of non-famous people are tough to sell and rarely command decent advances).

You may have personal reasons for wanting to work on someone else's story. Maybe you've come across a person with a compelling tale, and you want to help tell it. If you know the person can't afford to pay you for your time and talent, and you want to do it anyway, of course that's a valid decision. Just know that you may never get a financial payoff from it, no matter how convincing the person sounds when he or she says, "I'm telling you, this will be a bestseller."

Don't trust anyone outside of the publishing industry to know what will or will not be a bestseller. Heck, people in the publishing industry can't even predict that with much accuracy. But they do observe trends, and they do have experience with what the public will shell out money to buy and what they won't. A personal story may well be compelling, but still not have a market. Look on your own bookshelves and see how many memoirs or biographies you own of non-famous people. You may have one or two, but chances are that you don't have more than that.

Don't trust anyone outside of the publishing industry
to know what will or will not be a bestseller.

When I was actively pursuing screenwriting, people often came to me to tell me their great ideas for movies. They wanted to rattle off their idea in less than a minute, then send me off to sit in the chair and come up with every plot twist, every characterization, every everything, and give them half the money I'd eventually make by selling it myself.

Screenwriting is an even more difficult field than novel writing. It takes all kinds of miracles for a script to get sold and produced. I was never short on ideas; I had enough of my own ideas to last a lifetime. The problem was making any money off those ideas, and I was no more likely to sell someone else's idea than my own. Therefore, I had no incentive to spend months working out someone else's kernel of a concept, putting in the legwork to sell it, then getting half the money I would have if I had sold a script of my own.

Yet ads like these (quoted verbatim, typos and all) still abound on places like Craigslist.org:

> "I need a co-writer for my biography to write a proposal to get an advance from the publisher. This is spec only so don't bother to relpy if you can't do this on spec. You should have an agent and be published. This is an incedible true story.Involving Politics, Drug lords, Celebrities and International intrigue."

> "The story is a dramatic thriller based on a reality type show. I

have the story and the characters in place. I have experience writing stories, but have never written a screenplay. If you have experience in screen writing and want to have credit with a hit . . .this may be for you."

"hey. i am looking to direct my first film, but i need someone to write the story. i have ideas for what the story will be. i am just starting, so i'm not looking for a complicated script(no crowd scenes, public places scenes). but i want the story to be good."

You ever notice how everyone who has an "idea" for a book, script, etc. believes it's going to be a hit and make lots of money? Well, bully for them. Let them go back to school, learn how to write, and handle it themselves. Then they won't even have to share those millions of dollars they're sure are going to pour in.

As for you, my advice is to tell the people with these "generous" offers that you appreciate the thought, but that you're too busy working on your own projects. Unless they want to pay you up front for your time. After all, how are you supposed to eat while you're investing all this time on this blockbuster idea?

Every now and then, you'll come across someone who understands this notion. I've been paid $5,000 to ghostwrite a proposal. This means that even if the proposal never sells, I've been compensated for my time. If it does sell, then I get a fair percentage of the advance and royalties for writing the actual book . . . which I do not start until a contract is finalized and the on-signing check has cleared.

Just Get a Sucker

One of the more disturbing recent trends is the internet marketers' advice to non-writers that they should hire cheap labor to ghostwrite e-books and reports at a flat rate, buying work-for-hire rights.

Check this out: It's an excerpt from the sales pitch for the e-book *eBook Secrets Exposed* at www.ebooksecretsexposed.com:

"You don't even have to write your own ebook to make a lot of money (I'll show you 6 ways to get someone else to write your ebook for you – for next to nothing!)."

Translation: "I'll show you how to find a total sucker!"

Now let me tell you about Frank Kern. Frank is known as an expert on "microniches" on the Internet—finding small target markets and selling them info-products. As Frank revealed in a teleseminar, the Federal Trade Commission (FTC) busted him in 2003. In August 2001, he sold a product called "Instant Internet Empire," a collection of e-books about internet marketing with reprint rights. He included reprint rights to his sales letter, and many of those who bought it spammed people with that letter. The FTC shut down his bank accounts and froze his assets, calling it a pyramid scheme with deceptive advertising claims.

He changed his thinking. He decided not to sell any more products promising foolproof ways to skyrocket sales or make money by selling products to their own internet marketing community. Instead, he created a program teaching people how to sell info-products to other niche markets.

Fine. Except that it's terrible news for writers.

What he taught the internet marketing crowd was that they should create info-products to sell to very targeted audiences (like women who are about to be maids of honors, scrapbookers, people who want to learn how to play card games, or people who want to teach music lessons). Frank started playing this game by selling an e-book called *How to Teach Your Parrot to Talk in 30 Days or Less* on a simple web page he created: www.yourparrotwilltalk.com. Frank did not write this book. He hired a ghostwriter from Elance.com, a site where writers bid against each other for jobs. In general, the rates are ridiculously low because employers tend to seek out the cheapest labor they can find.

He said that about ten people bid on the job immediately, and he hired a woman for $650. He's already made about $27,000 from that e-book. He bought work-for-hire rights, which means that the writer gets no credit and has no claim to any further payment no matter what he does with this e-book in the future—he can transform it into an audiobook, print book, break it up into articles or reports, package it with other products, and so on . . . for the rest of his life, with no payment or credit to the writer. You tell me if that sounds fair to you.

Frank went on to hire many more writers to write e-books for other niche markets. Then he started a program called "The Underachiever Mastery System" and sold it for $1,497. He promised to sell only 700 copies and sold out almost immediately with a waiting list of thousands more. In other words, people lined up to learn how to use writers and make big bucks by paying them next to nothing and exploiting their hard work for unlimited future income. No royalties. And Frank's name is on the book's web page, not the writer's.

Obviously you need to weigh the benefits for yourself. I know there are writers who are hard-up for money and would take that $650 in a heartbeat. But ask yourself this: Why not just write your own e-book, sell it yourself, and keep all the profits? Sure, you'd have to learn a bit about how to market on the Internet, but I'd much rather do that than take a tiny fee and watch someone else make tens of thousands of dollars off my hard work.

```
Why not just write your own e-book, sell it yourself,
            and keep all the profits?
```

Freelance Bidding Sites

Well, okay, we've mentioned Elance. Now let's explain how this (and similar) sites work.

You sign up. You list your qualifications. You may pay a monthly fee to be listed, or you may get a chunk of your earnings taken out as a commission to the site. Either way, you're paying some sort of fee to the bidding site.

It's like eBay in reverse. On eBay, people bid on items, and the person with the highest bid wins the item. On Elance and similar sites, someone posts a job of some sort, and a bunch of freelancers submit a few sentences about themselves and their qualifications, along with a monetary bid for the assignment. The bids are usually well below industry norms, and in general, the person who placed the job knows this will be the case and is searching for low bids. He may not take the very lowest bidder (who may be totally unqualified), but it's likely that he'll take one of the lowest bidders.

After you've finished the job, the job placer can write feedback about you, which future job placers can see to determine if you're reliable. Similar sites include TheCentralMall.com, GetaFreelancer.com, and ContractedWork.com. Many other job bidding sites have come and gone since the late 1990s.

I know a few writers who were happy with Elance when they were building up their credits. I can't name a single person I know now who still uses sites like these regularly and makes any decent income from it, but that doesn't mean these people don't exist. What I'm suggesting, though, is that these are really bottom-of-the-barrel places to find jobs. Consider these listings on various freelance bidding sites:

- Twenty-five people bidding an average of $372 to write an e-book about racism, with some people bidding as low as $100.

- A post asking for 25 articles about golf for less than $250 total (less than $10 apiece for original articles!).

- A post asking for an e-book, a report, and an e-course about cocker spaniels for $500–750 total (with several bidders competing).

- Five bidders competed to write a research-based health e-book for $400.

- An average bid of $42 working on a computer manual.

On Elance and similar sites, someone posts a job of some sort, and a bunch of freelancers submit a few sentences about themselves and their qualifications, along with a monetary bid for the assignment.

Could you ever make a decent living accepting wages like this? I don't see how. And what disturbs me equally is that I'm sure many of the writers think they're doing this to build up their credits and reputation—however, if these are ghostwriting projects, there is no name credit, and the types of jobs that generally appear on sites like these are not exactly resume-boosters to mainstream publishers. "I ghostwrote an e-book about cocker spaniels" isn't going to do much to impress legitimate print publishers.

As long as there are people willing to work for peanuts and have their rights taken away to boot, there will be plenty of opportunists ready to exploit them. The time you spend writing for these pathetic jobs is time you could have spent working on your queries, proposals, books, and manuscripts that could bring in a lot more money and more reward.

I know what it's like to be starting out and to think that any work is better than no work, and I don't hold that against anyone. But beware of getting too caught up in taking the "easy" jobs. Sure, it's easier to get jobs that pay next to nothing, but you may just find that if you hold out and keep working at it, you'll be able to stop scrounging for jobs in dumpsters and start finding more lucrative work.

As long as there are people willing
to work for peanuts and have their
rights taken away to boot, there will be
plenty of opportunists ready to exploit them.

Stories for Unsold Anthologies and Unlaunched Publications

"I'm looking for stories about divorce for a new anthology. Payment is to be decided, but there will be pay!"

That's a pretty typical call for writers found around the Web. The editor of this anthology may have even set up a nice web site for the project and given it a title.

Sometimes the editor will be honest and tell you that the anthology doesn't have a publisher yet. This usually comes with a disclaimer like, "There is major agent interest" or "We have a publisher waiting to see the book." That means nothing. If the anthology hasn't been sold yet, there's no guarantee whatsoever that it ever will be, and you could very well be wasting your time if you write up an essay or story for it, no matter how good the pitch sounds.

I know of one particular anthology project where the editor solicited submissions for two years, and never found a publisher. Granted, she could go on to self-publish it, but where will the money to contributors come from? I doubt that she'll pay them out of her pocket. She could get into a "royalty-sharing" arrangement—the problem being, of course, that self-published and vanity-published books rarely make more than about one hundred sales, and that doesn't amount to much when you're dividing up the profits between more than twenty authors.

So if you see a call for anthology submissions, don't be afraid to ask: Is there a publisher in place for this book? Who is it?

The same goes for those who have decided they're going to start a magazine or e-zine and put out mass calls for submissions. If a reputable company is not backing the magazine, it may well be a pie-in-the-sky idea from a college student who thinks, "Well, if I just get a bunch of articles and get someone to do the graphic design, I'll attract major advertisers and get all the grocery stores to put my magazine in the front racks!"

```
I wouldn't write for anyone who has not determined a
        pay rate and can't supply a contract.
```

This is especially dangerous when the editors plan to pay on publication. What if you're dealing with one of these pie-in-the-sky dreamers whose idea never gets off the ground? Then you've done work on the premise that you'll get paid once the magazine is published . . . and the magazine is never going to be published.

I wouldn't write for anyone who has not determined a pay rate and can't supply a contract. Very likely, the "pay rate" could wind up being nothing, or close to it. A few times, I've written to someone who's solicited me and said that I'd be happy to consider submitting my work once a pay rate has been decided.

When working with a new company, I will also demand to be paid on acceptance, so I don't run into the situation where a publication doesn't get off the ground and my work languishes on the editor's hard drive.

Chapter 15

Spotting False Credentials

Liars on Message Boards

Examining Exaggerated Bios

Editors Don't Endorse Advertisers

Certainly you've heard of doctors, teachers, and even pilots who somehow got away with working without licenses. You know that people will sometimes puff up their resumes to get a job. But how does that translate to the writing world and how can you get wise to it?

The Message Board Mambo

Running the Bewares Board at AbsoluteWrite.com has given me an interesting insight into the way unethical people work the Web.

Here's a pretty typical scenario for us:

A member posts a complaint about a deadbeat publisher. She'll post a report that the publisher didn't pay up. A few days or weeks later, a flurry of new members will show up, one after the other, to stand up for this publisher.

"I've worked with so-and-so for years! You must just have a personal vendetta, because I've always been paid on time."

"Yeah, this is the best publisher in the world, people. Don't believe this junk for a minute!"

And so on.

Almost without fail, these people don't realize that I, as the site's administrator, can see their IP addresses and the email addresses they use to register. An IP address is a unique number that identifies your computer connection on the Internet. Depending on your type of connection, that number may change every time you sign on, or you may have the same IP address for long periods of time. In any case, your IP address will remain the same within the same browser session.

So I look, and I find that all these new members share the same IP address. What does this mean? It's all the same person. (Or more than one person sitting at the same computer.)

Sometimes the giveaway is even easier: Take this situation, for instance. A member came on our boards asking if anyone had experience with Stone Bench Associates, a purported literary agency. A few of our members advised caution because the company's web site had markings of a new and clueless agency. Soon, a new member showed up and posted:

> "All I can say is that the people who speak ill of Stone Bench Associates must have axes to grind. I have been working with the agency on my first book (on toxicology) and I have been nothing but pleased with our relationship. Perhaps these are people who submitted queries to Stone Bench and were rejected? That will do a lot for a writer's perspective.

> "First time writers need to understand that we are the lowest of the low. We are not likely to get the bigger name literary agencies to look at our manuscripts, let alone represent us. Do you know that most agencies reject 99% of submitted material? Stone Bench is TRYING to be different—to give first time writers a chance to break into the publishing world."

This was followed by a few insults to our board members and contact info for Stone Bench. Of course my "yeah, right" detector lit up, but I was actually stunned by how poorly this new member covered her tracks. She used her real email address to sign up—the email address of the owner of Stone Bench. Once I mentioned this, she never posted again.

```
Almost never is someone so inspired by a book that he
  joins a message board just to tell random strangers
                    about it.
```

The point is, most people show up on a message board, introduce themselves, join in some innocuous conversations, and so on. When someone's first post is to defend a company that's been mentioned as possibly unscrupulous, be very, very suspicious. Particularly if it's followed by other brand-new members jumping in to defend the first identity. You can generally see a person's post count either right in the post itself or in the person's profile.

The same goes for people who show up to give a great "review" of a product or service. When someone shows up to say, "Hi everyone! I just read this great new book for writers and I just wanted to tell you about it," nine times out of ten it's the author. The rest of the time it's the author's mom, sister, or best friend. Almost never is someone so inspired by a book that he joins a message board just to tell random strangers about it.

Email Groups

The same behavior often crops up in email groups. A new member will arrive and promptly tout a particular book or service. Groups are usually good at pointing out these Pinocchios, but always remain skeptical when someone shows up on the scene and launches straight into promotion mode on "someone else's" product.

One of the dead giveaways is the "I happened to" line: "I happened to see this book at my friend's house," "I happened to find this web site," etc. One of my own Absolute Write columnists tried this. He had an anonymous blog, and although he wanted people to read it, he didn't want them to know he had written it. So he wrote, "I happened to find this site . . ." and I edited it out before it made it to the newsletter. Dishonesty never bodes well for an author, even if it's not done maliciously. There are too many people who can see through such tactics and will eat you alive for it.

Another giveaway is the ordering information. If you recommend a book to a friend, do you launch into every possible way to order the book, from little-known publishers' web sites to toll-free phone numbers? Do you know its ISBN offhand? Do you recall the price, or even the name of the publisher? I didn't think so. As soon as you see this, laugh quietly to yourself and be glad you know better: "I just happened to read this great book that my sister gave me, and right now NoName Publisher is having a special, so you can get it at 10 percent off for just $21.48! Just use the search box to find ISBN 097220265x. It'll change your life!"

Know Your Guru

There are an awful lot of writers who write books and articles, teach courses, and run e-zines for writers. Some of them have the experience to back up their advice, but many of them don't.

If you're considering buying anything (a book, course, e-book, report, etc.) about writing, be sure the author has the credentials to teach you what you want to know.

I run Absolute Classes (www.absoluteclasses.com), a branch of Absolute Write that offers online courses for writers. As such, I've evaluated many course outlines and résumés from writers who want to teach courses. I'm sometimes amazed by what people think qualifies them to teach.

For instance, a person who had published precisely two reviews wanted to teach a course on how to become a book reviewer. A person whose only credits were from vanity presses wanted to teach a course on writing romance novels. A person who had never been published anywhere wanted to teach a course on short-story writing.

The thing is, you'd expect whoever hires the teachers, buys the books, or commissions the articles to check out a writer's credentials first, right? But you can't always rely on that.

The prospective romance instructor didn't tell me who her publishers were—she just listed a long string of books and positive reviews. I had to do the research—I went on Amazon and looked up her publishers. Then I Googled the publishers to find out what kinds of presses they were. Every one was a vanity press. Not all "gatekeepers" think to do this, or care to do this, however.

There are some who run writers' e-zines who will mention their hundreds or dozens of credits, but fail to specify where those credits come from. That's important if you're listening to a person's advice about publishing. Others will list credits of publications you've never heard of. No matter how many of them are listed, if you've never heard of them, that's not a good sign. They could well be no-pay or low-pay markets that do not have high editorial standards.

Others will bend the truth in their favor. I know one writer who mentioned a credit from a major national consumer magazine in her bio; when I congratulated her on it, she laughed and admitted it was a letter to the editor she wrote that they published.

You don't want to follow the advice of a person who writes about how to write and publish short stories if you can't find any evidence that this person has ever published a short story!

Run a Google search on the person's name and pay close attention to the types of links that come up. Are all of this person's credits about writing itself? In other words, has this person written and sold anything that doesn't have to do with how-tos for other writers? You don't want to follow the advice of a person who writes about how to write and publish short stories if you can't find any evidence that this person has ever published a short story!

There are many "gurus" in the screenwriting world who've never sold a script. I have no idea why publishers hired them to write books about screenwriting if they had no true industry experience. But there you have it.

If I want to learn how to write for women's magazines, I want to learn it from Jennifer Nelson—a writer who writes regularly for magazines like *Woman's Day, MORE,* and *Shape.* If I want to learn how to write a mystery novel, I want to learn it from Lawrence Block, who's written more than fifty mysteries and won major industry awards.

It can be tricky sometimes when you recognize a writer's name; you assume the writer must be legitimate because you've heard of him or her.

But some writers are far better at promoting themselves than they are at actually writing. Some of the best-known "gurus" online have no real credits to speak of, and people forget to check on that because they assume they're well-known writers. I bought a (self-published) book by one such guru earlier in my career. It seemed she knew what she was talking about, so I assumed she was experienced, and I followed her advice to the letter and got nowhere. Years later I realized how bad her advice was, but at the time, I never thought to question her authority. She seemed famous.

There are so many well-qualified teachers out there that there's just no reason to pay for the advice of under-qualified writers.

Ads Aren't Endorsements

One difficult part of editing Absolute Write is that I know readers trust me. Of course, that's normally a great thing—I want them to trust my advice, to feel like they know me. It becomes much more worrisome for me when they extend that trust to anyone who advertises in the publication.

In the magazine world, they sometimes talk about the separation between church and state: the editorial department being the "church," and the advertising department being the "state." The idea is that they are wholly separate entities; the editors have no idea what the ad team is doing, and the stories are not supposed to be influenced by who advertises.

That's mostly been the case at Absolute Write; the ad director handles that part of the business, and I normally don't even see the ads until they've already run. Therefore, I'm not personally endorsing any third-party advertisers unless specified otherwise. We discuss advertisers that I've "blacklisted," and if my ad director feels unsure about an ad, he'll run it by me. He tries to ensure that no bad deals pass through, but it's impossible to run a full background check on everyone who wants to advertise in our weekly newsletters.

A few times, we've had arguments over ads that I found questionable. For example, a writer teaching a seminar claimed lots of credits on her site, but Amazon didn't bear out even a tenth of the credits she listed. A work-from-home database company made sweeping claims that lit up my baloney detector. Most of the time, the ads look fine to me, but I still can't make guarantees.

"I was debating whether or not to try this service," a writer will email me. "Now that I see it in your newsletter, I know it's legit! Thanks!"

My face drops. If I have no experience with the company, I write back to say that I certainly hope the service is legit, but I haven't personally used it and am not endorsing it. I care a lot about my readers and my own reputation, as do most editors, but in the end, the only person whose credibility I can vouch for is my own.

Before I gained experience as a writer, I placed too much weight on what I assumed were endorsements. If a company's ad appeared in *Writer's Digest*, or a listing appeared in a well-known writers' directory, I didn't bother doing research on the company. (You may remember that this is how I landed with my first bum agent!) Despite the best intentions of ad departments or editors, they are not detectives and don't usually have the time and resources to perform thorough investigations on every advertiser. If you're considering paying for a service, you must look into it carefully no matter where the ad appeared.

Chapter 16

Protecting Yourself From Threats and Lawsuits

Understanding Libel and Slander

Comments in an Open Forum: Who's Responsible?

Rewording Is Still Plagiarism

Permission Sources for Copyrighted Work

Can You Record Conversations?

Dealing With Scary Lawyer Letters

If you work as a writer long enough, chances are high that someone, somewhere is going to threaten you with legal action. In this chapter, we'll go over some of the potential problems and what you can do about them.

Libel and Slander

Libel and slander both are forms of defamation; defamation is the legal term for any published false statement about a living person or organization (yes, you can defame a company!) that injures the subject's reputation. "Injury to reputation" generally is considered to be exposure to hatred, contempt, ridicule, or financial loss.

Libel is the written act of defamation, slander is the spoken act; no one can sue you for slander for what you write. Whether libel or slander, the defamation must be published—communicated to someone other than the subject of the defamation.

Defamation law is a complex subject, full of exceptions, "privileges," defenses, and the like. The following is a general overview.

Fact vs. Opinion. Most state courts recognize a distinction between statements of fact and opinion; "true" opinion cannot be proved or disproved and thus cannot be defamatory. Contrary to what many people believe, however, the mere fact that your statement is in the form of an opinion will not shield you from a defamation lawsuit. In other words, simply adding "in my opinion" to your statement is not enough, if the statement otherwise is defamatory; you must have disclosed facts to justify that opinion. WRONG: "My co-worker John Doe is a filthy cheat." This is defamatory: an unproven, pejorative ("filthy" and "cheat") statement about a private (non-public) individual. Adding "in my opinion" to the statement doesn't help. INSTEAD: "I saw John take five toner cartridges from the supply closet and put them in his car. I believe he is a cheat." This is your opinion based on disclosed facts, and (if true) is not defamatory.

If you want to write something negative about a person, company, or group, you either must have documentation to back up everything you write, or you must frame it clearly as your opinion that is based on facts.

Humor and Parody. As with true opinion, certain other statements are considered nonfactual because they are understood to be meant humorously or as satire. Authors often rely on this, but beware: If reasonable persons could find truth in the material and it would damage the subject's reputation, it may be defamatory.

Name Calling. Under the law in most states, mere name-calling ("he's a jerk") is not defamatory because epithets cannot be proved true or false, and reasonable persons understand that they are not meant to be assertions of fact.

Fiction. In fiction writing, the Supreme Court interprets the First

Amendment to hold an author and publisher liable for publishing a defamatory statement only upon a showing of negligence—that is, a plaintiff in a defamatory-fiction lawsuit must show that the publisher of a defamatory statement knew or should have known that a "fictionalized" character was objectively identifiable as a real person.

Public figures. If you write about public figures (politicians, movie stars, professional athletes, celebrities, etc.) you have additional protection: Public figures must show that the defamatory statement was published with "actual malice."

Defenses. In the United States, truth generally is an absolute defense to defamation: If what you say is true, it cannot be defamatory (a minority of states, however, allow the defense only if the statement was made in good faith). Most states also have a variety of "privileges" that may protect statements made in particular contexts, such as in court or in the legislature.

Just remember this: If you want to write something negative about a person, company, or group, you either must have documentation to back up everything you write, or you must frame it clearly as your opinion that is based on facts.

What If I Didn't Write It?

This one's close to my heart because I run an internet message board. Many times through the years, someone has threatened to sue me based on what someone else wrote on my message board. This also happens to bloggers who have comment fields open on their blogs and those with guestbooks available on their web sites, or anyone else who has some kind of open forum where people are allowed to post messages on the Web or in an email discussion list.

Luckily, there's the Communications Decency Act, passed in 1996. Section 230 of this act states, "No provider or user of an interactive computer service shall be treated as the publisher or speaker of any information provided by another information content provider." In other words, the webmasters, bloggers, and Internet service providers can't be treated as if they wrote the defamatory content.

This doesn't mean they can never be sued; it just means that it would be extremely unlikely for them to lose a suit based on what a third party wrote on their web pages or discussion lists. Fighting a libel suit can be extremely expensive, even if you've done nothing wrong.

Luckily, most lawyers won't bring suits against individuals where they know the plaintiff doesn't have a case. A few times, corporations have been sued: For example, AOL was subjected to a suit from a man whose home phone number was posted on an AOL bulletin board in connection with offensive messages about the Oklahoma City bombing (*Zeran v. AOL*). He received abusive phone calls as a result of the posting and tried several times to get AOL to take down the post. Zeran lost the case; this is how AOL describes it:

> "The case concerned the question of whether AOL may be liable for allegedly being unreasonably slow to remove a series of allegedly defamatory messages posted on AOL message boards by an unidentified third party. The United States District Court for Eastern District of Virginia granted judgment in favor of AOL, holding that Section 230 of the Communications Decency Act, known as the 'Good Samaritan' provision, protects providers of interactive computer services from liability for defamatory information posted on the network by someone else. The district court determined that AOL was not the legal publisher of the material for purposes of defending defamation and negligence claims."

The verdict was upheld on appeal. AOL calls this "a pivotal victory for online service providers because it protects them from liability for actions taken by their users," and site owners like me agree. However, it does present a challenge to the victims of defamation: In many cases, it's impossible to track down the person who actually did post the message, so they have trouble finding justice.

Webmasters, bloggers, and Internet service providers can't be treated as writers of defamatory content.

Usually, the best they can do is to alert the site owner or ISP (Internet service provider) and ask that the material be removed quickly, with a retraction or explanation if necessary. Victims may also wish to contact the Computer Crimes unit of their local police force to report the issue and attempt to track down the perpetrator. An officer can subpoena the web site's records to locate the person's IP address, then contact the person's ISP to try to find out who was using that IP address at the time the message was posted. It's not always simple, but it is possible.

Plagiarism

Some of us were taught in school that if you put something into your own words, you were A-okay. That's just not true.

You just can't take someone else's work, reword it a little, and call it your own. You must get permission from the copyright owner for all material—text, quotations, photographs, artwork—unless the material falls into the category of public domain material or "fair use" as described in chapter 9. Even if you received a forwarded email humor column with no author credit, that doesn't mean there's no author, or that the author ever wished to remain anonymous. Search for a line from the email on a search engine and do your best to track down the author and get permission—or don't use it.

Boston Globe columnist Mike Barnicle was suspended after lifting ten jokes from a George Carlin book. It's possible he took them directly from the book, but it's also possible the jokes wound up in an email forward and Barnicle thought they came from an unknown writer who would never be found.

Even if you don't need permission because the material is "fair use" or in the public domain, leaning too heavily on one source is definitely not good writing. If you write an article on writer's block, and all of your tips are takeoffs from ideas you read in my book *Outwitting Writer's Block,* you've misused my work whether you give me credit or not. Proper research includes multiple sources as well as your original thoughts.

You just can't take someone else's work, reword it a
little, and call it your own.

On the other hand, there's no need to include a citation for phrases and slogans that are not subject to copyright (see chapter 9). That is, if you write, "Two wrongs don't make a right," you need not cite it. You also don't have to track the sources for commonly accepted facts and ideas, like that obesity is on the rise in America, couples today wait longer to get married than in previous generations, and dinosaurs are extinct. If you give specific statistics, you have to provide a source, but if you just state a trend, you need not.

A danger that writers can run into is that the convenience of copying and pasting makes it easy to "lift" passages and later on forget where they came from. Whenever you copy anything into your manuscript, be sure to write down the credit immediately: Who's the author, where did you read it, and do you need permission to use it? Even if the work is in the public domain, you'll want to cite where it came from.

And remember that even if something is not published, it still is subject to copyright protection.

Using quotations is another difficult issue. You may be tempted to add in a quotation from Cher to spice up your article about fashion, but unless Cher was talking to you when she said it and agreed to your publication, you must obtain permission whether it was an article, book, television program, or her album liner notes. On the other hand, very short quotations generally are acceptable as "fair use" although technically the law limits "fair use" only for criticism, comment, teaching, scholarship, or research. If this applies to you, use this format: "Cher said in the May 2005 issue of Cosmopolitan . . ." or, "As Cher revealed to Atlanta radio host, Tim McAbbott . . ."

And remember that even if something is not published, it still is subject to copyright protection. Emails and letters that you receive cannot be used without permission of the sender (see chapter 9).

Written Releases and Permissions

In theory, getting permission to use copyrighted material should be easy— just find out who owns the copyright and ask. In practice, however, it can be tough. Publishers are easier to track down than authors, and they usually can put you in touch with the author. Libraries have many directories available, such as the *Literary Market Place,* to help you find publisher's names and addresses. The U.S. Copyright Office also will research copyright ownership for a fee.

In some cases, the publisher or copyright owner will have their own form for you to complete. Otherwise, you'll need to give (1) a complete description of the material to be used, including the precise portion of the material, pages, and/or photographs; (2) a description of how the material

PERMISSION SOURCES

PRINT MATERIALS

Copyright Clearance Center (CCC)
222 Rosewood Drive
Danvers, Maryland 01923
www.copyright.com
Although mainly for academic material, the CCC provides licensing for copyrighted materials in print and electronic form.

The Authors' Registry
www.authorsregistry.org

National Writers Union
www.nwu.org

U.S. Copyright Office, Library of Congress
www.copyright.gov
Where you can research registered copyrights.

MUSIC PUBLISHING RIGHTS (to use song lyrics)

American Society of Composers, Authors, and Publishers (ASCAP)
www.ascap.com

Broadcast Music Incorporated (BMI)
www.bmi.com

The Harry Fox Agency, Inc. (HFA)
Established by the National Music Publishers' Association, Inc.
www.nmpa.org/hfa.html

SESAC
www.sesac.com

DRAMATIC WORKS

Samuel French, Inc.
45 West 25th Street
NY, NY 10010-2751
(212) 206-8990
(212) 206-1429 Fax
www.samuelfrench.com

Dramatists Play Services, Inc.
440 Park Avenue South
NY, NY 10016
(212) 683-8960
(212) 213-1539 Fax
www.dramatists.com

Music Theatre International (Major musicals)
545 Eighth Avenue
NY, NY 10018-4307
(212) 868-6668
(212) 643-8465 Fax
www.mtishows.com

will be used, and in what media; (3) a description of how the material will be marketed, distributed, or sold; and (4) a place for the owner to sign their consent and an SASE for return.

Many copyright owners use licensing agencies to handle permissions, such as the Copyright Clearance Center. Unfortunately, getting permission from an agency usually involves paying at least a nominal fee. In many cases there will be no fee, or a nominal fee charged by the owner, but in other cases the fee will be prohibitive for your projected use. If so, find other materials that will serve your purpose.

If the copyright owner doesn't respond, don't take this as permission. You'll have to follow up until you get a response.

But what if you can't find out who the copyright owner is? The simple answer is this: you can't use the material. It's no defense in an infringement claim that you couldn't locate the author. Instead, try to find some other excerpt that suits your purpose.

Invasion of Privacy

You also can run into trouble for invasion of privacy. If you're writing a memoir or personal essay and you reveal private facts about someone (such as his sexual history, income level, or private health concerns), you're opening yourself up to a potential lawsuit.

Unfortunately, unlike property or contract law, privacy law is not separate or distinct. It is "common law" (court-made, not legislative), unique to America, and varies from state to state. In general, privacy law consists of four distinct "torts" or legal wrongs: intrusion upon seclusion; appropriation of name or likeness; public disclosure of private facts; and publicity placing a person in a false light. Generally only the latter two—public disclosure of private facts, and "false light," are relevant for writers.

Public disclosure of private facts occurs when a writer discloses private and embarrassing facts about a living person that are not of "public concern." First Amendment rights protect publication of items of legitimate public concern, such as the details of a crime. Ask yourself, is the story newsworthy? If so, the public's interest in knowing about the incident outweighs the privacy factor. If, however, the matter is not one of public concern, and is one that most people would find highly offensive, there is an invasion of privacy. For example, publicizing the fact that your brother-in-law has failed to pay his mortgage for three months, although true, would be an invasion of his privacy. Other examples would be details of a person's sexual problems or physical or mental ailments. Problems often arise when writing about a real-life event: In such cases, you should obtain written releases from the "ordinary people" who are only peripherally involved with the newsworthy event.

Matters of public record are not protected by privacy law. If a writer publishes a story disclosing facts obtained from a police publication or a court opinion, the matter is of public record and no lawsuit will be successful.

As with defamation, public figures (politicians, movie stars, professional athletes, etc.) have a somewhat lessened right to privacy because of the public's legitimate interest in their affairs. For example, a magazine may publish a profile of a politician without fear of being sued for invasion of privacy. The story can even include private facts about the public figure, but care must be taken that these otherwise private facts are within the scope of the story.

"False light" privacy lawsuits occur when a writer publishes facts about a person that create a deliberately false and misleading impression. Examples include when a newspaper publishes a story about convicted felons and includes the name or photograph of an innocent person, or when, in a story about a hate group, the writer includes the name of a person not a member of that group.

Once again, there is a different standard for when the published material is in the public interest or about a public figure. Even if the published material places the public figure in a false light, the public figure must prove that the publisher acted with malice or with reckless disregard for the truth. Thus if a newspaper publishes a false allegation that a politician accepted a bribe, but never attempted to verify the allegation, it could be sued for placing the politician in a false light.

False light privacy claims often arise under the same facts as defamation cases, and therefore not all states recognize false light actions. There is a subtle difference in the way courts view the legal theories—false light cases are about damage to a person's personal feelings or dignity, whereas defamation is about damage to a person's reputation.

Therefore, if you want to write a potentially sensitive detail of someone's life, make sure you've either attained permission first or sufficiently fiction-alized the person's identity. If the former, don't rely on verbal permission. The interview release form in the appendix of this book (form 2) is suitable for getting permission from interview subjects; however, if you are writing a "life story," a much more comprehensive agreement would be necessary.

If you want to write a potentially sensitive detail of someone's life, make sure you've either attained permission first or sufficiently fictionalized the person's identity.

Right of Publicity

Most states now have laws that protect living celebrities and, in some states, recently dead celebrities like Elvis Presley, from the commercial exploitation of their names, likenesses, or personas. News stories, biographies, and fiction, however, are protected by the First Amendment. To the extent you portray a celebrity in such works without defaming him or his family—and it is absolutely clear your work is fiction, news, or biography—you need not seek the celebrities' permission. You would, however, need permission to exploit purely commercial "spin-offs" of your work, such as T-shirts or posters. (In some cases—like that of Elvis—issues of trademark and copyright are also involved.) In general, however, if you are using a celebrity as a character in anything other than a cursory or purely factual way, it's often best to write and seek permission.

If you have any doubts about the use of real names in your work, consult a publishing attorney before you spend a year of your life writing the book.

Liability Insurance

This does bring up another important issue. Print magazines typically have lawyers who can vet whatever they publish before it goes to print to ensure that nothing is likely to get them sued. Online publications and individual editors and writers, however, are much less likely to have the budget for staff lawyers.

If you publish any sort of online publication, while you probably won't be held liable for posts on a message board or comments by readers, you indeed can be held liable for the content you've actually published as part of your e-zine or newsletter. In other words, if someone else writes an article and you put it on your web site or email newsletter, you can be responsible for that content. That's why it's important to fact-check material that you plan to publish, and not to let anything slip through if it contains possibly false and damaging information about a person or group. Those who publish e-zines are expected to follow laws the same way as the publishers of *Cosmopolitan* and *Sports Illustrated.*

Media liability insurance is not yet popular among individual writers and small site owners, but its time may be coming. I do not suggest that every writer or editor needs to have a liability policy; it depends on what you publish. If, for example, you write articles about home decorating, fishing tips, and food, it's pretty unlikely that anyone's going to sue you for libel. If you're an investigative writer, or publish a controversial e-zine, you're a much more likely target.

Media liability insurance, also known as "publisher's perils" insurance, can include coverage for libel, invasion of privacy, trademark and copyright infringement, errors and omissions, and more.

There are some downsides to insurance, however. For one thing, it is prohibitively expensive for individual authors and even many small publishers; for another, some insurers can force you to accept a settlement or print a retraction to keep your coverage. For a more detailed analysis of this issue, visit www.ojr.org/ojr/law/1077150111.php. The same web site (the Online Journalism Review) offers links to companies that offer media liability insurance here: www.ojr.org/ojr/law/1077147945.php.

Blacklisting

Nearly always, anyone who threatens to blacklist you has absolutely no power to do so. It's usually a threat to keep you quiet about something: missing payments, a stolen story, an agent's lack of sales . . . something you know that could be dangerous. If you go public with the information, the editor/publisher/producer/writer says, she'll make sure you "never work in this town again."

This is what happened to a writer-friend of mine, who flew into a blind panic over an unfortunate situation. She had interviewed a professional screenwriter, and at the time, she asked him if it would be okay to use his name as a referral when she approached a particular producer. He said it would be fine.

She wasn't ready to submit her script for a few months, though, and in the interim, he forgot who she was. When the producer called him to check on her reference, he foamed at the mouth and said that he had never given her any such permission. He tracked her down and told her that he was going to blacklist her, making sure that she would pay for using his name like this.

It was so frightening for her that she went into "virtual hiding" for a while, offering to leave our writing group so we didn't get blacklisted, too, by virtue of being listed on the same web site as she was. But it was a false alarm. Just a month or two later, she got hired to write her first assigned feature script, won a bunch of contests, and came to realize that even if this guy had made some calls, no one had paid any attention to him. What did he really think? That all of Hollywood was going to enter her name into some "don't buy from this writer" database and ignore good material from her just because he said she had used his name as a reference without permission? Please. Unless you've been convicted of a felony (and probably not even then), no one's going to pay any attention.

That's not to say there have never been internal blacklists. Indeed, when a group of writers raised a legal stink over contracts at *The New York Times*, it appeared that the *Times* sent a memo to their editors to advise them not to work with those writers. But at that point, none of the writers were willing to work under the current contracts anyway.

But have no fear about the dregs of literary "society." Fee-charging agents, vanity publishers, and nonpaying editors do not have the clout to thwart you from writing for any legitimate publisher or producer. If they had any real connections, they wouldn't be where they are.

The fear of being termed a troublemaker is what prevents many writers from speaking out about scams. They've been told that editors will find out that they complained about a vanity press or scoundrel of an agent, and won't want to work with them because they're "whiners" or "dissenters." Not true. I've been causing plenty of trouble for scammers in the writing world for years—I even went on television to speak out against vanity presses—and since that time, I've written for Simon & Schuster, McGraw-Hill, Penguin Putnam, and others. Nobody batted an eye. Dee Power, one of the most vocal ex-PublishAmerica authors to speak out about that company, sold her next book to Dearborn.

> The fear of being termed a troublemaker is what
> prevents many writers from speaking out about scams.

The "real" publishing world is usually either totally unaware that this dark underbelly even exists, or they simply hold it in contempt and dismiss it. Therefore, they're not going to hold it against authors who speak out against con artists and publishing lowlifes. If they hear about it at all, they're likely to have more respect for the writers who speak out. Real publishers and agents don't appreciate the leeches who pretend to be on their level.

Tape Recording

If you do interviews by phone, it comes in handy to have a phone recorder. You may always record if your subject consents. If you don't ask permission, most state laws allow you to record a conversation to which you are a party without informing the other parties you are doing so. Federal wiretap statutes also permit one-party-consent recording of telephone conversations in most circumstances.

However, as of the publication date of this book, eleven states forbid the recording of private conversations without the consent of all parties: California, Connecticut, Delaware, Florida, Massachusetts, Maryland, Michigan, Montana, New Hampshire, Pennsylvania, and Washington. State laws change frequently, so be sure to check the status of your state's anti-wiretap law *before* recording.

To be on the safe side, when you begin taping, ask (on tape) for the interviewee to state his name and confirm that it's okay to tape the call. And save your tapes! If a source ever complains of being misquoted, it's important for you to be able to go back to the tape and prove that you didn't change the source's words. (By the way, if in a face-to-face interview your recorder or camera is in plain view, the consent of all parties is presumed.) Most states also permit the recording of speeches and conversations that take place where the parties may reasonably expect to be recorded.

What happens if you are in a state that permits one-party taping but the subject resides in a state that does not permit it? It depends on the state; some may choose to enforce their law, others will not. Generally, when state law conflicts, federal law will apply, and federal law permits surreptitious recording of conversations when one party consents, "unless such communication is intercepted for the purpose of committing any criminal or tortious act in violation of the Constitution or laws of the United States or of any State."

Best advice: If either party resides in a state that does not permit one-sided recording, don't do it. Ask permission.

What Do Scary Letters Mean?

Lawyers send scary letters. That's part of their job. Writers who are not accustomed to the corporate world can get spooked by lawyer letters pretty easily.

Understand that lawyers are paid to send these letters, and that lawyers are not judges. A lawyer may know full well that his demand would never stand up in court, or that his client has no real case, or that his client can't afford to go to court. But if the client says, "Write a letter and scare off this writer," that's what a lot of lawyers will do. They'll use words like "cease and desist" and "defamation" and "damages," and many writers will immediately yield. Depending on the situation, that might be appropriate—or it might be a form of bullying you into submitting to something you don't have to do.

Anyone can accuse you of libel, slander, copyright infringement, trademark infringement, or a number of other crimes, but even if the accusation comes on a lawyer's letterhead, that doesn't make it true. Of course, corporations are usually in a better position to hire lawyers, which they know . . . and use to their advantage. A writer who can't hire a lawyer of her own to evaluate a scary letter is easier to intimidate.

If you get such a letter, don't panic. Take a deep breath and analyze the claim objectively. Did you make a mistake? Or is the claim spurious? Either way, you'll have to decide whether you wish to handle it yourself or consult a lawyer.

This decision should always be made on the basis of what is at stake. If you are sure the claim is minor or the result of a genuine misunderstanding, then you might want to handle it yourself. Otherwise, it always is best to consult a publishing lawyer. If you can't afford one, there are dozens of legal organizations dedicated to providing free legal assistance to writers and artists: Go to www.vlany.org/res_dir.html for a listing.

Chapter 17

"They Stole My Idea!" and Other Things Not to Worry About

Scam Agents Are Big in Japan

You Don't Pay Back an Advance

Checking Royalty Statements

Using Brand Names in Your Writing

Well, here's a change of pace: a chapter of things you can stop worrying about right now.

What If the Editor Steals My Idea?

Every time you send out a query, proposal, or manuscript, you are taking a small risk. Don't let that risk paralyze you with fear.

It is true that there's always a chance that an editor will love your idea, but not your entire manuscript, and will hire someone else to write about the topic you've chosen.

"The toughest problem I faced as an acquiring editor was getting great queries from writers whose clips told me they would have as much chance of writing an acceptable story as I would have of climbing K2 without oxygen or Sherpas," one national magazine editor told me. "Do you pay a nominal 'idea fee,' just to be decent? Do you 'steal' the idea (keeping in mind that ideas for stories aren't in fact owned)? Do you put the idea out of mind—and pray a better writer queries on it? That, in fact, was always my choice."

Most editors, especially those at reputable publications, are like this editor. Some magazines are known for offering "story fees" or "idea fees," meaning that they'll pay a small amount for the idea, but hire a different writer to fulfill the assignment. But very few will just take a writer's ideas without payment or credit.

Now, you have to remember what I mentioned earlier about how unusual it is to come up with an idea that's actually unique; while you may have a hard time believing that someone else had the same idea you did, it's a lot more likely than you might suspect.

But for a publisher to actually take your writing and publish it without notifying you, paying you, or crediting you . . . that's so unlikely that I don't want you to spend even a minute worrying about it, because it can make you nuts.

Editors and publishers know that if they actually stole a writer's work (not just a general "idea," but the words a writer used), they'd be doing something illegal and would likely get sued. The cost of a lawsuit is a much greater risk than the cost of just paying the writer for the work in the first place, so even if ethical issues don't stop them from stealing, financial issues surely should. There's too much on the line; plagiarism and intellectual property theft are expensive suits to lose. In addition, no publisher wants to ruin its reputation like that.

What is more common is that once a piece is published online, others may copy it without your permission. These "others" are generally small site owners or bloggers who have no understanding of copyright and often believe that when something is online, it's in the public domain (not under anyone's copyright). For the most part, this is easy to clear up and won't infringe on your profits much, if at all.

But as far as sending your work to editors at publishing houses, magazines, newspapers, and so on, just do it. Don't overthink it. You really just have two choices: Send your work out and take the small risk, or be paranoid and never get anything published because you're too afraid someone will steal your stuff. Take whichever option sounds more appealing.

> Editors and publishers know that if they actually stole a writer's work (not just a general "idea," but the words a writer used), they'd be doing something illegal and would likely get sued.

What If the Agent Steals My Manuscript?

This fear often comes up once someone has realized they've sent work to a scam agent. The writer freaks out, demands that the agent return the manuscript, and freaks out some more when the agent doesn't comply. (Usually this just means that either the scam agent is too cheap to mail back the manuscript, or the agent didn't even keep the manuscript in the first place.)

> Here's the good news: Scam agents are so inept that they're incapable of selling your work even if they did want to steal it.

Most scam agents are not even trying to sell writers' work. They collect their fees from writers, then make little or no effort to get the work published. Often, they've never even read the work. Making a sale to a publisher takes actual effort and skill. A scam agent takes the much easier road and simply profits from hopeful writers.

"But what if the agent sold the rights to my book in Japan? I'd never know!" a writer worries. Again, if you're dealing with scam agents, they wouldn't even know how to sell a book in America, let alone in Japan. Selling foreign rights usually requires that a book be printed in North America first; then overseas publishers watch the sales and take an interest. Japan has enough unpublished manuscripts of its own without having agents from the United States come peddle unsold first-time writers' work in foreign languages. Japan is no more interested in publishing the slush pile than America is—in fact, they're less likely to do so because the work would have to be translated into Japanese.

This would also entail taking a financial risk on the scammer's part. Do you think a scammer who's already on Easy Street just collecting writer fees is going to spend money to copy manuscripts and Air Mail them to overseas editors who likely won't bite? That would be an actual business risk, and the scammers don't need to take them. They can just sit back, let writer payments pour in, and do no work at all.

And again, even scam agents know that this could mean huge lawsuits if the publisher or author ever found out, and they're generally not trying to run afoul of the law to this extent.

If you're dealing with a legitimate agent, the agent has no motivation to "steal" your work. The agent already makes commissions by selling clients' work, and would not risk his or her reputation on such a stunt.

It's just such an unlikely scenario that it's not something to spend time thinking about.

What Happens to My Books If I Die?

Copyrights are private property, and if you own the copyright to your work (that is, you didn't sell or give away the copyright to anyone), the copyright is still "yours" for seventy years after your death (if the work was created after 1978, which is when this law was updated).

Therefore, it's up to you what happens to the copyright after you die. If you want to be sure that your spouse, children, grandchildren, co-author, or friend can earn money from your writing after you die, all you need to do is bequeath your copyrights to whomever you want in your will or trust. While it's a simple procedure, it needs to be worded correctly, so make sure you consult a lawyer or paralegal who understands intellectual property law.

You may appoint a "literary executor" of your will in addition to the general executor. This literary executor may be your agent or manager, or anyone you trust to make the right decisions regarding the sale and distribution of your work.

What If I Don't Sell Enough to Make Back My Advance?

An advance is a sum of money that's paid against future earnings. In other words, if you get a $10,000 advance, your book will need to sell enough copies to cover $10,000 in royalties before you begin earning more money from that book.

However, even if the book doesn't sell a single copy after it's published, you do not have to repay any portion of the advance. The advance is the publisher's "gamble." The publisher takes an educated guess about how much money they expect a particular book to make, and the advance they pay is a reflection of that. Usually, that's the amount they expect you will make in royalties. Be aware that the majority of books never earn out their advances. The good news is that the advance money is still yours regardless of sales.

I Know I Sold More Than That!

This is a pretty common scenario: I get an email from someone who is steaming mad because she just got her first royalty check (typically from a vanity press), and it's much lower than she expected.

She tells me, "They said I sold five books. No way! I know I sold more than that!"

At this point, I try to walk delicately around the subject. How does the writer know she sold more than that? If the book is not stocked in bookstores or specialty stores and has not been ordered by libraries, there's a good shot that the only copies that have sold are ones the author personally sold, or were ordered by nice relatives.

I'm not saying that there are no suspect accounting practices at vanity houses. There are. Several authors tried to organize a class action lawsuit against 1st Books (now known as AuthorHouse) because of royalty payment disagreements, and I helped a writer to prove that she hasn't received money she's owed from PublishAmerica (I saved a receipt when I bought her book, and she never received a royalty payment after that date).

What I am saying, however, is that the discrepancy probably isn't large, if there is one. Authors sometimes assume that if their books are on sites like Amazon and Bn.com and their publishers' site, they must be selling. It's just not true; it's very unlikely for a reader to happen upon a vanity press web site and go looking for books to buy. It's almost as unlikely for a reader to hop onto Amazon and plug in an unknown author's name or book title, or find it by happenstance.

That said, let's go over some steps you can take to tell how your book is selling, whether it's commercially published or otherwise.

Checking Sales

If your book is listed with Ingram, you can call their automated status phone number and find out how many copies of your book are in their warehouses, on back-order, have sold this year, and have sold last year. Just call (615) 213-6803 and have your ISBN ready.

There is no easy way to tell what your Amazon rank means. It's not a simple correlation between the rank and the actual number of books sold, because it's weighted by a few factors: The rank takes into account how many books have sold lately as well as how many have sold in the book's lifetime. A book that previously had a rank in the millions can jump into the ten-thousands overnight by selling just a few copies in one day. The rank will drop again quickly, though, if sales don't continue picking up.

A book on Amazon that has never sold a single copy there starts with no rank. Not "zero"—there's just no listing whatsoever. A book that has sold one copy moves into the two-million-or-so range.

> There is no easy way to tell what your
> Amazon rank means.

It seems that recent sales affect rank more than total sales, meaning that a book that has sold one hundred copies in its lifetime on Amazon, but hasn't sold any copies in the last few months, will probably rank lower than a book that's sold only ten copies on Amazon, but all of those sales were in the last two weeks.

Amazon's ranking system has undergone several changes through the years, and may have changed again by the time you read this book, but currently, books are re-ranked every hour. To get an idea of your book's true rank, you must follow it over several weeks (or months) and average it, not pay much attention to the daily dips and surges.

While it's exciting to see your book jump thousands of slots at a time, it probably just means that it made a sale or two during the previous hour. Pay more attention to the average, not the range. My book may have a lifetime high rank of 100, but occasionally plummet to the 500,000 range; however, if it's typically around 70,000, that's its "true" rank.

> A book on Amazon that has never sold a single copy there starts with no rank at all. Not "zero"—there's just no listing whatsoever.

Having said that, I can't tell you exactly what a rank of 70,000 means. Morris Rosenthal has an article online called "What Amazon Sales Ranks Mean," and it's about the best I've seen on the topic. Like the rest, Morris's data isn't perfectly scientific and involves a lot of extrapolation and educated guessing, but he estimates that a book with an average rank of 1,000 is selling about 100 copies a week, a book with an average rank of 10,000 sells about 18 copies a week, a book with an average rank of 100,000 sells about 3 copies a week, and a book with an average rank of 1 million sells about 0.6 copies per week (or about one every other week). To see his article in its entirety, visit www.fonerbooks.com/surfing.htm.

What You Can't Do

Now, many authors' next natural reaction once they believe their royalty statements are incorrect is to try to contact booksellers to find out how many of the authors' books they've sold.

I tried this myself, albeit for another reason—I ran a successful promotion and saw my book rank rise to #4 on Amazon's charts. Naturally, I was dying to find out just how many sales that translated to. My publisher wouldn't know for a while, so I wrote to Amazon and asked if they could tell me how many of my books had sold in the past few days. They couldn't tell me, they explained. It was proprietary information.

"But," I argued, "It's my book, and I'm not trying to find out for any nefarious purposes . . . I just want to know how well I did."

No dice. They would not, under any circumstances, tell me how many books I had sold that week, that month, or that lifetime. Other writers who were having royalty disputes also contacted Amazon to ask about their sales; no matter the reason, Amazon doesn't give out that information to authors.

Neither do printers. Writers with print-on-demand books with vanity and fringe houses have tried contacting printers such as Lightning Source to ask how many of their books were printed. The printers, however, are not under any kind of contract with the writer: Their contracts are with the publishers. Therefore, only the publisher can find out how many copies were printed. The printer has no obligation to even respond to writers and could breach their contracts with the publishers if they did so.

So there are really just two ways to know for sure:

If your contract with the publisher includes an auditing clause, you can use it. Generally, this states that you or someone you hire can audit the publisher's records to make sure that royalties have been properly reported.

Alternatively, you could file a lawsuit against the publisher alleging a breach of contract, and your lawyer could then subpoena the publisher's records.

Now, what I'm telling you is that you must decide what your objective is. If your book is commercially available and you are reasonably sure you've been cheated out of a significant amount of royalties, you may have a financial reason to audit or hire a lawyer. If your book is with a vanity press and the difference is less than a hundred books, you probably won't make back enough money to justify your expenses and effort in fighting. However—and this is a big however—often writers decide that the principle of the matter is more important than the financial outcome.

The problem with scammers is that they know most writers won't put up a big fight over $20 in lost royalties, so they know they can get away with it . . . at least until writers organize and decide to fight back. If they've screwed you out of $20, they've probably screwed all their other writers, too, and all those $20 checks add up for the company.

The reason I'm putting this one in the "don't worry about this" category is not to dismiss those with legitimate complaints. It's just that I often hear this worry from people who have no real reason to suspect that their royalties are incorrect. They're just sure that they must have sold more than those five copies. Sometimes they've misread their Amazon ranks and believe that the rank is the number of books sold (so they see a rank of 800,000 and think it means they've sold 800,000 books on Amazon). Sometimes their friends have told them they're all going to buy copies (but they never actually do). Sometimes they think they were supposed to get royalties on the copies they bought themselves (check the contract: Some companies pay royalties on author-purchased copies, but many do not).

> A lack of sales of a vanity-published title
> doesn't reflect the quality of the book as much
> as it reflects the barriers the book has
> against reaching the buying public.

More often than not, it's just that the author has bumped into a sad reality check and isn't ready to believe it. As Preditors and Editors founder Dave Kuzminski says, "The royalty check and the reality check arrive in the same envelope." Most experts believe that POD books through vanity presses and fringe presses sell fewer than one hundred copies on average in their entire lifetimes. That's a hard statistic for most hopeful authors to believe, and even if they've heard it, they suspect they'll be the exceptions.

Whether a book is good or bad isn't usually the issue; vanity POD books just have a tremendous uphill battle in the commercial marketplace due to bookstore policies, pricing issues, review policies, and so on. A lack of sales of a vanity-published title doesn't reflect the quality of the book as much as it reflects the barriers the book has against reaching the buying public.

Trademarks

A few times, new writers have asked me if they're allowed to use trademarked brand names in their stories; in other words, can they write that a character drank Sprite or that she wore Red Door perfume? Indeed you can, and the companies will probably even appreciate it.

What you can't do, however, is publish or produce works related to trademarked or copyrighted characters. The best example of this is known as "fan fiction." You may love Buffy the Vampire Slayer, the Superman comics, or Star Trek, but someone owns those copyrights: You can't sell your own Star Trek novel, or your own Superman comic, or produce your own Buffy episode.

There does exist a strong "subculture" of fan fiction writers, and it's a long-standing tradition that copyright holders rarely go after those who write and publish fan fiction freely online or in underground zines. The truth is that most know fans do this out of love for a series and the material they write doesn't detract from sales of the "official" material. (In fact, it may increase interest.) However, it is a fine line to walk.

I know a writer who spent many months adapting someone else's novel into screenplay form, planning to sell this adaptation. He was shocked when another writer informed him that he didn't have the right to do that, and would have had to approach the author or the publisher to ask for an option on the film rights before he showed the script to anyone. Considering the author was a best-seller, most likely, the film option was already spoken for; even if it weren't, it's unlikely an unproduced screenwriter would be awarded that right. If you're interested in adapting someone's work or writing a related work, you'd first need to contact the author or publisher to find out who holds those rights, then you'd need to negotiate an agreement for the rights you seek.

A lesser-known novelist might be willing to let a writer option film rights for a limited time for just a few hundred dollars; best-selling authors may expect hundreds of thousands of dollars for the same deal. *Getting Permission: How to License and Clear Copyrighted Materials Online and Off* by Richard Stim (Nolo Press) delineates the process of seeking permission and even includes forums for you to use.

Once a work is in the public domain, you can write adaptations or related works without worrying about payment or rights. Do whatever you like with *Moby Dick* or any of Shakespeare's works, for example. But be absolutely certain a work is in the public domain and that the author's estate no longer retains rights to it. That can be a complicated process, so I can't provide "quick and dirty" recommendations here. I recommend that you check out the book T*he Public Domain: How to Find and Use Copyright-Free Writings, Music, Art & More* by Stephen Fishman (Nolo Press) if you're interested in a complete guide.

Links Without Permission

Every now and then, a writer will come to me and complain that a site they didn't like linked to one of their articles. But there's not much you can do about this. Any site can link to any site they like (provided they're not linking to private or paid-subscription content).

I remember once that a writer was upset because her article was linked on an "anti-feminist" site, which she believed made it look like she agreed with their principles. If you have strong reason to oppose having your link on a particular site, of course you can write to the editor or webmaster to ask that it be removed, but there's not much you can do to enforce this unless they're charging for access to your work.

In general, a few sentences of summary or the opening of your article, with a link to the full text in its original format, is allowable under the fair use doctrine. You can't demand payment for this kind of use.

People Who Refuse to Learn

Now that you know more about what to look out for regarding writing scams and bad deals, you may want to run out and warn all your writer-friends whenever you see a bad opportunity pop up. Some of them will appreciate that you're looking out for them; other people will run head-long into every possible scam they can find and there's nothing you can do to stop them.

There are some who remain purposefully blind to any potential problems, or who are so desperate to find publication that they'll remain perpetually optimistic that they will be the exception to all the other scammed clients. They cling to a fantasy because reality is too hard to deal with. They're tired of rejections, and they just want someone to sweep them away and tell them that they're the greatest writers ever and make all their dreams come true. Those are the toughest writers to get through to, and the ones most likely to remain loyal to scammers despite all logic and damning evidence. After all, the scammers gave them encouragement. The real world was never so kind. They'd rather be placated with lies, even if it costs them dearly, than to lose the fantasy that someone believed in them.

A few of my writer-friends have come to me in anguish because they couldn't steer a friend away from a vanity press or bad agent. I think our responsibility as human beings is to send out those warning flags, respond with compassion when we know we're saying something that may burst a writer's bubble, then let go. When you've done all you can and someone is still determined to make a bad choice, it no longer belongs on your conscience.

Lead by example. Show other writers that you really can make it legitimately, that you don't need special connections or famous names. You can provide hope to those writers who are on the edge, debating whether to fall for the pretty words and empty promises or keep at the hard work it takes to earn real success as a writer.

Above all, keep your own goals in mind. Only you know what will satisfy you. If commercial success is your aim, you don't get there through dirty back alleys and shortcuts with signs that say, "New writers! Over here!" You get there through perseverance, humility, research, reading, and lots of writing. You get there by earning it, not by buying it.

If others won't come up to your level, wish them well in their pursuits and hope they never come crashing to reality. You, on the other hand, side-step those minefields and build your own path to writing success.

Afterword

While you've just learned that the writers' world has plenty of nasty characters, I hope what you've read hasn't discouraged you. As long as you know how to arm yourself against sharks and scams, the writing field can be a pleasure.

The majority of the editors and agents I've worked with have been wonderful people who would never want to harm writers. Many of them have become my friends, and some of them are even active in the fight against scammers.

Just understand that as a new writer, you look like a tasty target to unscrupulous people. Scammers prey on the hopeful, and they bank on the fact that many new writers will let their dreams cloud their judgment. You don't need to be a cynic to make your way as a writer, but you need to be cautious. Value your work and know its worth. Stay suspicious of any shortcuts to success.

I wish you a long, happy writing career with immunity from those who would derail your dreams. Write on!

APPENDIX OF FORMS

Disclaimer

The following forms are provided for illustration only, and without any warranty, express or implied, as to their legal effect and completeness. You should use these forms only to familiarize yourself with the applicable legal language and as a guideline for drafting or reviewing your own documents. Additionally, the laws in different countries, states, and other jurisdictions vary. If you are in any doubt about the language of a contract you are presented, consult with a knowledgeable agent or attorney.

FORM 1 – LITERARY AGENCY AGREEMENT

FORM 2 – INTERVIEW RELEASE

FORM 3 – PERMISSIONS AGREEMENT

FORM 4 – CONTRIBUTOR'S AGREEMENT

FORM 5 – TRADE PUBLISHING AGREEMENT

FORM 6 – FILM OPTION AND LITERARY PURCHASE AGREEMENT

FORM 1

Literary Agency Agreement

Dated as of _____, 20__.

This Agency Agreement ("Agreement") is entered into by and between BigTime Agency, LLC ("Agent") and Charles Dickens ("Author") with regard to the following Work(s):

_____

1. Scope of Representation.

Author hereby appoints Agent as his exclusive literary agent in representing and negotiating the sale, lease, license, or other disposition of the rights to Author's Work or Works. As used here, Author's "Works" shall refer to:

[specific Work or Works, e.g., "A Tale of Two Cities"]

OR

[all works of authorship which Author has created or creates during the term of this Agreement, or in which Author has any title or interest, including but not limited to books, articles, playscripts, screenplays, teleplays, treatments and outlines, and any and all rights in and to such work.]

All offers for such sale, lease, licensing, or other disposition of Author's rights shall be subject to Author's prior, written approval. Author warrants that, during the term of this Agreement, the Author will employ no other Literary Agent to represent the Author for the Works.

2. Term.

Subject to the provisions for termination as hereinafter provided herein in section 10 hereof, the initial term of this Agreement shall be for one (1) year, and for successive one (1) year periods thereafter, unless either party gives the other written notice, at least sixty (60) days prior to the end of the initial term, or any extended term, that the employment is to terminate. "Term," as the word is used in this Agreement, refers to the full term of this Agreement as it may be extended as described here.

3. Commission.

In consideration of Agent's services hereunder, Author shall pay Agent, and authorizes Agent to deduct and retain as a commission for services rendered the sum of 15 percent (15%) of gross revenue whenever received, due and payable to Author in connection with any and all dispositions of rights in the Works (the "Contract" or "Contracts") resulting from efforts of Agent signed during (or within the six (6) months following) the Term. If Agent should engage a co-agent or sub-agent to assist in the disposition of film, television, or performance rights, or for rights to be exercised outside the United States and Canada, the commission shall be 20 percent (20%) of gross compensation to Author, and Agent shall be responsible for paying such sub or co-agent from Agent's commission.

4. Disbursements.

Author authorizes Agent to collect and receive on Author's behalf all gross monies and other consideration due and payable to Author in connection with the Contracts. Agent shall pay over to author all such collections, less commissions and approved expenses as provided in this Agreement, within five (5) business days of the funds clearing Agent's bank account.

5. Expenses.

Subject to Author's advance approval in writing, Author shall reimburse Agent for unusual or extraordinary expenses incurred by Agent.

6. Communication and Statements.

Agent and Author shall promptly send each other copies of (a) any legal notice under any Contract and (b) any important communication from any publisher under any Contract and any material correspondence. In January of each year, Agent shall provide Author with an annual statement showing all Author's Payments, Agent's Commissions and other itemized deductions for the previous calendar year.

7. Audit.

Author or Author's designated certified public accountant shall have the right to audit Agent's accounting records, and to make copies and extracts therefrom, with respect to expenses and disbursements incurred pursuant to carrying out the purposes of this Agreement. Author shall pay for all costs in connection with such an examination unless errors of accounting amounting to 5 percent (5%) or more of the total sum paid to Author shall be found to Author's disadvantage, in which case the cost shall be borne by Agent. At Author's option, the records of account may be performed through examination of photocopies or facsimiles of Agent's applicable records.

8. Powers.

Agent shall not execute or sign any agreement or grant of rights with respect to the Works. Author's signature shall be required for any such agreement. Notwithstanding the above, Author hereby authorizes and instructs Agent to include a customary "agency clause" incorporating the terms of this Agreement in any Contract(s) which Agent may negotiate, and the parties agree to execute such additional documents as may be necessary to give full force and effect to this Agreement.

9. Bankruptcy.

In the event Agent enters into proceedings relating to bankruptcy, whether voluntary or involuntary, Agent agrees to furnish, by certified mail, written notification of the bankruptcy (including the date on which the bankruptcy petition was filed, and the name and location of the court in which the petition was filed within five (5) days of the initiation of the proceedings relating to bankruptcy filing.

10. Termination.

After the initial term of this Agreement, either party may terminate this Agreement at any time upon thirty (30) days prior notice. Author also may terminate this Agreement immediately in the event of the filing for bankruptcy (whether voluntary or involuntary), insolvency, liquidation, death, or disability of Agent.

11. Dispute Resolution.

In the event of any dispute under this Agreement, the parties agree that common sense should prevail, and that if necessary an independent person or persons mutually agreed upon by both parties shall be called upon to make a decision which is binding upon both parties. If the parties cannot agree on an arbitrator within thirty (30) days of a written arbitration request by either party, the parties may pursue remedies in law or equity in any court of competent jurisdiction.

12. Entire Agreement.

Agent and Author agree that this Agreement contains the entire agreement between them and may not be modified or amended except in writing signed by both parties.

13. Notices

All notices shall be in writing and shall be deemed to have been given when same are sent by first-class mail or delivered to the parties at the addresses set forth below, with the exception that any notice of termination must be given by certified mail, return receipt requested or other means evidencing receipt.

[Author Signature] _____

[Author Name] _____

[Author Address] _____

[Agent Signature] _____

[Agent Name] _____

[Agent Address] _____

FORM 2

This is a general release, suitable for getting permission from interview subjects; however, if you are writing a life story or biography, a much more comprehensive agreement might be necessary.

Interview Release

By my signature below, I hereby confirm that I have had extensive conversations with _____ ("Writer") with respect to a book/article (the "Work) for general publication which he/she is writing about _____ (the "Topic"), and that Writer has explained to me that some or all of what I said during the interviews might appear in the work.

1. I acknowledge and understand that my statements may form the basis for conclusions and discussions regarding the Topic, and other issues relating to the Work. I also realize that Writer may transfer ownership of his/her work or may authorize others to publish the material and that it may appear in magazines, other articles, treatises, collections, subsequent editions, and other written forms as well as in audio or audiovisual presentations, including educational and commercial television programs and movies.

2. I acknowledge that I have voluntarily disclosed to Writer personal and intimate information and opinions about myself and other individuals, and I hereby confirm that none of the information disclosed by me during these discussions was acquired as a result of a confidential relationship, violates any restriction or covenant made by me, discloses any trade secrets, or is in any way contrary to law.

3. I understand that Writer will expend extensive and valuable time and effort in preparing a manuscript based on his/her interviews with me and has relied on my consent to use this interview material.

4. In consideration of (only those items checked apply):

[ ] copies of the published work

[ ] _____dollars, receipt of which is hereby acknowledged

[ ] the opportunity to contribute to and to support the objectives of the Work and for other valuable consideration

I hereby consent to the publication of any or all of the material disclosed by me during the interviews; my identification as a subject or source; and the use of my name and likeness and relevant biographical data in the published material and in any promotion or advertising of it.

5. I hereby release and discharge Writer and his/her assigns and licensees and all further sublicensees and transferees from any and all claims, demands, liabilities, causes of action, or damages arising out of the abovementioned use of my name and likeness and the publication of any material from the interviews.

IN WITNESS WHEREOF, I have signed this Release this _____ day of _____, 20__

[Signature]_____

[Name] _____

[Address] _____

FORM 3

Permissions Agreement

This Permissions Agreement (Agreement) is entered into by and between [name and address of party granting permission] ("Licensor"), and the [name and address of party requesting permission] ("Licensee"), to be effective as of the ____day of _____, 20__.

Licensor and Licensee hereby enter into this Agreement regarding the use of the following:

_____("Licensor's Work").

1. Rights Granted.

Licensor hereby grants to Licensee, its successors, assigns, and sublicensees, a nonexclusive license to publish and sublicense Licensor's Work in all languages, for the legal term of copyright, throughout the world [or more limited rights].

2. Use of Licensor's Work.

The Licensor's Work shall not be altered, adapted or modified in any manner without the prior written permission of Licensor, and Licensee shall attribute Licensor's Work as follows: [Insert precise form of copyright and/or trademark notice, acknowledgments, and any other notices that the Licensor requires the Licensee to include in the Licensee's Work.]

3. Compensation.

In consideration of the rights licensed in this Agreement, Licensee agrees to pay Licensor as follows: [insert terms of payment]

4. Warranties and Indemnity.

The Licensor is the sole author of Licensor's Work and sole owner of the rights granted in this Agreement, has not assigned, pledged, or otherwise encumbered them and has the right to enter this Agreement and can convey the rights granted to Licensee. Licensor shall indemnify and hold Licensee harmless from any claim, loss, or liability arising from a breach of the foregoing warranty. Licensee agrees to indemnify and defend Licensor from any claim, loss, or liability arising from Licensee's use of the Licensor's Work.

IN WITNESS WHEREOF, I have signed this Release this ____ day of _____, 20__

[Licensor Signature]_____

[Licensor Name]_____

[Licensor Address]_____

[Licensee Signature] _____

[Licensee Name]_____

[Licensee Address]_____

FORM 4

This is a writer-friendly magazine contributor's agreement.

Contributor's Agreement

Dear [writer]:

This is to confirm the agreement ("Agreement") between you and _____
_____, publisher of *Telephone Sanitizer Magazine* ("Publisher").

1. Work.

You agree to contribute an original column or article (the "Work"), identified as follows:

_____

2. Rights Granted.

You grant to Publisher the following intellectual property rights in the
Work:

A. Worldwide First Serial Rights (exclusive first publication of the Work
in a print periodical). If, however, Publisher does not publish the Work
within twelve (12) months of acceptance, this right shall revert to you.

B. For a period of three (3) years from the date of this Agreement, the
nonexclusive right to publish the Work on Publisher's World Wide Web
site and sell the Work throughout the world in digital format (digital
format includes Internet, disk, electronic download, CD, or any other
digital format known or unknown at this time). Publisher shall publish
the Work only in secure and/or password-enabled electronic formats
that protect your copyright as far as is reasonable and possible using
current encryption methods, except with the prior written agreement of
the Contributor.

C. A nonexclusive worldwide right to include the Work in anthologies,
reprint editions, adaptations, or collections of articles.

D. The nonexclusive right to use selections from the Work in the advertising and promotion of Publisher and Publisher's web site.

E. All rights to the Work not specifically granted above are reserved by you. You retain copyright to the Work.

3. Warranty.

You warrant that to the best of your knowledge the Work does not violate or infringe any copyright, trademark, contract, or proprietary rights of others, or contain anything libelous or defamatory, and you agree to indemnify and hold Publisher harmless against any final judgment resulting from the falsity of the foregoing warranties.

4. Compensation.

A. First Serial Rights. Within thirty (30) days of receipt of the Work, Publisher shall notify you whether it accepts or rejects the Work for publication. If the Work is accepted, Publisher will pay you the sum of $_____ _____ (the "Payment") in compensation for the rights granted Publisher under Section 2A above. Such payment will be made to you within thirty (30) days of acceptance. If Publisher finds the Work is not acceptable for publication, Publisher shall pay you a "kill fee" equal to 25 percent (25%) of the Payment within thirty (30) days of notice of such rejection. In such event, all rights shall revert to you.

B. Electronic and Digital Rights. If Publisher publishes the Work in digital or electronic form in a product of the Publisher for which the customer is charged a fee, Publisher shall pay you 10 percent (10%) of the Payment within thirty (30) days of such publication.

C. One-time Reprint Rights. If Publisher chooses to reprint the Work as set forth in Section 2C above, it shall pay you 25 percent (25%) of the Payment within thirty (30) days of such publication, for each such publication.

5. Editorial Changes.

Publisher may revise, edit, condense, or otherwise alter the Work, and may code the work in HTML as needed for Web presentation, but will make no substantive changes in text, title, or graphic content without your permission.

6. Miscellaneous.

A. No modification to this Agreement shall be binding unless made in writing and signed by the parties hereto.

B. This agreement shall be deemed executed under the laws of the state of _____.

C. The parties acknowledge that each party has read and understood this contract before execution.

Please keep one copy of this agreement for your files and send a signed and dated copy back to us. We thank you for your contribution.

Very truly yours,

Accepted: _____

[Contributor Name] _____

[Contributor Address] _____

[Contributor SS#] _____

FORM 5

Trade Publishing Agreement

AGREEMENT made this day of_____, 20 _____

between _____(hereafter known as "Publisher")

and _____(hereinafter referred to as "Author"),

whose mailing address is _____

concerning a work presently known as: _____

(hereinafter referred to as "the Work")

SECTION 1. Rights Granted.

1.1   Author hereby grants, transfers, and assigns to Publisher for the full term of copyright and all extensions thereof including any supplementary materials and revised editions, including but not limited to the right, by itself or with others, throughout the world, to print, publish, republish, distribute, and transmit the Work and to prepare, publish, distribute, and transmit derivative works based thereon, in English and in other languages, in all media or expression, digital and print, now known or later developed, and to license or permit others to do so. Publisher's rights shall include but not be limited to:

1.1.1 The exclusive right to publish and sell the Work in the English language in North America (the United States, its possessions and territories, Canada and Mexico), the Philippines, the British Commonwealth, and the Republics of Ireland and South Africa;

1.1.2   Foreign-language rights throughout the world;

1.1.3   Periodical or newspaper rights prior to or following book publication, including syndication rights throughout the world;

1.1.4   Non-dramatic audio recording rights throughout the world;

1.1.5   Motion picture, television, radio, stage dramatic, and musical rights throughout the world;

1.1.6   Commercial and merchandising rights throughout the world.

1.2   All rights to the Work not specifically granted to Publisher in this Agreement are reserved by Author. Author also retains the rights to all characters created in the Work.

SECTION 2. Delivery of the Work.

2.1   Author shall deliver to Publisher by _____ [date] one copy of the complete manuscript for the Work approximately _____ words in length and acceptable to Publisher in content and form and computer disk(s) or files compatible with Publisher's computerized system on which the Work is stored. Publisher shall use its best efforts to advise Author within forty-five (45) days of its receipt of the complete Work whether or not the Work is acceptable to Publisher. If the Work is not acceptable to Publisher, Publisher shall give Author a request for changes and revisions. Author shall have sixty (60) days from Author's receipt of such a request to deliver to Publisher a revised Work that is acceptable to Publisher.

2.2   In the event Publisher has requested a revised Work, Publisher shall use its best efforts to advise Author within forty-five (45) days of its receipt of the revised Work whether or not the revised Work is acceptable to Publisher. If the Work as resubmitted is deemed unacceptable, the Agreement may be terminated at the option of Publisher as set forth in paragraph 12.2 hereof.

2.3   If Author does not receive any notice from Publisher within the forty-five (45) day periods set forth in paragraphs 2.1 and 2.2 above, Author may at any time thereafter give written notice by certified mail or overnight delivery service to Publisher demanding notice of acceptance or rejection, such notice to specify that failure to respond within fifteen (15) days from the receipt of such notice shall be deemed acceptance. If Author receives no response from Publisher within fifteen (15) days from Publisher's receipt of such demand, the manuscript shall be deemed accepted by Publisher.

2.4   The Work shall be Author's next book and Author shall not offer rights to another book to another publisher nor accept an offer for another book from another publisher until a complete manuscript for the Work has been delivered to Publisher and Author has complied with the option provision of section 13. This provision shall apply to books co-authored by Author as well as to books written solely by Author.

SECTION 3. Quoted Material.

The Work shall contain no material including but not limited to art, illustrations, and quotes from other copyrighted works without a written consent of the copyright holder. Author will obtain such consents at his or her own expense and file them with Publisher at the time the Work is delivered. Any obligations associated with permissions, such as free copies, will be the obligation of Author.

SECTION 4. Editorial Changes and Proofs.

4.1   After the Work has been accepted by Publisher, no material change may be made without Author's prior written approval. Publisher, however, may copyedit the Work in accordance with its standards of punctuation, spelling, capitalization, and usage. Publisher shall send the copyedited Work to Author, who shall make any revisions and corrections and return it within two weeks of receipt.

4.2   Author shall review and return within two weeks of receipt, proofs or other production materials submitted by Publisher. For print editions, Author shall pay all charges in excess of 5 percent (5%) of the cost of composition for changes (other than corrections of printer's errors or changes made at Publisher's request) that Author makes in the Work after type has been set in conformity with the copyedited manuscript and all charges for changes requested by Author in second or subsequent printings. These costs will be charged to Author's royalty account, except Author shall upon request pay directly such charges that are in excess of 15 percent (15%) of the original cost of composition.

SECTION 5. Publication.

5.1   Publisher shall publish a print version of the Work in such style and manner as Publisher deems appropriate within eighteen (18) months from the date of Publisher's acceptance of the Work.

5.2   Publisher will consult in advance with Author concerning the format and style of all trade editions, and concerning the text, graphic material, and style of the dust jacket.

5.3   In the event of a sale of periodical rights for publication prior to book publication, book publication shall be delayed until such periodical publication is completed.

5.4   Upon print publication of the Work, Publisher shall give forty-five (45) free copies of the Work to Author, who may purchase, for personal use only, additional copies of the Work at a discount of 40 percent (40%) from the then-current United States catalog list price.

SECTION 6. Copyright.

6.1   Publisher shall include a copyright notice in all publications of the Work in conformity with the United States Copyright Act, as amended, and the Universal Copyright Convention, in the name of Author, and require its licensees to do the same. Publisher shall register the copyright on the Work at Publisher's cost in Author's name with the United States Copyright Office promptly after first publication and may record this Agreement with the United States Copyright Office.

6.2   Any textual or illustrative material prepared for the Work by Publisher at its expense may be copyrighted separately as Publisher deems appropriate.

SECTION 7. Royalties.

7.1   As an advance against all royalties and all proceeds from the disposition of subsidiary rights due Author under this Agreement, Publisher shall pay to Author the sum of _____ payable:

7.1.1 $_____ upon execution of this Agreement;

7.1.2 $_____ upon Publisher's acceptance for publication of the complete Work.

7.2   Publisher shall pay to Author royalties on sales, less returns, the following percentages of the Work's retail price:

7.2.1 On all hardcover copies sold through ordinary channels of trade in the United States, its possessions, and Canada	1 to 5,000 copies: 10% 5,001 to 10,000 copies: 12½% in excess of 10,000 copies: 15%
7.2.2 On all trade paperback copies sold through ordinary channels of trade in the United States, its possessions, and Canada	10½%
7.2.3 On all mass-market copies sold through ordinary channels of trade in the United States, its possessions, and Canada	7½%
7.2.4 From sales of a hardcover edition elsewhere	10%
7.2.5 From sales of a trade paperback or other softcover edition (including mass market paperback edition) elsewhere	7½%
7.2.6 From sales or licenses of the Work or materials from the Work in electronic form, whether directly by the Publisher or indirectly with others	10%
7.2.7 From sales of any edition, print or electronic, through direct to consumer marketing (including direct mail), but not including sales made through Publisher's own web site	5%
7.2.8 From sales of the Work at discounts of 56% or more from list price or sold in bulk for premium or promotional use or special uses outside the ordinary channels of trade	5%
7.2.9 From "on demand" publishing of the Work	10%
7.2.10 From sales of non-dramatic audio/video recording and audio/video adaptation	7½%
7.2.11 From "remainder" sales at more than the cost of manufacture	10%

7.3   No royalties shall be paid on print or digital copies sold to Author, distributed for review, advertising, publicity, or sales promotion, sold at or below the cost of manufacture, or damaged or destroyed.

7.4   Only copies sold under paragraph 7.2.1 shall be counted in determining the royalty escalations described in paragraph 7.2.1.

SECTION 8. Subsidiary Rights.

8.1   The subsidiary rights to the Work granted to Publisher, and the allocation of proceeds received by Author and Publisher from the grant of such rights to third parties, are:

	Author's Percentages:	Publisher's Percentages:
8.1.1 Periodical or newspaper publication prior to book publication	90%	10%
8.1.2 Periodical or newspaper publication following book publication, including syndication rights	50%	50%
8.1.3 Permissions, including publication of portions of the Work in anthologies	50%	50%
8.1.4 Condensations and abridgements	50%	50%
8.1.5 Book club publication	50%	
8.1.6 Publication of editions for premium or special use or for direct sale to consumers	50%	50%
8.1.7 English-language publication outside the United States and Canada (including the right to sub-license the other rights granted in this Agreement to English-language publishers)	80%	20%
8.1.8 Paperback reprint editions	50%	50%
8.1.9 Hardcover reprint editions	50%	50%
8.1.10 Audio recordings of all or parts of the Work or of adaptations of the Work	50%	50%

(continued on page 276)

(continued from page 275)

	Author's Percentages:	Publisher's Percentages:
8.1.11 The right to record and transmit and display the Work, or parts of the Work, by any means, electronic or otherwise, in the form in which the Work is published by Publisher, including the right to include the Work or quotations from the Work in information storage and retrieval systems and databases and in multimedia products	50%	50%
8.1.12 The right to produce and distribute multimedia products adapted from the Work	50%	50%
8.1.13 Non-exclusive public reading rights, including the right to authorize the reading of parts of the Work on radio or television (it being understood that Publisher may grant such rights for publicity purposes without charge and without payment to Author)	50%	50%
8.1.14 Braille, large-type, and other editions for the handicapped (Publisher may grant such rights to recognized non-profit organizations for the handicapped without charge and without payment to Author	50%	50%

8.2   If Publisher desires to exercise any of the rights described above (as opposed to licensing them to third parties), other than those rights for which royalty rates are already provided in this section 8, Author and Publisher shall negotiate in good faith the royalties payable thereon.

SECTION 9. Accounting.

9.1   Following the first publication of the Work by Publisher, an accounting of Author's earnings under the terms of this Agreement, accompanied by payment of amounts due on such accounting, shall be rendered no later than April 1 and October 1 of each year of the periods ending the preceding December 31, and June 30, respectively.

9.2   Publisher may take a credit for any returns for which royalties have been previously paid. If the balance due Author for any royalty period is less than $10, no payment shall be due until the next royalty period at the end of which the cumulative balance has reached $10. Publisher may retain a 20 percent (20%) reserve for future returns for no more than three royalty periods, provided the accounting statements indicate the amount of the reserve and how it has been applied. Any offsets against royalties or sums owed by Author to Publisher under this Agreement or any other agreement between Author or Publisher may be deducted from any payments due Author under this Agreement or any other Agreement between Author and Publisher.

9.3   Upon written request and reasonable notice to Publisher, Author's certified public accountant may, within one year of any royalty statement, examine Publisher's records of accounts as they relate to the sales and inventory of the Work for the purpose of certifying the accuracy of Publisher's accounting to Author. The audit shall be during regular business hours and Publisher shall reasonably assist in the audit. Author shall pay for all costs in connection with such an examination unless errors of accounting amounting to 5 percent (5%) or more of the total sum paid to Author shall be found to Author's disadvantage, in which case the cost shall be borne by Publisher. At Author's option, the records of account may be performed through examination of photocopies or facsimiles of Publisher's applicable records.

SECTION 10. Author's Warranties and Indemnity.

10.1   Author warrants to Publisher that:

10.1.1   Author is the sole author of the Work and sole owner of the rights granted in this Agreement; has not assigned, pledged or otherwise encumbered them; and has the right to enter this Agreement and can convey the rights granted to Publisher.

10.1.2   The Work is original except for material for which written third party permissions have been obtained; the Work has not been previously published and is not in the public domain, and does not infringe upon or violate any copyright, trademark, or trade secret; statements in the Work asserted as fact are true or based upon generally accepted research practices

10.1.3   To the best of Author's knowledge, the Work contains no material that is libelous, in violation of any right of privacy or publicity, harmful so as to subject Publisher to liability to any third party, or otherwise contrary to law.

10.2   Author shall indemnify and hold Publisher and its distributors and licensees harmless against all liability, including expenses and reasonable attorneys' fees, from any claim finally sustained against Publisher resulting from a breach by Author of the foregoing warranties. Each party will give prompt notice to the other if any claim is made and Author will cooperate with Publisher, who will direct the defense thereof. Pending any settlement, final resolution, or clear abandonment of the claim, Publisher may engage counsel of its choice and may withhold in a reasonable amount sums due Author under this or any other Agreement between the parties. The provisions of this paragraph shall survive termination of this Agreement.

SECTION 11. Termination by Author.

11.1   If Publisher does not publish the Work within the time specified in section 5 for reasons other than delays of Author in returning the copyedited manuscript or proofs, Author's failure to comply with requests made by Publisher's counsel, or delays caused by circumstances beyond Publisher's control, and if Publisher at any time thereafter receives written notice from Author demanding publication, Publisher shall within ninety (90) days of Publisher's receipt of such written demand either publish the Work or revert to Author in writing all rights to the Work granted to Publisher in this Agreement, subject to any outstanding licenses, which shall be assigned to Author, and Author shall retain any advance payments made under this Agreement prior to such reversion as liquidated damages for Publisher's failure to publish the Work.

11.2   If the Work is out of print and Publisher receives from Author a written request for a reversion of rights, Publisher shall within thirty (30) days of Publisher's receipt of such request do one of the following: (i) announce that it will reissue an edition of the Work under one of its imprints within six (6) months from the date of the request; (ii) enter a license providing for the publication in the United States of an edition of the Work within one (1) year from the date of the license; or (iii) revert in writing to Author the rights granted to Publisher in this Agreement. If Publisher does announce that it will reissue an edition of the Work but has not reissued an edition within six (6) months after Publisher's receipt of a request for reversion, the rights shall on such date automatically revert to Author.

11.3   Any reversion shall be subject to grants of rights made to third parties prior to the date of the reversion and the right of Author and Publisher to participate in the proceeds from such grants.

11.4   The Work shall be considered "out of print" if it is not available in the United States through regular retail channels in an English language book form edition (not print-on-demand, digital, or other mechanical means of reproduction) and listed in the publisher's catalog.

SECTION 12. Termination by Publisher.

12.1   If Author does not deliver the complete manuscript and/or computer disk(s) or files for the Work within three (3) months of the delivery date in paragraph 2.1 or, if requested to do so, does not deliver a revised, complete manuscript and/or computer disk(s) or files for the Work within the time specified in paragraph 2.1, Publisher shall not be required to publish the Work and shall have the right exercisable at Publisher's discretion at any time thereafter to recover from Author any advances made to Author under this Agreement. When such advances are fully repaid, this Agreement shall terminate.

12.2   If the complete manuscript and/or computer disk(s) or files as first submitted by Author are unacceptable and Author, after receiving Publisher's request for changes and revisions, in good faith makes a timely delivery of a revised, complete manuscript and/or computer disk(s) or files for the Work that satisfies all the provisions of this Agreement except the requirement of being acceptable to Publisher in content and form, Publisher shall not be required to publish the Work and Publisher shall give Author notice of its decision not to publish. In that event, Author shall be at liberty to submit the manuscript to others. Author shall make every effort to sell the Work elsewhere, and Author shall be obligated to repay all advances and other charges, previously paid hereunder, but such obligation shall be limited to repayment from the first (and all) proceeds of any contracts with others concerning the Work or any rights thereto.

SECTION 13. Option.

In further consideration of this Agreement Author grants to Publisher an option on Author's next book-length work ("the option book"), such option to be exercised as follows. Author shall submit to Publisher an outline and three sample chapters for the option hook before offering rights to the option book to any other party. Publisher shall have thirty (30) days from its receipt of the outline and sample chapters for the option book to advise Author whether it wishes to publish the option book and upon what financial terms, such thirty- (30-) day period to commence no earlier than sixty (60) days following Publisher's acceptance of the Work. If within such thirty- (30-) day period Publisher does not advise Author that it wishes to publish the option book, Author may offer the option book to other parties without further obligation to Publisher. If within such thirty- (30-) day period Publisher does advise Author that it wishes to publish the option book but within thirty (30) days of Publisher so advising Author, Author and Publisher have not agreed on financial terms for such publication, Author may offer the option book to other publishers without further obligation to Publisher. This option provision shall apply to the next book co-authored by Author as well as the next book solely authored by Author.

SECTION 14. Competing and Future Works.

14.1 During the term of this Agreement, Author has not prepared and published, and shall not prepare or publish, or participate in the preparation or publication of, any competing work that is substantially similar to the Work, or which is reasonably likely to injure the sales of the Work. Notwithstanding the above, Author may draw on and refer to material contained in the Work in preparing articles for publication and papers for delivery at professional meetings, provided that credit is given to the Work and Publisher.

14.2 Author may not copy or sell copies of Work other than those procured through Publisher. Author may purchase unlimited electronic format books for Author's resale use at conferences, signings, local booksellers, etc., at full price from Publisher, and will receive royalties on said purchase. Any other sales must be through Publisher or Publisher-approved vendor.

14.3 If Author has a web site, Author may use up to one chapter, or the prologue and one chapter, of the final, approved version of the Work as a promotional teaser on the web site. Author's web site must include a link to Publisher's web site.

SECTION 15. Revised Edition.

15.1   The term "Revised Edition" shall mean a substantial modification of the Work, including, but not limited to, rewriting, reorganizing, and adding additional material, as Publisher deems appropriate. If Publisher determines that a revision of the Work is desirable, Publisher shall request that Author prepare the Revised Edition and Author shall advise Publisher within sixty (60) days of receipt of such notice whether Author will prepare the Revised Edition. If Author elects to prepare the Revised Edition, Author shall prepare and deliver a manuscript for the Revised Edition within twelve (12) months following the date on which Publisher notified Author that it wishes to publish the Revised Edition.

15.2   If Author does not agree to prepare the Revised Edition, Publisher shall have the right to arrange with others for the preparation of the Revised Edition. In such case, Publisher shall have the right to deduct from Author's royalties any fees or royalties paid to the reviser(s) provided that Author's royalties shall not be reduced by more than 50 percent (50%) for the first such revised edition. If a second Revised Edition is prepared by other than Author, Publisher shall have the right to deduct from Author's royalties any fees or royalties paid to the reviser(s) of the second Revised Edition provided that Author's royalties shall not be reduced by more than 75 percent (75%) for the second such Revised Edition. No royalties shall be paid to Author with respect to further Revised Editions not prepared by Author. The Revised Editions may be published under the same title and may refer to Author by name, but credit may be given to the reviser(s) in the Revised Edition(s) and in advertising and promotional material with respect thereto.

15.3   Except as otherwise provided herein, the provisions of this Agreement, including royalty terms (but excluding the advance provided herein) shall apply to each successive revised edition, and royalties for Revised Editions shall be calculated cumulatively with sales of the original edition.

SECTION 16. Force Majeure.

The failure of Publisher to publish or reissue the Work shall not be a breach of this Agreement or give rise to any right of termination or reversion if such failure is caused by restrictions of governmental agencies, labor disputes, inability to obtain materials necessary for manufacture of the Work, or any other reason beyond Publisher's control; in the event of delay from such cause, the publication or reissue shall be postponed for a period of time reasonably related to such cause.

SECTION 17. General Provisions.

17.1   Author shall keep at least one copy of the manuscript for the Work and any other materials submitted to Publisher under this Agreement. Publisher shall upon Author's written request, made within one (1) year after first publication by Publisher, return to Author the copy of the manuscript used for typesetting, if a print edition was published; Publisher shall not be required to retain such manuscript for more than one (1) year. If editing of the Work is done solely on disk or electronically, Publisher shall not be required to return the edited manuscript to Author. Publisher shall not be responsible for the loss or damage to any manuscript or other materials except in the event of gross negligence.

17.2   No advertisements (other than advertisements for other publications or audio recordings of Publisher) shall be included in any edition of the Work published by Publisher or under license from Publisher without Author's written consent.

17.3   Publisher may use Author's name, likeness, and biographical data on any editions of the Work published by Publisher and in any advertising, publicity, or promotion for the Work and may extend these rights in connection with grants of subsidiary rights made by Publisher.

17.4   If Publisher is required by law to withhold and pay to any U.S. or foreign government taxing authority any portion of the amounts due Author under this Agreement, such payments shall be deducted from the amounts due Author hereunder.

17.5   If any foreign taxes, bank charges, or agents' commissions are imposed on any payments due Publisher from the exercise of any right granted in this Agreement, the appropriate allocation of proceeds between Publisher and Author from the exercise of such right shall be made on amounts received after such charges have been paid.

17.6   In the event of the bankruptcy, insolvency, or liquidation of Publisher, this Agreement shall terminate and all rights granted to Publisher shall revert to Author automatically and without the necessity of any demand or notification.

17.7   This Agreement shall be binding upon and inure to the benefit of the heirs, executors, or administrators and assigns of Author and the successors and assigns of Publisher and may not be assigned by either without the written consent of the other, with the following exceptions. Author may assign Author's right to receive payment under this Agreement upon written notice to Publisher. Publisher may upon written notice to Author assign this Agreement to any company that acquires or succeeds to all or a substantial portion of the assets of Publisher.

17.8   If under any provision of this Agreement, Publisher is required to obtain Author's approval, such approval shall not be unreasonably withheld or delayed. If Publisher fails to receive a response from Author within such time as Publisher may reasonably designate to accommodate its schedule for publication, promotion, or the exercise of rights when any approval is requested, the approval requested shall be deemed granted.

17.9   This Agreement contains the entire understanding of Author and Publisher with reference to the Work; there are no warranties other than those expressly stated in this Agreement. No waiver or modification of any provision of this Agreement shall be valid unless in writing and signed by both parties. No waiver of any breach shall be deemed a waiver of any subsequent breach. If any provision of this Agreement is held to be invalid or unenforceable, the remaining provisions shall not be affected.

17.10   Regardless of its place of physical execution or performance, the provisions of this Agreement shall in all respects be construed according to, and the rights and liabilities of the parties hereto shall in all respects be governed by, the laws of the State of _____.

17.11   The caption headings of this Agreement are inserted for convenience only and are without substantive effect.

17.12   This Agreement shall be of no force and effect unless signed by both parties within sixty (60) days of the date first stated above.

17.13   [OPTIONAL: Agency clause] Author hereby authorizes Author's agent, _____, of _____, to be Author's sole and exclusive agent with respect to all matters arising out of this Agreement and directs Publisher to make all payments due or to become due to Author hereunder to such agent and until receipt by Publisher from Author of notice canceling the agent's authority hereunder, Publisher may conclusively rely upon such authority. Receipt by Author's agent of payments due hereunder shall constitute a full and valid discharge for such payments under the terms of this Agreement. Author hereby irrevocably assigns and transfers to the _____ Agency and the _____Agency shall retain a sum equal to 15 percent (15%) of all money due and payable to and for Author's account under this Agreement.

IN WITNESS WHEROF, the parties have signed this Agreement to be effective as of the date first stated above.

[Signature]_____

By: _____

Author's Name & Address:_____

[Signature]_____

Publisher's Name & Address: _____

Author's Tax Identification No. _____

Author's citizenship: _____

Author's birth date: _____
(This information necessary for copyright purposes)

FORM 6

There are many types of film and television option agreements, from one-page letters to multi-page documents complete with copyright assignment forms. Ideally, an option agreement should include two separate documents, both the option itself and the purchase agreement to be used if the option is exercised. The following form is a compromise: It incorporates both option and purchase terms in one document, but contemplates the signing of a full purchase agreement if the option is exercised. This form assumes a low-budget film with neither the producer nor writer being a member of the Writer's Guild of America.

Film Option and Literary Purchase Agreement

This AGREEMENT is made and entered into as of _____ by and between _____ (hereinafter "Writer") and _____ (hereinafter "Producer").

WHEREAS, Writer is the sole and exclusive proprietor, throughout the world of that certain original Property written by Writer, titled _____(the "Property").

1. OPTION.

In consideration of payment of one thousand dollars ($1,000), receipt of which is hereby acknowledged, Writer hereby grants Producer a six (6) month exclusive Option (the "Option") to purchase all motion picture, television, ancillary, and exploitation rights in and to the Property and in the copyright thereof and all renewals and extensions of copyright, in order to develop and produce an original motion picture based on the Property ("the Picture") and exploit the Picture and all rights acquired herein, provided that any sums paid under this section 1 or any other provision of this Agreement with respect to the Option shall be credited against the first sums payable on account of such purchase price. If Producer shall fail to exercise this Option, then the sums paid to Writer hereunder with respect to the Option shall be and remain the sole property of Writer.

2. OPTION PERIOD.

The Option shall be effective during the period commencing on the date hereof and ending one year later (the "Initial Option Period"). The Initial Option Period may be extended for an additional six (6) months by payment of one thousand dollars ($1,000) on or before the expiration date specified above (the "Second Option Period").

3. EXERCISE OF OPTION.

3.1   If Producer elects to exercise the Option, Producer (at any time during the Initial or Second Option Period) shall serve upon Writer written notice of the exercise by addressing such notice to Writer at his address by certified mail, return receipt requested with postage prepaid, in the United States mail. The deposit of such notice in the United States mail as hereinabove specified shall constitute service thereof, and the date of such deposit shall be deemed to be the date of service of such notice. The Option may be exercised only by notice in writing as set forth.

3.2   If Producer exercises this Option, Writer, without cost to Producer shall execute, acknowledge, and deliver to Producer, or shall cause the execution, acknowledgment, and delivery to Producer of such further instruments as Producer may reasonably require in order to confirm unto Producer the rights, licenses, privileges, and property that are the subject of the within Option. If Writer shall fail to execute and deliver or to cause the execution and delivery to Producer of any such instruments, Producer is hereby irrevocably granted the power coupled with an interest to execute such instruments and to take such other steps and proceedings as may be necessary in connection therewith in the name and on behalf of Writer and as Writer's attorney-in-fact. Writer shall supply all supporting agreements and documentation requested by Producer.

4. PURCHASE PRICE OF PROPERTY.

4.1   As consideration for all rights granted and assigned to Producer including the production of one or more theatrical or television motion pictures, and for Writer's representations and warranties, Producer agrees to pay to Writer, and Writer agrees to accept, the following compensation (the "Purchase Price"):

4.1.1 If a motion picture is produced based on the Property with a final production budget more than $500,000 but less than $1 million, Writer shall be paid the sum of $10,000.

4.1.2 If a motion picture is produced based on the Property with a final production budget more than $1 million but less than $2.5 million, Writer shall be paid the sum of $34,740.

4.1.3 If a motion picture is produced based on the Property with a final production budget more than $2.5 million, Writer shall be paid the sum of $58,000.

4.2 The Purchase Price shall be paid by Producer as follows: $_____ within thirty (30) days of exercise of the option as set forth in section 3; the remainder within thirty (30) days of the first day of principal photography.

4.3 In addition to the aforesaid Purchase Price, Writer shall receive Additional Compensation as follows:

4.3.1 For any sequel produced based on the Property, in whole or in part, Producer will pay or cause Writer to be paid one-half of the Purchase Price; and for any remake produced based on the Property, in whole or in part, Producer will pay or cause Writer to be paid one-third of the Purchase Price. The compensation described in this section 4.3.1 shall be paid to Writer upon commencement of principal photography of any such sequel and/or remake.

4.3.2 For any television series produced based on the Property, Producer will pay or cause to be paid to Writer the following royalties per initial production upon completion of production of each program: programs up to thirty (30) minutes, $1,500; over thirty (30) minutes but not more than sixty (60) minutes, $1,750; over sixty (60) minutes but not more than ninety (90) minutes, $2,000; over ninety (90) minutes, $2,500; and in addition to the foregoing, as a buy-out of all royalty obligations, 100 percent (100%) of the applicable initial royalty amount, in equal installments over five (5) reruns, payable within thirty (30) days after each such rerun, or subject to the WGA minimum, whichever is greater.

4.4 All of the sums set forth as compensation in this paragraph are for the total amount of monies payable by Producer.

5. CREDIT.

In determining whether Writer is awarded sole, shared, or no writing credit for the Property, reference shall be made to the principles of the WGA credit arbitration rules. Although Producer is not a WGA signatory, and Writer is not a member of the WGA, to the extent possible, the principles of the WGA credit arbitration rules shall be followed by the parties. In the event of a credit dispute, the arbitrator of such a dispute shall follow the WGA credit rules.

6. RIGHT TO ENGAGE IN PREPRODUCTION.

Writer acknowledges that Producer may, during the Option Period, undertake production and preproduction activities in connection with any of the rights to be acquired hereunder including, without limitation, the preparation and submission of treatments and/or screenplays based on the Property.

7. ASSIGNMENT.

This Option Agreement and the rights granted hereunder may be assigned by Producer to any other person, firm, or corporation, without the consent of Writer.

8. OPTION REVERSION.

If Producer does not timely exercise the Option during its original or extended term, the Option shall terminate and all rights in the Property shall immediately revert to Writer. Writer shall retain all sums paid. Producer shall immediately execute and deliver to Writer any assignments and documents required to effectuate the Reversion. If Producer shall fail or be unable to do so, Producer hereby grants Writer a power coupled with an interest to execute and deliver such documents as Producer's attorney-in-fact.

9. WARRANTY AND INDEMNIFICATION.

9.1   Writer represents and warrants to Producer that Writer has not adapted the Property from any other literary, dramatic, or other material of any kind, nature, or description, nor, excepting for material that is in the public domain, has Writer copied or used in the Property the plot, scenes, sequence, or story of any other literary, dramatic, or other material; that the Property does not infringe upon any common law or statutory rights in any other literary, dramatic, or other material; that insofar as Writer has knowledge, no material in the Property is libelous or violative of the right of privacy of any person and the full utilization of the rights in the Property that are covered by the within Option would not violate any rights of any person, firm, or corporation; and that the Property is not in the public domain in any country in the world where copyright protection is available.

9.2   Writer represents and warrants to Producer that Writer is the exclusive proprietor, throughout the world, of the rights in the Property that are covered by the within Option; that Writer has not assigned, licensed, nor in any manner encumbered, diminished, or impaired these rights. Writer further represents and warrants that no attempt hereafter will be made to encumber, diminish, or impair any of the rights herein granted and that all appropriate protections of such rights will continue to be maintained by Writer.

9.3   Writer agrees to indemnify Producer against all judgments, liability, damages, penalties, losses, and expense (including reasonable attorneys' fees) that may be suffered or assumed by or obtained against Producer, its successors, licensees, and assigns, by reason of any breach or failure of any warranty or agreement herein made by Writer. This paragraph shall survive termination of this Agreement.

10. FURTHER AGREEMENT.

In the event the Option is exercised by Producer, the parties intend to enter into a more formal agreement consistent with the terms of this Purchase Agreement and containing such other terms and conditions as are customary in option agreements in the motion picture and television industry.

11. MISCELLANEOUS.

11.1   Terms used herein in the masculine gender include the feminine and neuter gender, and terms used in the singular number include the plural number, if the context may require.

11.2   The headings of paragraphs, sections, and other subdivisions of this Agreement are for convenient reference only. They shall not be used in any way to govern, limit, modify, construe this agreement or any part or provision thereof, or otherwise be given any legal effect.

11.3   This Agreement contains the full and complete understanding and agreement between the parties with respect to the within subject matter, and supersedes all other agreements between the parties whether written or oral relating thereto, and may not be modified or amended except by written instrument executed by both of the parties hereto. This agreement shall in all respects be subject to the laws of_____ applicable to agreements executed and wholly performed within such State. All the rights, licenses, privileges, and property herein granted to Producer are irrevocable and not subject to rescission, restraint, or injunction under any or all circumstances.

11.4　In the event of any dispute or disagreement regarding this Agreement, the parties agree that common sense should prevail, and that if necessary an independent person or persons mutually agreed upon by both parties shall be called upon to make a decision which is binding upon both parties. If the parties cannot agree on an arbitrator within thirty (30) days of a written arbitration request by either party, the parties may pursue remedies in law or equity in any court of competent jurisdiction.

IN WITNESS THEREOF, the parties hereto have signed this Option Agreement as of the day and year first hereinabove written.

_____

WRITER
[full name and address]

_____

PRODUCER
[full name and address]

Index